CAMBRIDGE LIBRARY COLLECTION

Books of enduring scholarly value

Classics

From the Renaissance to the nineteenth century, Latin and Greek were compulsory subjects in almost all European universities, and most early modern scholars published their research and conducted international correspondence in Latin. Latin had continued in use in Western Europe long after the fall of the Roman empire as the lingua franca of the educated classes and of law, diplomacy, religion and university teaching. The flight of Greek scholars to the West after the fall of Constantinople in 1453 gave impetus to the study of ancient Greek literature and the Greek New Testament. Eventually, just as nineteenth-century reforms of university curricula were beginning to erode this ascendancy, developments in textual criticism and linguistic analysis, and new ways of studying ancient societies, especially archaeology, led to renewed enthusiasm for the Classics. This collection offers works of criticism, interpretation and synthesis by the outstanding scholars of the nineteenth century.

Alcestis of Euripides

T.W.C. Edwards's edition of Monk's 1816 translation of Euripides's *Alcestis* was published in 1824. Edwards used the earlier work to form the basis of a parallel pedagogic text, adding copious notes for the use of students of ancient Greek. *Alcestis* is Euripides's earliest surviving play; a 'problem play' that shares much with tragedy, but has a happy ending. Admetus marries Alcestis who offers to die in his place after he angers the goddess Artemis. She is rescued from death by Heracles who returns her in disguise to her husband. Admetus refuses to marry this unknown woman, having vowed celibacy after what he believed was his wife's death, but she is revealed as Alcestis to much rejoicing. The play was originally performed at the Athenian Dionysia in 438 BC, where it formed the final part of an otherwise lost tetralogy of plays, replacing the traditional satyr play.

Cambridge University Press has long been a pioneer in the reissuing of out-of-print titles from its own backlist, producing digital reprints of books that are still sought after by scholars and students but could not be reprinted economically using traditional technology. The Cambridge Library Collection extends this activity to a wider range of books which are still of importance to researchers and professionals, either for the source material they contain, or as landmarks in the history of their academic discipline.

Drawing from the world-renowned collections in the Cambridge University Library, and guided by the advice of experts in each subject area, Cambridge University Press is using state-of-the-art scanning machines in its own Printing House to capture the content of each book selected for inclusion. The files are processed to give a consistently clear, crisp image, and the books finished to the high quality standard for which the Press is recognised around the world. The latest print-on-demand technology ensures that the books will remain available indefinitely, and that orders for single or multiple copies can quickly be supplied.

The Cambridge Library Collection will bring back to life books of enduring scholarly value (including out-of-copyright works originally issued by other publishers) across a wide range of disciplines in the humanities and social sciences and in science and technology.

Alcestis of Euripides

Literally Translated into English Prose from the Text of Monk with the Original Greek, the Metres, the Order, and English Accentuation

T.W.C. EDWARDS

CAMBRIDGE UNIVERSITY PRESS

Cambridge, New York, Melbourne, Madrid, Cape Town, Singapore,
São Paolo, Delhi, Dubai, Tokyo

Published in the United States of America by Cambridge University Press, New York

www.cambridge.org
Information on this title: www.cambridge.org/9781108015400

© in this compilation Cambridge University Press 2010

This edition first published 1824
This digitally printed version 2010

ISBN 978-1-108-01540-0 Paperback

THE

ALCESTIS OF EURIPIDES,

LITERALLY TRANSLATED INTO ENGLISH PROSE;

FROM

THE TEXT OF MONK.

ΕΥΡΙΠΙΔΟΥ ΑΛΚΗΣΤΙΣ.

THE

ALCESTIS OF EURIPIDES,

LITERALLY TRANSLATED INTO ENGLISH PROSE;

FROM

THE TEXT OF MONK:

WITH

THE ORIGINAL GREEK, THE METRES, THE ORDER, AND
ENGLISH ACCENTUATION.

TO WHICH ARE SUBJOINED

NUMEROUS EXPLANATORY NOTES.

FOR THE USE OF STUDENTS.

BY

T. W. C. EDWARDS, M. A.

Κἄπειτα θάλαμον εἰσπεσοῦσα, καὶ λέχος,
ἐνταῦθα δὴ ᾽δάκρυσε, καὶ λέγει τάδε·
῾Ω λέκτρον, ἔνθα παρθένει᾽ ἔλυσ᾽ ἐγὼ
κορεύματ᾽ ἐκ τοῦδ᾽ ἀνδρὸς, οὗ θνήσκω πέρι,
χαῖρ᾽· οὐ γὰρ ἐχθαίρω σ᾽· ἀπώλεσας δ᾽ ἐμὲ
μόνην· προδοῦναι γάρ σ᾽ ὀκνοῦσα, καὶ πόσιν,
θνήσκω· σὲ δ᾽ ἄλλη τις γυνὴ κεκτήσεται,
σώφρων μὲν οὐχὶ μᾶλλον, εὐτυχὴς δ᾽ ἴσως.
ΑΛΚΗΣΤ. 176—183.

ΑΔ.῾Ω φιλτάτης γυναικὸς ὄμμα, καὶ δέμας
ἔχω σ᾽ ἀέλπτως, οὔποτ᾽ ὄψεσθαι δοκῶν;
ΑΛΚΗΣΤ. 1152—1153.

LONDON:

MATTHEW ILEY, SOMERSET ST. PORTMAN SQ.

SOLD BY TALBOYS, OXFORD; NEWBY, CAMBRIDGE; AND
BELL AND BRADFUTE, EDINBURGH.

1824.

TO

JOHN SCOTT, M.D.

FELLOW OF THE ROYAL COLLEGE OF PHYSICIANS,

&c. &c. &c.

BEDFORD SQUARE, LONDON.

DEAR SIR,

    THE warm interest you have ever taken in the success of my Works, from the period of their first appearance, and the kind exertions you have made to promote that success, I feel with the liveliest pleasure,—and acknowledge with the most unfeigned thankfulness.

    The elevated rank you hold in society, in your Profession, and in the world of letters has greatly enhanced the value of your friendship, and determined me to lay myself under further obligations to you, by constituting you Patron of the following Play, The Alcestis of Euripides.

    In it I have endeavoured to profit by the judicious hints you some time ago had the condescension to give me, respecting idiomatic phrases and the use of particles, particularly of expletives, which in Greek Poetry are often redundant to the sense, although necessary to the rhythm. As, however, I profess to abide in my Translations as nearly as I can by the original, and as, in general, I offer some meaning for every word of the text, I have still been unable to adhere so closely to the strict signification of those and other parts of speech, as either your friendly suggestions or my own ardent wish prompted. Far less, then, I lament to say, has it been in my power, with all my striving, to put in practice the most excellent advice with which I was recently honored by the Lord Bishop of St. David's, namely, "To adopt as much as possible the phraseology of Shakespeare." The desirableness of so doing is great, but the difficulty of accomplishing it is greater!

    Most happy should I have been to have had the ability (for the will was not wanting) to effect my Versions in a manner more worthy of your patronage, and of the approbation of the Right Reverend Prelate above named: but in the absence of such ability, I must content myself with the consciousness of having possessed the will, and with the certainty that both you and he, not less distinguished for your acquirements and zeal in the cause of learning, than remarkable for a spirit of candor, will examine the

*following pages with the lenity they require,—and that ye will
throw a veil over minor imperfections— recollecting that the object
of the Work is the facilitation of a very difficult, but most useful,
branch of classical knowledge.*

*The language is that in which your favorite Hippocrates of
Cos wrote his Aphorisms, upwards of seventy generations ago:
it is the language, through the medium of which we moderns have
derived much instruction, and have reaped varied delight, and have
received the message of the gladdest of tidings.*

*If the heroes, and sages, and geniuses of antiquity have long
since crumbled to dust, so we to dust must crumble:—but in the
message of glad tidings we have the consoling hope that the crumbled and scattered dust of our earthly tenements shall be re-vivifi-
ed, and be again united to the soul to be dis-united no more.*

*This thought and this consoling hope serve as a check to our
pride upon the one hand, and as a spur to the faithful discharge of
our several duties on the other. But some men there are who stand
in little or no need either of check or spur, being naturally of mild
and unassuming manners; and incapable, from an innate love of
virtue, of practising vice: these merit the greatest commendation;
and fortunate would it be for the world that folks of this descrip-
tion were more numerous. Where, however, nature proves defec-
tive, education will frequently succeed in restraining the passions,
and in bettering the heart. Indeed few can read the writings of
Euripides, particularly his Alcestis, without feeling the strongest
inducement to lean to the side of virtue, and to detest vice; so full
are they of morality, and of tenderness, and of exquisite sensibili-
ty, that even the most hardened are melted to tears at the represen-
tation of so much suffering and of so much wo: they possess, besides, the power of charming those who peruse them, not merely
once, but again and again.*

*This pleasure you have often experienced:—that you may
very long continue to experience it, and to enjoy all the happiness
arising from domestic comfort, a cultivated mind, the blessing of
health, the smile of fortune, the esteem of your countrymen, the
consciousness of having done your duty, and the pious hope of eter-
nal felicity, is the hearty wish of,*

Dear Sir,

Your obliged and obedient Servant,

G.W.C.Edwards.

London, Sept. 23rd 1824.

TO
THE READER.

THERE are many, who, possessing in reality very little knowledge, yet wishing withal to be thought extremely erudite, are constantly yelping that *" the interests of sound learning are in danger,"* whenever they hear of any Work, of which the object is to render the attainment of any branch of literature easy : and these are joined in the cry by another set, whose bread indeed depends on their making a vast secret of the scanty knowledge they have themselves picked up, (*viz.* a smattering of the Greek and Roman languages, with little or nothing besides,) dealing it out in miserably small portions at a very enormous price.

All such persons are unworthy of the name they assume: for, *in the first place*, an intimate acquaintance with the Classics is, in itself, an acquisition of comparatively small value: and what, then, must the worth of a smattering be? An acquaintance with the Classics, I say, is comparatively of very small value of itself, being merely an Introduction to Grammar and to Refinement of Taste: whereas, sound learning, as I understand the expression, means a thorough knowledge of all or most of the Arts and Sciences. *In the second place*, these yelpers are unworthy of the name they assume, because literature, which is calculated to ennoble the mind, and to inspire liberal ideas, ought not, like the petty secrets of some scurvy trade, or the tricks of jugglers, to be wrapped in mystery and darkness; but it ought to be made plain and easy of acquirement, that "they who run may read."

I have long made up my own mind upon this subject, and whenever I hear the cry of *"sound learning in danger,"* I know from what quarter it comes, because no man of sound learning ever raised such a cry.

Any attempt, (how unsuccessful soever it may prove,) to facilitate the acquirement of useful knowledge, is, in my opinion, laudable: and I am well convinced that this is the sentiment of every liberal-minded and well-informed man, without exception.

Impressed with this conviction, I continue to come from time to time before the public:—and I have the pleasure of knowing, that notwithstanding the humbleness of my efforts, and the opposition of no informidable party, I am, upon the whole, well received. The liberal make every allowance for the very great difficulty which there necessarily is in translating Greek Poetry into Literal English Prose; and for the silliness of diction, as well as (I beg pardon of the yelping guardians of sound learning,) total absence of genius in many parts of the original.

In the following Edition of the Alcestis, the Greek Text has been copied from Monk's second Edition of that Play, which I believe is the last that has appeared, printed at Cambridge in 1818.

As there are, however, in Monk's Text, several gross mis-spellings, (as κύτπον for κτύπον, verse 87,—μηθίστη for μιθίστη, verse 175,—ΠΡΑ-ΚΛΗΣ for ΗΡΑΚΛΙΙΣ, verse 492;) and many mis-accentuations, (as ὐδὶν for ὐδὶν, verse 136; ἰστιν for ἰστὶν, verse 140, and similarly in verses 45 and 147; ποτε for ποτὶ, verses 340 and 715; τίν᾽ for τιν᾽, verse 497; ᾽ναξ for ῎ναξ, verse 555; μεν for μὶν, verse 797; καί for καὶ, verse 1034; and σπονδας for σπονδὰς, verse 1035; with very many others,) I have, of course, corrected these:—and the *uncini* or *brackets*, which disfigure Monk's text, I have discarded.

In verse 77, where, on no authority whatever, the learned professor gives πρόσθεν for πρόσθε, that the penult of μελάθρων, which follows, may remain short, I have retained πρόσθε, fully convinced that the vulgate lection is the best, and that the poet intended the penult of μελάθρων to be long. Again, in verse 905, where Monk after mature consideration thought proper to transpose the words, and to read ἄχθος μέτριον, to the entire destruction of the rhythm, I have re-transposed them, and edited, consentingly with all MSS. and editions before Monk's, μέτριον ἄχθος. The word νέκυς, of verse 94, I have rejected,—entertaining no doubt whatever of its spuriousness.

Monk's punctuation, too, I have frequently altered:—and although I have followed him in the distribution of character, I have done so in several instances at the expense of the sense: for who can tolerate, for example, Semichorus for Chorus, verses 77 and 79; and Chorus for Semichorus, verses 86 and 89? And yet Barnes and Monk have deemed this arrangement the best,—in opposition to the most unquestionable authority, and the voice of common intellect.

In verse 605, I have restored ὀικεῖς, disapproving *in toto* of Monk's ὀικεῖ, for which there does not appear to me to be the smallest necessity, and certainly no warrant whatever.

The verb κλαίω, *fleo*, which Monk (consentingly, it is true, with Porson,) has uniformly written κλάω, *frango*, as being (they tell us) more strictly Attic, I have continued to spell in the old way: and the coalescence of καὶ with a long syllable aspirated, as in the words χῆ, χὸι, (as Monk gives them) for καὶ ἡ and καὶ ὁι, I consider (but this is mere matter of opinion) to be more properly written and printed χʹη and χʹὸι.

Where καὶ coalesces with an initial diphthong as in κᾷτα for καὶ εῖτα, I have with Monk and Porson (on the recommendation of Dawes) retained the ι subscript, and in all other instances, as κάπειτα for καὶ ἔπειτα, I have with them rejected it, contrary to the practice of Brunck and many other celebrated editors.

Respecting the Translation and other parts of the Work, I have nothing new to offer,—but take the liberty of referring to the Preface of the King Œdipus of Sophocles, and of the other Plays I have already published, for a full developement of my plan.

London, Sept. 23rd 1824.

SUMMARY

OF

FACTS AND CIRCUMSTANCES CONNECTED WITH THE PLAY.

ÆSCULAPIUS, a beloved son of Apóllo, and physician of old, who was considered by the ancients to be so intimately acquainted with the medicinal properties of every plant, that he was called the inventor and god of medicine, having, by his extraordinary skill, restored many recently dead persons to life, Plúto, whose rights were thereby infringed, and whose subjects were in consequence diminished in number, complained to Júpiter of conduct so subversive of the natural order of things. The father of the gods being incensed, struck Æsculápius with lightning, and killed him: whereupon Apóllo, to be revenged for the death of his son, slew the Cýclops who had made the thunderbolts.

This daring act of injustice and of contempt, Júpiter punished by banishing his son Apóllo from heaven, and sentencing him to the drudgeries of a menial on the earth for a limited time. In conformity, therefore, to the will and command of his father, Apóllo went into exile : — and, having come into Greece, hired himself to Admétus, king of Phéræ, in Théssaly, cheerfully submitting to rank as a servant, and faithfully discharging the duties of a shepherd for nine years.

During this sojourn of Apóllo in the house and service of Admétus, he was treated with much kindness, and became so warmly attached to the family by the ties of gratitude and the feelings of respect, that he felt inclined to confer on his master some extraordinary favor in token of his regard, and as a mark of his entire satisfaction with the treatment he had experienced.

As Admétus was most singularly averse to death, the greatest favor that could in any way be bestowed on him, was the means of escape from this king of terrors and terror of kings:—accordingly Apóllo solicited the Fates in his behalf, and obtained from them, that Admétus should never die, provided that always, when it came to his turn to die, some other person would die in his stead.

Admétus, after the death of his first wife, had married Alcéstis, called also Alcéstë, daughter of Pélias, king of Iólchos. Two children, Eumélus and Periméné, were the offspring of this marriage, and had not arrived at puberty when it came to their father's turn to die.

Authors are not agreed as to the precise sort of death which threatened Admétus, but they all affirm that he found it very difficult to procure a substitute,—his aged father Phérës, and his mother Clýmene, having each of them peremptorily refused to redeem their son's life at the price of their own. But his noble queen Alcéstis, although yet in the flower of her youth, most generously volunteered to die for her husband.

The principal incidents of the Play are Alcéstis's death and funeral, with her restoration to life and to Admétus by Hércülës, who came to the palace of Phéræ on a visit at this truly mournful, but eventually happy season; and who by dint of prowess and of sheer strength, succeeded in rescuing from the grasp of death and of the grave, the most worthy wife of the son of Phérës.

The pusillanimity of Admétus, and his ingratitude and insolence to his father, are impressive of contempt for him personally,—notwithstanding the great stress laid by the Chorus on the hospitableness of his disposition. And had Alcéstis said less of herself and of her act, she would have appeared to more advantage.

Another great defect in the Fable, is the silence of Alcéstis after resuscitation; although the poet accounts for it in a way not altogether unsatisfactory.

ΤΑ ΤΟΥ ΔΡΑΜΑΤΟΣ ΠΡΟΣΩΠΑ.

ΤΑ ΠΡΟΣΩ΄ΠΑ ΤΟΥ ΔΡΑ΄ΜΑΤΟΣ.	THE PERSONS OF THE DRAMA.
ΑΠΟΛΛΩΝ - - - - - -	APOLLO
ΘΑΝΑΤΟΣ - - - - - -	DEATH
ΧΟΡΟΣ ΑΝΔΡΩΝ ΦΕΡΑΙΩΝ - - -	CHORUS OF MEN OF PHERÆ
ΘΕΡΑΠΑΙΝΑ - - - - - -	FEMALE ATTENDANT
ΑΛΚΗΣΤΙΣ - - - - - -	ALCESTIS
ΑΔΜΗΤΟΣ - - - - - -	ADMETUS
ΕΥΜΗΛΟΣ - - - - - -	EUMELUS
ΗΡΑΚΛΗΣ - - - - - -	HERCULES
ΦΕΡΗΣ - - - - - -	PHERES
ΘΕΡΑΠΩΝ - - - - - -	MAN-SERVANT.

B

ΥΠΟΘΕΣΙΣ ΑΛΚΗΣΤΙΔΟΣ.

ΑΠΟΛΛΩΝ ᾐτήσατο παρὰ τῶν Μοιρῶν, ὅπως ὁ Ἄδμητος, τελευτᾷν μέλλων, παράσχῃ τινὰ τὸν ὑπὲρ αὐτοῦ τεθνηξόμενον, ἵνα ἴσον τῷ προτέρῳ χρόνῳ ζή-σῃ· καὶ Ἄλκηστις ἡ γυνὴ ἐπέδωκεν ἑαυτὴν, μηδετέρου τῶν γονέων ἐθελήσαν-τος ὑπὲρ τοῦ παιδὸς ἀποθανεῖν. Μετ᾽ οὐ πολὺ δὲ, τῆς συμφορᾶς ταύτης γε-νομένης, Ἡρακλῆς παραγενόμενος, καὶ μαθὼν παρά τινος θεράποντος τὰ πε-ρὶ τὴν Ἄλκηστιν, ἐπορεύθη ἐπὶ τὸν τάφον· καὶ τὸν Θάνατον ἀποστῆναι ποι-ήσας, ἐσθῆτι καλύπτει τὴν γυναῖκα· τὸν δὲ Ἄδμητον ἠξίου λαβόντα τη-ρεῖν· εἰληφέναι δὲ αὐτὴν πάλης ἆθλον ἔλεγε· μὴ βουλομένου δὲ ἐκείνου, ἀ-ποκαλύψας, ἔδειξεν ἣν ἐπένθει.

THE ORDER, AND ENGLISH ACCENTUATION.

ΥΠΟΘΕΣΙΣ ΑΛΚΗΣΤΙΔΟΣ.

ΑΠΟΛΛΩΝ ᾐτήσατο πάρα των Μοίρων, ὅπως ὁ Ἄδμητος, μέλλων τελευτᾷν, παράσχῃ τίνα τον τεθνηξόμενον ὕπερ αὐτου, ἵνα ζήσῃ ἴσον τω πρότερω χρόνω· καὶ Ἄλκηστις ἡ γύνη, μηδέτερου των γόνεων ἐθελησάντος· ἀπόθανειν ὕπερ του παιδος, ἐπέδωκε ἑαυτην. Δε ου πόλυ μέτα, της ταύτης σύμφορας γενόμενης, Ἡρακλης παραγινόμενος, καὶ μάθων πάρα τίνος θεράποντος τα πέρι την Ἄλκηστιν, ἐπορεύθη ἐπι τον τάφον· και ποιήσας τον Θάνατον ἀποστῆναι, καλύπ-τει την γυναικα ἐσθῆτι· δε ἠξιου τον Ἀδμήτον λαβόντα τηρειν· δε ἔλεγε εἰληφέναι αὐτην ἆθ-λον πάλης· δε εκείνου μη βουλόμενου, ἀποκαλύψας, εδειξε ἣν ἐπένθει.

TRANSLATION.

ARGUMENT OF THE ALCESTIS.

APOLLO desired of the Fates, that Admétus, who was about to die, might give some one as a substitute to die for him, that so he might live for a term equal to his former life:—and Alcéstis his consort, neither of his parents being willing to die for their son, gave herself up. But not long after the time when this calamity took place, Hér-culës having arrived, and having learnt from a servant the particu-lars concerning Alcéstis, went to her tomb, and, having made Death retire, covers the lady with a robe: and he requested Admétus to re-ceive and keep her for him; and said he had borne her off as a prize in wrestling: but when he would not, having unveiled her, he disco-vered to him her whom he was lamenting.

Line 1.The Fates, called Μοῖραι by the Greeks, and by the Latins, *Parcæ*, were three most powerful Goddesses, daugh-ters of Nox and Erebus, who were said to preside over the birth, life, and death of mankind. Their names, according to most authors, Pausánias indeed except-ed, were Clótho, Láchesis, and Atropos. Clótho, the youngest of the sisters, and whose office it was to regulate the time of coming into the world, was represen-ted holding in her hand a distaff, from which Láchesis span out the thread of human existence—teeming with action and fraught with vicissitude: Atropos, the eldest of the three, and who held in her hand a pair of scissars, snipped the thread at the moment appointed—and the pulse of life instantly ceased. Apól-lo is said to have made these Goddesses

drunk—and thus to have obtained from them their compliance with his request in favor of Admétus. How much soever the Fates might have regretted the im-prudence of their own conduct, and the impropriety of the concession they had made, yet they were in honor bound not to retract their promise.

Line 2. παράσχῃ τινὰ ὑπὲρ αὐτοῦ, *might provide some person for him — might sub-stitute some one in his stead — might fur-nish a deputy:* — ἵνα ἴσον τῷ προτέρῳ χρόνῳ ζήσῃ, literally, *that he might live a time e-qual to his former time: that he might live as long as he had already lived.*

Line 7. τὸν Ἄδμητον ἠξίου λαβόντα τηρεῖν, *he requested Admétus, having received her, to keep her,* i. e., *to receive and keep her.*

Line 8. μὴ βουλομένου ἐκείνου, *he* (name-ly, *Admétus*) *not being willing.*

ΕΥΡΙΠΙΔΟΥ ΑΛΚΗΣΤΙΣ.

ΑΠΟΛΛΩΝ.

Ὦ δώματ' Ἀδμήτει', ἐν οἷς ἔτλην ἐγὼ
θῆσσαν τράπεζαν αἰνέσαι, θεός περ ὤν·
Ζεὺς γὰρ, κατακτὰς παῖδα τὸν ἐμὸν, αἴτιος,
Ἀσκληπιὸν, στέρνοισιν ἐμβαλὼν φλόγα·
οὗ δὴ χολωθεὶς, τέκτονας δίου πυρὸς   5
κτείνω Κύκλωπας· καί με θητεύειν πατὴρ
θνητῷ παρ' ἀνδρὶ, τῶνδ' ἄποιν', ἠνάγκασεν.
Ἐλθὼν δὲ γαῖαν τήνδ', ἐβουφόρβουν ξένῳ,
καὶ τόνδ' ἔσωζον οἶκον ἐς τόδ' ἡμέρας·

THE ORDER, AND ENGLISH ACCENTUATION.

ΑΠΟΛΛΩΝ.

Ω Ἀδμήτεία δώματα, ἐν οἷς ἐγὼ ἔτλην αἰνέσαι θῆσσαν τραπέζαν, περ ων θεός· γαρ Ζευς αἴτιος, κατάκτας τον ἐμὸν παῖδα Ἀσκλήπιον, ἐμβαλων φλόγα στερνοίσι· ου δη χολώθεις, κτείνω Κυκλώπας τέκτονας δίου πύρος· και με πάτηρ ηνάγκασε θητεύειν πάρα θνήτω ἀνδρι, αποίνα τώνδε. Δε ἐλθων τήνδε γαῖαν, εβουφόρβουν ξένω, και εσώζον τόνδε οἶκον εις τόδε ήμερας·

TRANSLATION.

[SCENE. *The Palace of Admétus at Phéræ: Apollo, with his bow, passing and gazing.*]

APOLLO.

O! MANSIONS of Admétus, in which I endured to assent-to the bond-servant's table, although I was a God:—for Júpiter was the cause, having slain my son Æsculápius,—by hurling the lightning's-flame at his breast: whereat then enraged, I kill the Cýclops, the forgers of Jove's fire:—and me did my father compel to serve‚as-a-hireling to a mortal man, a punishment for these doings. So, having come to this land, I tended-herds for my host, and have preserved the house until this day:

1. ὦ δώματ' Ἀδμήτει', *O Admétéan mansions:—*in place of Ἀδμήτει', Lascar has Ἀδμήτοι'.—Admétus, son of Phéres and of Clýmenè, was king of Phéræ in Thessaly. He received Apóllo in the capacity of shepherd when his father Jove had banished him from heaven. By help of Apóllo, Admétus obtained the hand of Alcéstis, daughter of Pélias, king of Iólchos; who required the suitor whom he should approve for son-in-law, to come in a chariot drawn by a lion and a wild boar. Apóllo, as a mark of the sense he entertained of the great attention paid to him by Admétus, continued to feel a lively interest in the welfare of the family. Of ἔτλην in this verse, the signification is, " *I brooked* or *endured*."

2. Suidas has given δουλικὴν τροφὴν, *servant's fare,* as the interpretation of θῆσσαν τράπεζαν, *mensam servilem.* The adjective θῆσσαν, which is here put for θητικὴν or μισθωτικὴν, is formed from θὴς, as Κρῆσσα is from Κρής. The literal English

of αἰνέσαι is " *to have praised* or *commended:*"—it also signifies " *to have assented to* or *to have acquiesced in,*" as Monk remarks in his note on this verse. In line 12 below, ἤνεσαν means "*they granted.*"

4. Æsculápius, god of botany and medicine, was son of Apóllo by Corónis, or (as some say) by Larissa.

5. οὗ, understand ἕνεκα :—τέκτονας δίου πυρὸς, literally, *manufacturers* or *framers of the heavenly fire.* The Cýclops, so named from their having only one eye, *viz.* in the middle of the forehead, were originally three in number, and had their forge in the interior of Ætna, under the superintendance of Vulcan.

7. ἄποινα, the accusative disjunct, like ψυχὰν τέρψιν, ver. 363, below; the context in both instances having reference to the objective case.

8. Another reading here, is ἐλθὼν δ' ἐς αἶαν τήνδε:—but prepositions, as Monk observes, are for the most part suppressed after verbs of motion.

ὁσίου γὰρ ἀνδρὸς ὅσιος ὢν ἐτύγχανον,   10
παιδὸς Φέρητος, ὃν θανεῖν ἐρρυσάμην,
Μοίρας δολώσας· ἤνεσαν δέ μοι θεαὶ,
Ἄδμητον Ἅιδην τὸν παραυτίκ᾽ ἐκφυγεῖν,
ἄλλον διαλλάξαντα τοῖς κάτω νεκρόν.
Πάντας δ᾽ ἐλέγξας καὶ διεξελθὼν φίλους,   15
πατέρα, γεραιάν θ᾽, ἥ σφ᾽ ἔτικτε, μητέρα,
οὐχ εὗρε, πλὴν γυναικὸς, ὅστις ἤθελε,
θανὼν πρὸ κείνου, μηκέτ᾽ εἰσορᾷν φάος·
ἢ νῦν κατ᾽ οἴκους ἐν χεροῖν βαστάζεται
ψυχοῤῥαγοῦσα· τῇδε γάρ σφ᾽ ἐν ἡμέρᾳ   20
θανεῖν πέπρωται, καὶ μεταστῆναι βίου.
Ἐγὼ δὲ, μὴ μίασμά μ᾽ ἐν δόμοις κίχῃ,
λείπω μελάθρων τῶνδε φιλτάτην στέγην.
Ἤδη δὲ τόνδε Θάνατον εἰσορῶ πέλας,

THE ORDER, AND ENGLISH ACCENTUATION.

γὰρ ἐτύγχανον ὢν ὅσιος ὁσίου ἀνδρὸς, παιδὸς Φερήτος, ὃν ἐρρύσαμην θάνειν, δολώσας Μοίρας· δὲ θέαι ἤνεσαν μοι, Ἀδμήτον ἐκφυγειν τὸν Ἅιδην παραύτικα, διαλλάξαντα ἄλλον νέκρον τοις κάτω. Δὲ ἐλέγξας καὶ διεξελθων πάντας φίλους, πάτερα, τε γεραίαν μήτερα, ἢ ἔτικτε σφε, οὐκ εὕρε, πλὴν γυναικος, ὅστις ἤθελε, θάνων πρὸ κείνου, εἰσοραν φάος μήκετι· ἢ νυν κάτα οἴκους ψυχοῤῥαγούσα βαστάζεται ἐν χέρειν· γὰρ πεπρώται σφε ἐν τῇδε ἡμερα θάνειν, καὶ μεταστῆναι βίου. Δὲ ἐγώ, μὴ μίασμα κίχη με ἐν δόμοις, λείπω φίλτατην στέγην τῶνδε μελάθρων. Δὲ εἰσορω ἤδη πέλας τόνδε Θάνατον,

TRANSLATION.

for pious it was, and belonged to a pious man, the son of Phérës, whom I rescued from dying by deluding the Fates:—for those Goddesses did grant unto me, that Admétus should escape the death that was before him, by giving-in-his-stead another dead to the powers beneath.

But having tried and gone through all his friends, his father, and his aged mother, her who bare him, he found not one, save his wife, who was willing, by dying for him, to look on the light no more:—her who now within the palace, breathing out her soul, is borne in their arms: for it is destined for her on this day to die, and to depart from life!

But I, lest the pollution come upon me in the house, leave the most dear abode of the palace. And I see already at hand that fellow Death,

---

10. ὁσίου γὰρ ἀνδρὸς ὅσιος ὢν ἐτύγχανον, literally, *for it* (namely, οἶκος, *the mansion*) *happened being pious, a pious man's:* that is, *being the property of a pious man it was pious.* For ἐτύγχανον, Aldus has ἐτύγχανε.

11. Lascar edited ἐρυσάμην, with one ρ. Monk says, ' usitátior structúra ésset, ὃν ἐρρυσάμην μὴ θανεῖν, ut in Oréste, v. 591, εἰ μὴ κελεύσας ῥύσεται με μὴ θανεῖν: · vel in Electrâ, 540, αὐτὸν ἐξέκλεψα μὴ θανεῖν.'

12. Μοίρας δολώσας—*having tricked the Fates, viz., by plying them with wine, and charming them with music.*

13. ᾅδην Aldus,—et editiónes, praéter Lascárem qui 'Ἅιδην et παρ᾽ αὐτίκ᾽. Ἅιδην τὸν παραυτίκα, instántem mórtem:—in quâ locutióne nîl est quod reprehéndas; 'Ἅιδης énim simplicitèr pro mórte persaépe

dictum est: ut in Hippolyt. 1050, 1363. Iphig. Taur. 486. Soph. Œdip. Colon. 1439. Æschyl. Agam. 676. MONK.

17–18. The vulgate reading here is ὅτις ἤθελε θανεῖν, with which μηκέτ᾽ hardly makes sense, and therefore in lieu of it, Barnes and Musgrave conjectured μηδ᾽ ἔτι. Heath retained μήκετ᾽—imagining ὥστε to be understood. Reiske amended the text as it now stands.

20. ψυχοῤῥαγοῦσα, *ánimam ágens, ushering fórth her life* or *soul, that is, expiring,* or *breathing her last breath.*

23. For τῶνδε in this verse, Lascar, Aldus, and all before Musgrave, have τήνδε agreeing with στέγην.

24. τόνδε Θάνατον εἰσορῶ, literally, *I see this Death,* that is, *I here see Death.*

ἱερέα θανόντων, ὅς νιν εἰς Ἀίδου δόμους   25 ∪∪-|∪-||--|∪-||--|∪-

μέλλει κατάξειν· ξυμμέτρως δ᾽ ἀφίκετο,   --|∪-||--|∪-||∪-|∪∪

φρουρῶν τόδ᾽ ἦμαρ, ᾧ θανεῖν αὐτὴν χρεών.   --|∪-||--|∪-||-|∪-

ΘΑΝΑΤΟΣ.

Ἄ, ἄ, ἄ, ἄ.   --|--

Τί σὺ πρὸς μελάθροις; Τί σὺ τῇδε πολεῖς,   ∪∪-|∪∪-||∪∪-|∪∪-

Φοῖβ᾽; Ἀδικεῖς αὖ, τιμὰς ἐνέρων   30 -∪∪|--||--|∪∪-

ἀφοριζόμενος, καὶ καταπαύων;   ∪∪-|∪∪-||-∪∪|--

Οὐκ ἤρκεσέ σοι μόρον Ἀδμήτου   --|∪∪-||∪∪-|--

διακωλῦσαι, Μοίρας δολίῳ   ∪∪-|-..||--|∪∪-

σφήλαντι τέχνῃ; Νῦν δ᾽ ἐπὶ τῇδ᾽ αὖ   --|∪∪-||∪∪-|--

χέρα τοξήρη φρουρεῖς ὁπλίσας,   35 ∪∪-|--||--|∪∪-

ἢ τόθ᾽ ὑπέστη, πόσιν ἐκλύσασ᾽,   -∪∪|--||∪∪-|--

αὐτὴ προθανεῖν Πελίου παῖς;   --|∪∪-||∪∪-|-*

ΑΠ. Θάρσει· δίκην τε, καὶ λόγους κεδνοὺς ἔχω.   --|∪-||∪-|∪-||--|∪-

ΘΑ. Τί δῆτα τόξων ἔργον, εἰ δίκην ἔχεις;   ∪-|∪-||--|∪-||∪-|∪-

---

THE ORDER, AND ENGLISH ACCENTUATION.

ἱέρεα θανόντων, ὅς μέλλει κατάξειν νιν εἰς δόμους Ἀίδου· δὲ ἀφίκετο ξύμμετρως, φρούρων τόδε ἦμαρ, ᾧ χρέων αὐτην θάνειν. ΘΑ. Α, α, α, α. Τι συ προς μελάθροις; Τι πόλεις συ τῇδε, Φοῖβε; Αυ ἀδικεῖς, ἀφοριζόμενος και καταπαύων τίμας ἐνέρων; Οὐκ ἤρκεσε σοι διακωλῦσαι μόρον Ἀδμήτου, δόλιω τέχνῃ σφηλάντι Μοίρας; Δε νυν αυ ὅπλισας χέρα τοξήρη φρούρεις ἐπι τῇδε, ἣ τότε ὑπέστη, ἐκλυσάσα πόσιν, αὐτη παις Πελίου πρόθανειν; ΑΠ. Θάρσει· ἔχω τε δίκην, και κέδνους λόγους. ΘΑ. Τι ἔργον δῆτα τόξων, εἰ ἔχεις δίκην;

TRANSLATION.

priest of the dead,—who is about to waft her down to the mansions of Plúto:—and he is come exactly-to-the-time, observing this day, upon which it is destined for her to die.

DEATH. [*Entering, robed in black, with a sword in his hand, accosts Apóllo.*] Ha! ha! ha! ha! What doest thou at the palace? Why loungest thou here, Phoébus? Art thou again at thy deeds of injustice, abridging and obstructing the honors of the powers beneath? Was it not enough for thee to stay the fate of Admétus, having by fraudful artifice deluded the Destinies? But now again, armed as to thy hand with thy bow, dost thou keep guard over her, who at that time undertook, in order to redeem her husband, herself the daughter of Pélias, to die for him?

APOLLO. [*With frankness and sincerity.*] Be of courage: I adhere both to justice and to honorable terms.

DEATH. What occasion then for thy bow, if thou adherest to justice?

---

25. ἱερῇ dant ómnes: restítui, (monénte Elmsleío,) véram accusatívi fórmam ἱερέα, cújus dúo últimæ sýllabæ in únam coaléscunt. MONK.

26. ξυμμέτρως, *congruénte intervállo.*

28. It is to me, I must own, matter of much surprise that Potter or any other should have given "Orcus" as the translation of Θάνατος, when no word in our language, except "Death," can rightly express the meaning of the original. In Aldus —and so in most of the early editions, this person is termed Χάρων.

29. Reiske wished to read πολεῖ in the middle voice, but unnecessarily; for, as Monk observes, πολέω, (when used as a neuter verb,) signifies, *vérsor, frequéntor.*

30. ἀδικεῖς αὖ; literally, *Doest thou injustice again? Actest thou again unjustly?* Monk gives "*attributes* or *prerogatives*' as the interpretation of τιμάς.

33–34. Μοίρας δολίῳ σφήλαντι τέχνῃ, *having by guileful art deceived the Fates.* See the note at verse 12, above.

36. For τόθ᾽, the vulgate lection is τόδ᾽.

37. Aldus, and most MSS. have αὐτήν: Lascar and Musgrave αὐτή. Wakefield changed the breathing and edited αὑτή.

ΑΠ. Ξύνηθες ἀεὶ ταῦτα βαστάζειν ἐμοί.   40

ΘΑ. Καὶ τοῖσδέ γ' οἴκοις ἐκδίκως προσωφελεῖν.

ΑΠ. Φίλου γὰρ ἀνδρὸς ξυμφοραῖς βαρύνομαι.

ΘΑ. Καὶ νοσφιεῖς με τοῦδε δευτέρου νεκροῦ;

ΑΠ. Ἀλλ' οὐδ' ἐκεῖνον πρὸς βίαν σ' ἀφειλόμην.

ΘΑ. Πῶς οὖν ὑπὲρ γῆς ἐστι, κοὐ κατὰ χθονός;   45

ΑΠ. Δάμαρτ' ἀμείψας, ἣν σὺ νῦν ἥκεις μέτα.

ΘΑ. Κἀπάξομαί γε νερτέραν ὑπὸ χθόνα.

ΑΠ. Λαβὼν ἴθ'· οὐ γὰρ οἶδ' ἂν εἰ πείσαιμί σε—

ΘΑ.—κτείνειν ὃν ἂν χρῇ; Τοῦτο γὰρ τετάγμεθα.

ΑΠ. Οὔκ· ἀλλὰ τοῖς μέλλουσι θάνατον ἐμβαλεῖν.   50

ΘΑ. Ἔχω λόγον γε, καὶ προθυμίαν σέθεν.

ΑΠ. Ἔστ' οὖν ὅπως Ἄλκηστις εἰς γῆρας μόλοι;

ΘΑ. Οὐκ ἔστι· τιμαῖς κἀμὲ τέρπεσθαι δόκει.

ΑΠ. Οὔτοι πλέον γ' ἂν ἢ μίαν ψυχὴν λάβοις.

THE ORDER, AND ENGLISH ACCENTUATION.

ΑΠ. Ξυνῆθες ἐμοὶ ἀεὶ βαστάζειν ταῦτα.—ΘΑ. Γε καὶ ἐκδίκως προσώφελειν τοῖσδε οἴκοις. ΑΠ. Γὰρ βαρύνομαι ξύμφοραις φίλου ἀνδρός. ΘΑ. Καὶ νόσφιεις με τοῦδε δεύτερου νέκρου; ΑΠ. Ἀλλα οὐδε ἀφείλομην ἐκεῖνον σε πρὸς βίαν. ΘΑ. Πως οὖν ἐστι ὕπερ γης, καὶ ου κάτα χθόνος; ΑΠ. Ἀμείψας δαμάρτα, μέτα ἣν σὺ νυν ἥκεις. ΘΑ. Καὶ ἀπάξομαι γε ὕπο νέρτεραν χθόνα. ΑΠ. Λάβων ἴθι· γὰρ οὐκ οἶδα εἰ αν πεισαίμι σε; ΘΑ. Κτείνειν ὃν αν χρῇ; Γὰρ τοῦτο τετάγμεθα. ΑΠ. Οὐκ· ἀλλα ἐμβαλειν θάνατον τοις μελλοῦσι. ΘΑ. Γε ἔχω λόγον σέθεν, καὶ προθύμιαν. ΑΠ. Ἐστι οὖν ὅπως Ἀλκηστις μόλοι εἰς γήρας; ΘΑ. Οὐκ ἔστι· δόκει καὶ ἐμε τερπέσθαι τίμαις. ΑΠ. Αν οὔτοι γε λάβοις πλέον η μίαν ψύχην.

TRANSLATION.

APOLLO. It is habitual to me ever to bear it. DEATH. Yes—and contrary-to-justice, to aid these mansions.

APOLLO. For I am afflicted at the misfortunes of a man who is dear to me. DEATH. And wilt thou debar me of this second dead?

APOLLO. But neither took I him from thee by force— DEATH. How then is he above ground, and not beneath the earth?

APOLLO. Having in his stead given his wife, after whom thou art now come. DEATH. And I will bear her off, too, to the land below!

APOLLO. Taking her, begone: for I do not know whether I can persuade thee—DEATH.—to slay him whom I ought? For this were we commanded.

APOLLO. No: but to scatter death on those about to die!

DEATH. Yes, I comprehend thy discourse, and drift.

APOLLO. Is it possible then that Alcéstis can arrive at old-age?

DEATH. [Denyingly.] It is not: consider that I, likewise, am delighted with my due honors.

APOLLO. Thou canst no how, at all events, take more than one life!

---

40. ξύνηθες ἐμοὶ, *it is usual* or *customary for me*, i. e., *it is my manner*. Apóllo generally carried his bow in his hand, and upon no occasion did he appear without this weapon: in confirmation of it Monk very aptly quotes, 'núnquàm húmero posíturus árcum.' Hor. Carm. III. iv. 60.

43. νοσφιεῖς με; *wilt thou sever me from* or *wilt cause me to be destitute of?*

45. Monk has followed Aldus. Lascar has χθονὸς κάτω :—Musgrave, κάτω χθονός.

47. νερτέραν ὑπὸ χθόνα,—literally, *under the nether earth:*—so in the Hércules In furiate, verse 335, we find ἥξω πρὸς ὑμᾶς, νερτέρα δώσων χθονί.

48. Some of the learned have objected to ἂν in this verse, proposing ἄρ' as an amendment, but unnecessarily.

49. The common lection is χρὴν, badly: Schaefer restored χρῇ.

ΘΑ. Νέων φθινόντων, μεῖζον ἄρνυμαι κλέος.　55　∪-|∪-‖--|∪-‖∪-|∪∪
ΑΠ. Κἂν γραῦς ὄληται, πλουσίως ταφήσεται.　--|∪-‖--|∪-‖∪-|∪∪
ΘΑ. Πρὸς τῶν ἐχόντων, Φοῖβε, τὸν νόμον τίθης.　--|∪-‖--|∪-‖∪-|∪-
ΑΠ. Πῶς εἶπας; Ἀλλ᾽ ἦ καὶ σοφὸς λέληθας ὤν;　--|∪-‖--|∪-‖∪-|∪-
ΘΑ. Ὠνοῖντ᾽ ἂν, οἷς πάρεστι, γηραιοὺς θανεῖν.　--|∪-‖∪-|∪-‖--|∪-
ΑΠ. Οὔκουν δοκεῖ σοι τήνδε μοι δοῦναι χάριν;　60　--|∪-‖--|∪-‖--|∪∪
ΘΑ. Οὐ δῆτ᾽· ἐπίστασαι δὲ τοὺς ἐμοὺς τρόπους.　--|∪-‖∪-|∪-‖∪-|∪-
ΑΠ. Ἐχθροὺς γε θνητοῖς, καὶ θεοῖς στυγουμένους.　--|∪-‖--|∪-‖∪-|∪-
ΘΑ. Οὐκ ἂν δύναιο πάντ᾽ ἔχειν, ἃ μή σε δεῖ.　--|∪-‖∪-|∪-‖∪-|∪-
ΑΠ. Ἦ μὴν σὺ παύσει, καίπερ ὠμὸς ὢν ἄγαν·　--|∪-‖--|∪-‖∪-|∪-
τοῖος Φέρητος εἶσι πρὸς δόμους ἀνήρ,　65　∪-|∪-‖∪-|∪-‖∪-|∪-
Εὐρυσθέως πέμψαντος ἵππειον μέτα　--|∪-‖--|∪-‖--|∪∪
ὄχημα Θρήκης ἐκ τόπων δυσχειμέρων,　∪-|∪-‖∪-|∪-‖∪-|∪∪
ὃς δὴ, ξενωθεὶς τοῖσδ᾽ ἐν Ἀδμήτου δόμοις,　--|∪-‖--|∪-‖--|∪-
βίᾳ γυναῖκα τήνδε σ᾽ ἐξαιρήσεται·　∪-|∪-‖∪-|∪-‖∪-|∪-
κοὔθ᾽ ἡ παρ᾽ ἡμῶν σοι γενήσεται χάρις,　70　--|∪-‖--|∪-‖∪-|∪∪
δράσεις θ᾽ ὁμοίως ταῦτ᾽, ἀπεχθήσει τ᾽ ἐμοί.　--|∪-‖--|∪-‖--|∪-

---

THE ORDER, AND ENGLISH ACCENTUATION.

ΘΑ. Νέων φθινόντων, ἄρνυμαι μεῖζον κλέος. ΑΠ. Καὶ ἂν ὄληται γραῦς, πλούσιως ταφήσεται. ΘΑ. Τίθης τον νόμον, Φοῖβε, προς των ἐχόντων. ΑΠ. Πως εἶπας; Ἀλλα ἦ λέληθας ων και σόφος; ΘΑ. Οἷς πάρεστι αν ὠνοίντο θανειν γηραίους. ΑΠ. Οὔκουν δόκει σοι δοῦναι μοι τήνδε χάριν; ΘΑ. Οὐ δῆτα· δὲ ἐπίστασαι τους ἐμους τρόπους. ΑΠ. Ἐχθρους γε θνητοῖς, και στυγούμενους θέοις. ΘΑ. Οὐκ αν δυναιο ἐχειν πάντα, ἃ μη δει σε. ΑΠ. Ἦ μην συ παύσει, καίπερ ων ἀγαν ὠμος· τοῖος ἀνηρ εἰσι προς δόμους Φερητος, Εὐρύσθεως πεμψαντος μέτα ἱππειον ὄχημα ἐκ δυσχειμερων τόπων Θρηκης, ὃς δη, ξενωθεις ἐν τοῖσδε δόμοις Ἀδμήτου, βίᾳ ἐξαιρήσεται τήνδε γυναῖκα σε· και οὔτε γενήσεται ἡ χάρις σοι πάρα ἡμων, τε ὁμοίως δράσεις ταῦτα, τε ἀπεχθήσει ἐμοι.

TRANSLATION.

Death. When the young die, I reap the greater glory. Apollo. And if she die old, she will be sumptuously entombed!

Death. Thou layest down the law, Phoébus, in favor of the rich! Apollo. How didst thou say? But forgattest thou thyself, being the while witty? Death. Those, who have the means, would purchase to die old! Apollo. Doth it then seem good unto thee to grant me this favor?

Death. No, in troth: and thou knowest my ways! Apollo. Hostile at least to mortals, and detested by the Gods!

Death. Thou canst not have all things, which thou oughtest not!

Apollo. [*Predictingly.*] Yet assuredly thou wilt relax, although thou art mighty stubborn: such a man will come to the house of Phérës, Eurýstheus having sent him after a chariot of horses from the wintry regions of Thrace, who in fact, after being-received-a-guest in this house of Admétus, shall by force take this woman away from thee: and there will not be any obligation to thee from us,—but nevertheless thou wilt do this, and wilt be hated by me. [*Exit Apóllo displeased.*]

56. πλουσίως ταφήσεται, *she will be richly entombed,*—alluding to the custom of interring the aged with greater magnificence and pomp than the young.

57. τῶν ἐχόντων, those possessing, understand χρήματα, *riches* or *wealth.*

59. οἷς πάρεστι, *to whom there is present,* understand χρήματα, *wealth.* In this line for ὠνοῖντ᾽, Aldus and his followers have

ὄνοιντ᾽,—which some indeed negligently render as if written ὄναιντ᾽.

64. ἦ μὴν σὺ παύσει, *thou wilt nevertheless stop short—thou wilt give over or desist—thou wilt cease yet.*

66-67. ἵππειον ὄχημα, literally, *a horse chariot,* that is, *a chariot and its horses,* or rather, *the chariot horses:* namely, those of Díomede, king of Thrace.

ΘΑ. Πόλλ' ἂν σὺ λέξας οὐδὲν ἂν πλέον λάβοις. |- -|◡ -||- -|◡ -||◡ -|◡ -

Ἢδ' οὖν γυνὴ κάτεισιν εἰς Ἀίδου δόμους· |- -|◡ -||◡ -|◡ -||- -|◡ -

στείχω δ' ἐπ' αὐτὴν, ὡς κατάρξωμαι ξίφει· |- -|◡ -||- -|◡ -||- -|◡ -

ἱερὸς γὰρ οὗτος τῶν κατὰ χθονὸς θεῶν,   75   ◡◡ -|◡ -||- -|◡ -||◡ -|◡ -

ὅτου τόδ' ἔγχος κρατὸς ἁγνίσῃ τρίχα.   ◡ -|◡ -||- -|◡ -||◡ -|◡◡

ΧΟΡΟΣ.

ΗΜΙΧ. Α'. Τί ποθ' ἡσυχία πρόσθε μελάθρων;   ◡◡ -|◡◡ -||- ◡◡|- -

Τί σεσίγηται δόμος Ἀδμήτου;   ◡◡ -|- -||◡◡ -|- -

ΗΜΙΧ. Β'. Ἀλλ' οὐδὲ φίλων τις πέλας· οὐδείς,   - -|◡◡ -||- ◡◡|- -

ὅστις ἂν εἴποι πότερον φθιμένην   80   - ◡◡|- -||◡◡ -|◡◡ -

βασίλειαν χρὴ πενθεῖν, ἢ ζῶσ'   ◡◡ -|- -||- -|- -

ἔτι φῶς τόδε λεύσσει Πελίου παῖς   ◡◡ -|◡◡ -||- ◡◡|- -

Ἄλκηστις, ἐμοὶ πᾶσί τ' ἀρίστη   - -|◡◡ -||- ◡◡|- -

δόξασα γυνὴ   - -|◡◡ -

πόσιν εἰς αὐτῆς γεγενῆσθαι;   85   ◡◡ -|- -||◡◡ -|◡ *

THE ORDER, AND ENGLISH ACCENTUATION.

ΘΑ. Πόλλα αν συ λέξας, αν λάβοις οὐδεν πλέον. Ἢδε γύνη οὐν κατείσι εἰς δόμους Ἀίδου· δε στείχω ἐπι αὐτην, ὡς κατάρξωμαι ξίφει· γαρ ἱερος οὗτος των θέων κάτα χθόνος, τρίχα κράτος ὅτου τόδε ἔγχος ἅγνισῃ. ΗΜΙΧ. Α'. Τι πότε ἡσυχία πρόσθε μελάθρων; Τι δόμος Ἀδμήτου σεσιγήται; ΗΜΙΧ. Β'. Ἀλλα οὐδε τις φίλων πέλας· οὐδεις, ὅστις αν εἴποι πότερον χρη πένθειν φθίμενην βασιλείαν, η Ἀλκήστις, παις Πέλιου, ἔτι ζῶσα λεύσσει τόδε φως, δοξάσα ἐμοι τε πάσι γεγενήσθαι ἀρίστη γύνη εἰς πόσιν αὐτης.

TRANSLATION.

DEATH. [*Sneeringly.*] Much as thou hast said, thou wilt gain nought the more! This woman, then, shall descend to the mansions of Plúto: and I am advancing on her, that I may begin the rites with my sword; for sacred is he to the Gods beneath the Earth, the hair of whose head this blade hath consecrated. [*Exit Death,—proceeding with determined step in behind the royal mansion.*]

1. SEMICHORUS. [*Entering from the left of the stage, the second from the right.*] Why ever this stilness before the palace? Why is the house of Admétus hushed-in-silence?

2. SEMICHORUS. But there is not any one of friends near: nobody who can tell us whether we have to deplore the departed queen, or whether Alcéstis, daughter of Pélias, being still alive views the light; having appeared to me and to all, to have been the best of wives to her husband!

---

72. Wakefield conjectured πόλλ' ἂν σὺ λέξαις, *multa tamétsi tu díxeris*, a mode of speech utterly foreign to the Greeks!

73. The vulgate lection here is ἢ δ' οὖν. Blomfield would rather have ἢ γ' οὖν.

74. κατάρξωμαι, that is, κατάρξωμαι τοῦ ἱερόυ, *sácra auspicábor, I will begin the business of consecration*,—by cutting off Alcéstis's hair in front: this hair was afterwards thrown on the blazing fire of the altar, a first and most acceptable offering to the powers below.

75. ἱερὸς τῶν θεῶν, literally, *sacred of the Gods*, i. e., *their holy property*.

76. For ἁγνίσῃ almost all have ἁγνίσει.

77. Monk has, in my opinion, display-

ed great want of judgment in prefixing ΗΜΙΧ. Α', instead of ΧΟ. to this verse on the simple recommendation of Barnes; and still more, in his assignment of person in Στροφὴ α'. I have retained Monk's allotment of character throughout, but my ear would not allow me to adopt his supposed emendation πρόσθεν for πρόσθε, in this line, a mark of vitiated taste and of fondness of innovation—as glaring as his ἄχθος μέτριον, verse 905, below.

80. MSS. and editions have ἂν ἐνέποι.

81. Aldus's reading and that of all others, except Lascar and Matthíæ, is τὴν βασίλειαν, with the omission of τόδε in the next line,—but badly.

ΧΟ. Κλύει τις ἢ στεναγμὸν, ἢ   [Στροφὴ α'.] ‿ -|‿ -‖‿ -|‿ -   α'
χερῶν κτύπον κατὰ στέγας;   ‿ -|‿ -‖‿ -|‿ -   β'
ἢ γόον, ὡς πεπραγμένων;   -‿‿ -‖‿ -|‿ -   γ'
Ὀυ μὰν, ὀυ δέ τις ἀμφιπόλων   --|‿ ‿‿|- ‿‿|-   δ'
στατίζεται ἀμφὶ πύλας.   90   ‿ -|‿ -‖‿ ‿‿ -   ε'
Ἐι γὰρ μετακύμιος ἄτας,   --|‿ -‖‿ - ‿ -‖|-   ζ'
ὦ Παιὰν, φανείης.   - - - ‿|: - -   η'

ΗΜΙΧ. Α'. Ὀύ τ' ἂν φθιμένης γ' ἐσιώπων·   - -|‿ ‿ -‖‿ ‿ -|- *
ὀυ γὰρ δὴ φροῦδός γ' ἐξ ὀίκων—   - -|- -‖|- -|: -
ΗΜΙΧ. Β'. Πόθεν; Ὀυκ ἀυχῶ. Τί σε θαρσύνει; 95   ‿ ‿ -|- -‖‿ ‿ -|-
ΗΜΙΧ. Α'. Πῶς ἂν ἔρημον τάφον Ἀδμητος   - ‿‿|- -‖‿ ‿ -|- -
κεδνῆς ἂν ἔπραξε γυναικός;   - -|‿ ‿ -‖‿ ‿ -|‿ *

ΧΟ. Πυλᾶν πάροιθε δ' ὀυχ ὁρῶ   [Ἀντιστρ. α'.] ‿ -|‿ -‖‿ -|‿ -   α'
πηγαῖον, ὡς νομίζεται,   - -|‿ -‖‿ -|‿ ‿   β'
χέρνιβ', ἐπὶ φθιτᾶν πύλαις·   100   -‿‿ -‖‿ -|‿ -   γ'
χαῖτα τ' ὀύτις ἐπὶ προθύροις   - -|- ‿‿|- ‿‿|-   δ'
τομαῖος, ἃ δὴ νεκύων   ‿ -|‿ -‖‿ ‿ ‿ -   ε'
πένθει πίτνει· ὀυ νεολαίᾳ   - -|‿ -‖‿ ‿ ‿ -‖|-   ζ'
δουπεῖ χεὶρ γυναικῶν.   - - - ‿‖|- -   η'

THE ORDER, AND ENGLISH ACCENTUATION.

ΧΟ. Κλύει τις η στεναγμον, η κτυπον χέρων κάτα στέγας, η γόον, ὡς πεπράγμενων; Ου μαν, δε ουτις αμφίπολων στατίζεται ἀμφι πύλας. Ω Παίαν, γαρ ει φανείης μετακύμιος ἀτας· ΗΜΙΧ. Α'. Ου τοι γε αν εσιώπων φθίμενης· γαρ γε φροῦδος ου δη εξ ὀίκων—ΗΜΙΧ. Β'. Πόθεν; Ουκ αύχω. Τι θαρσύνει σε; ΗΜΙΧ. Α'. Πως αν Αδμητος αν επράξε ερημον τάφον κέδνης γυναικος; ΧΟ. Δε ουκ ὁρω παροίθε πύλαν πηγαιον χέρνιϐα, ὡς νομίζεται επι πύλαις φθίτων τε επι πρόθυροις ουτις τομαιος χαιτα, ἁ δη π.τνει πένθει νέκυων χειρ γυναικων ου δουπει νεολαίᾳ.

TRANSLATION.

Chorus. Hears any-one either a wailing—or the beating of hands in the palace,—or lamentation, as though the event-had-taken-place? [*Responsively.*] No, indeed; nor is any of the servants stationed about the gates! [*With fervour.*] O Apollo,—for I wish that thou wouldest appear amidst the waves of this calamity. 1. Semichorus. They would no how, at-least, be silent, were she dead:—for certainly the corpse is not yet gone from the house. 2. Semichorus. Whence this surmise? I presume not *to entertain it?* What emboldens thee *to think so?* 1. Semichorus. How could Admétus have made a private funeral of his so excellent consort?—Chorus. But I see not before the gates the spring-water bath—as is the custom at the gates of the dead:—and in the porches there is no shorn hair, which generally falls in grief for the deceased:—the hands of women sound not for the youthful-bride!

86-7-8. In most editions these three verses constitute two trimeter iambics, with ἢ Θρῆνον for ἢ γόον. In MSS. also we find HMIX. prefixed to verses 86 and 89. For χερῶν Lascar has χερὸς,—and for γόον, Aldus, and MSS. partially, have γόων.

87. Monk has κύτπον,—by an error at press. In v. 89, he has ὀυ μὰν ὀυδέ τις—

94. After ὀίκων some MSS. have νέκυς,

which Monk incloses in brackets. I have omitted it. Musgrave conjectured φροῦδος γὰρ δὴ νέκυς ἐξ ὀίκων—and Matthiæ, γὰρ δὴ φροῦδος νέκυς ἐξ ὀίκων, carrying ὀυ back to the preceding verse.

100. χέρνιψ hic est vas illud fictile (ὄστρακον) aquâ lustráli plénum, quod stábat ánte aédes—in quibus exponerétur mórtuus: ἀρθάνιον vocabátur. Monk.

c

ΗΜΙΧ. Α΄. Καὶ μὴν τόδε κύριον ἦμαρ—   105 | - -|◡ ◡ -||◡ ◡ -|◡ *
ΗΜΙΧ. Β΄. Τί τόδ᾽ αὐδᾷς ; | ◡ ◡ -|-
ΗΜΙΧ. Α΄.—ᾧ χρῆν σφε μολεῖν κατὰ γαίας. | - -|◡ ◡ -||◡ ◡ -|- *
ΗΜΙΧ. Β΄.᾽Εθιγες ψυχῆς, ἔθιγες δὲ φρενῶν. | ◡ ◡ -|-||◡ ◡ -|◡ ◡ -
Χρὴ, τῶν ἀγαθῶν διακναιομένων, | - -|◡ ◡ -||◡ ◡ -|◡ ◡ -
πενθεῖν ὅστις   110 | - -|- -
χρηστὸς ἀπ᾽ ἀρχῆς νενόμισται. | -◡ ◡ -|- -||◡ ◡ -|◡ *

ΧΟ. ᾽Αλλ᾽ οὐδὲ ναυκληρίαν   [Στροφὴ β΄.] | - -|◡ -||- ◡|-   α΄
ἔσθ᾽ ὅποι τις αἴας | - ◡|- ◡||- ·   β΄
στείλας, ἢ Λυκίαν, | - -|◡ ◡ -|-   γ΄
εἴτ᾽ ἐπὶ τὰς ἀνύδρους   115 | - ◡ ◡|-◡ ◡|-   δ΄
᾽Αμμωνίδας ἕδρας, | - -|◡ ◡ -|-   ε΄
δυστάνου παραλῦσαι | ···-|◡ ◡ -|-   ζ΄
ψυχὰν, μόρος γὰρ ἀπότομος | - -|◡ -||◡ ◡ ◡|◡ ◡   η΄
πλάθει, θεῶν δ᾽ ἐπ᾽ ἐσχάραις; | - -|◡ -||◡ -|◡ -   θ΄
οὐκ ἔχω 'πὶ   120 | - ◡|- ◡   ι΄
τίνα μηλοθυτᾶν πορευθῶ. | ◡ ◡ -|◡ ◡ -||◡ -|-   κ΄

THE ORDER, AND ENGLISH ACCENTUATION.

ΗΜΙΧ. Α΄. Καὶ μὴν τόδε κύριον ἦμαρ—ΗΜΙΧ. Β΄. Τί τόδε αὐδᾷς ; ΗΜΙΧ. Α΄.—ᾧ χρην σφε μόλειν κάτα γαίας. ΗΜΙΧ. Β΄. ᾽Εθιγες ψύχης, δε ἔθιγες φρένων. Πένθειν, των ἀγαθων διακναιόμενων, χρη ὅστις νενόμισται χρήστος ἀπο ἀρχης. ΧΟ. ᾽Αλλα οὐδὲ ἐστι αἴας, ὅποι, τις στείλας ναυκλήριαν, η ἐπι Λύκιαν, εἴτε τας ἀνύδρους ᾽Αμμωνίδας ἕδρας, παραλῦσαι ψύχαν δυστάνου, γαρ ἀπότομος μόρος πλάθει, δε οὐκ ἔχω ἐπι τίνα μηλόθυταν ἐπι ἐσχάραις θεῶν πορεύθω.

TRANSLATION.

1. SEMICHORUS. And yet this is the appointed day—
2. SEMICHORUS. [*Interruptingly.*] What is that thou sayest?
1. SEMICHORUS.—in which she must go beneath the Earth!
2. SEMICHORUS. [*With great pathos.*] Thou hast touched my soul; ay, thou hast touched my heart. To mourn, when the good are afflicted, is befitting in him who from the beginning has been accounted good!

CHORUS. But there is not on the Earth any where, to which, one having sent naval-equipment,—either unto Lýcia, or to the thirsty site of Ammon's fane,—can redeem the life of the unhappy woman; for abrupt fate is approaching,—and I know not unto what one of those that sacrifice at the altars of the Gods I can go!

105. Aldus and most others have καὶ μὴν τόδε δὴ κύριον ἦμαρ in this verse, and καὶ τί τόδ᾽ αὐδᾷς ; in the next: on which reading Monk says, "δὴ et καὶ manifésto sunt interpoláta—quo ad similitúdinem legítimi systématis versículi cogeréntur."

109. The Scholiast explained διακναιομένων by φθειρομένων. Hesýchius read διακναίόμενον in the accusative singular, and gave διαπονούμενον as the signification.

114. All MSS. have Λυκίας. Monk's apology for Λυκίαν, is:—" Λυκίαν flagitáre vidétur constrúctio :—præpositio sémel tántùm, et in áltero senténtiæ mémbro, exprímitur."

115—16. τὰς ἀνύδρους ᾽Αμμωνίδας ἕδρας,

literally, *the arid Ammonian seats,* that is, *the temple of Júpiter Ammon in the parched and thirsty deserts of Líbya,* in Africa. Júpiter Ammon had another temple and oraclé in Æthiópia. The vulgate lection here is ᾽Αμμωνίαδας ἕδρας.

117. For παραλῦσαι most editions have παραλύσαι. Wakefield conjectured παραλύσει,—but, as Monk observes, the optative is the only true construction.

118. Vúlgo ἄποτμος,—quod, cùm métro antistróphico párùm quádret, felícitèr córrigit Blomfiéldius ἀπότομος.—Aptíssimè dícitur Alcéstidis fátum *prærúptum:* infrà vv. 1003-04, de *necessitáte,* οὐδέ τις ἀποτόμου λήματός ἐστιν αἰδώς. Μοnk.

Μόνος δ', ἂν, εἰ φῶς τόδ' ἦν   ['Αντιστρ. β'.]   ⏑–|⏑–||–⏑|–   α'
ὄμμασιν δεδορκὼς   –⏑|–⏑||––   β'
Φοίβου παῖς, προλιποῦσ'   ––|–⏑⏑|–   γ'
ἦλθεν ἕδρας σκοτίους   125   –⏑⏑|–⏑⏑|–   δ'
'Αἰδαό τε πύλας'   ––|–⏑⏑|–   ε'
δμαθέντας γὰρ ἀνίστη,   ––|–⏑⏑|––   ζ'
πρὶν αὐτὸν εἷλε Διόβολον   ⏑–|⏑–||⏑⏑⏑|⏑⏑   η'
πλᾶκτρον πυρὸς κεραυνίου.   ––|⏑–||⏑–|⏑–   Ϟ'
Νῦν δὲ τίν' ἔτι   130   –⏑|⏑⏑⏑   ι'
βίου ἐλπίδα προσδέχωμαι;   ⏑⏑–|⏑⏑–||⏑–|⏑   κ'

Πάντα γὰρ ἤδη τετέλεσται   –⏑⏑|––||⏑⏑–|⏑–*
βασιλεῦσιν,   ⏑⏑–|⏑–*
πάντων δὲ θεῶν ἐπὶ βώμοις   ––|⏑⏑⏑–||⏑⏑–|–*
αἱμόῤῥαντοι θυσίαι πλήρεις,   135   ––|––||⏑⏑–|––
οὐδ' ἔστι κακῶν ἄκος οὐδέν.   ––|⏑⏑–||⏑⏑–|⏑–*
'Αλλ' ἤδ' ὀπαδῶν ἐκ δόμων τις ἔρχεται   ––|⏑–||––|⏑–||⏑–|⏑⏑
δακρυῤῥοοῦσα· τίνα τύχην ἀκούσομαι;   ⏑–|⏑–||⏑⏑⏑|⏑–||⏑–|⏑⏑

THE ORDER, AND ENGLISH ACCENTUATION.

Δε μόνος ει παις Φοίβου ην δεδόρκως ὄμμασι τόδε φως, αν ἦλθε, προλιποῦσα σκότιους ἕδρας τε πύλας Αἰδαο· γαρ ανίστη δμαθέντας, πριν πλᾶκτρον κεραυνίου πύρος Διόβολον εἷλε αὐτον. Δε νυν τίνα ἐλπιδα βίου ετι προσδεχώμαι; Γαρ ἤδη πάντα τετέλεσται βασιλεῦσι, δε ἐπι βώμοις πάντων θέων αἱμορράντοι θύσιαι πλήρεις, οὐδε ἐστι οὐδεν ἀκος κάκων. Ἀλλα ἤδε ἔρχεται τις οπάδων εκ δόμων δακρυρροούσα· τίνα τύχην ακούσομαι;

TRANSLATION.

Because only if the son of Phoébus were beholding with his eyes the light, could she come,—having left the darksome habitations and the portals of Plúto:—for he up-raised the dead, before that the impact of the lightning's fire, striking him from Júpiter, cut him off.

But now what hope of life can I any longer entertain? For already has every thing been done by the king; and at the altars of all the Gods the bleeding victims are abundant—nor is there any remedy for these evils! [*Looking up.*] But here comes one of the female attendants from out the house, weeping! [*Anxiously.*] What event shall I hear?

124. Φοίβου παῖς, *the son of Apóllo,* (viz. *Æsculápius,*) a skilful physician, who, it was said, restored many persons to life; for which Júpiter, at the instance of Plúto, struck him dead with the thunder.

125. Monk suspected, and I think not without reason, that ἦλθεν should be ἦλθ' ἄν. He appropriately quotes verse 926 below,—where the syntax requires συνέσχ' ἄν, although all MSS. have συνέσχεν. He hints too that σκοτίας might perhaps be more correct than σκοτίους.

126. Aldus and most others have "Αδα τε. Monk writes as follows: " crédo Eurípidem sumpsísse Homéricam fórmam, Il. ψ'. 71, πύλας 'Αΐδαο περήσω. Cérte ab Iónicâ genitivórum terminatióne in mélicis non usquequáque abstinuère Trági-

ci. Oréstis 812, et Eléctræ, 465, ἀελίοιο: Tróadum 838, Πριάμοιο, &c. Sin hoc displiceat, légere póssis 'Αΐδα τε πύλας, et in stróphico, ver. 116, "Αμμωνος ἕδρας, quod támen vidétur recépto lónge detérius."

129. πλᾶκτρον vel πλῆκτρον, *pléctrum,* is properly the quill wherewith musicians were wont to strike the strings of their instruments; but in a wider sense it signifies whatever inflicts a blow or stroke. See Morell's Thesaúrus, revised and enlarged by Maltby.

130. Of this line and the next we find various readings. Aldus has νῦν δὲ τίνα βίου ἐλπίδα προσδέχομαι;

133. βασιλεῦσι,—the plural for the singular, as in other instances. Monk cites κοιρᾶνοις, verse 216, below: but inaptly.

Πενθεῖν μὲν, εἴ τι δεσπόταισι τυγχάνει,　　　| - - | ◡ - || ◡ - | ◡ - || ◡ - | ◡ -

ξυγγνωστόν· εἰ δ' ἔτ' ἐστὶν ἔμψυχος γυνή,　140　| - - | ◡ - || ◡ - | ◡ - || - - | ◡ -

εἴτ' οὖν ὄλωλεν, εἰδέναι βουλοίμεθ' ἄν.　　　| - - | ◡ - || ◡ - | ◡ - || - - | ◡ ◡

ΘΕΡΑΠΑΙΝΑ.

Καὶ ζῶσαν εἰπεῖν καὶ θανοῦσαν ἔστι σοι.　　　| - - | ◡ - || - - | ◡ - || ◡ - | ◡ -

ΧΟ. Καὶ πῶς ἂν αὐτὸς κατθάνοι τε καὶ βλέποι;　| - - | ◡ - || - - | ◡ - || ◡ - | ◡ -

ΘΕ. Ἤδη προνωπής ἐστι, καὶ ψυχορραγεῖ.　　　| - - | ◡ - || - - | ◡ - || - - | ◡ -

ΧΟ. Ὦ τλῆμον, οἵας οἷος ὢν ἁμαρτάνεις.　145　| - - | ◡ - || - - | ◡ - || ◡ - | ◡ -

ΘΕ. Οὔπω τόδ' οἶδε δεσπότης, πρὶν ἂν πάθη.　　| - - | ◡ - || ◡ - | ◡ - || ◡ - | ◡ -

ΧΟ. Ἐλπὶς μὲν οὐκέτ' ἔστι σώσασθαι βίον;　　| - - | ◡ - || ◡ - | ◡ - || - - | ◡ ◡

ΘΕ. Πεπρωμένη γὰρ ἡμέρα βιάζεται.　　　　　| ◡ - | ◡ - || ◡ - | ◡ - || ◡ - | ◡ ◡

ΧΟ. Οὔκουν ἐπ' αὐτῇ πράσσεται τὰ πρόσφορα;　| - - | ◡ - || - - | ◡ - || ◡ - | ◡ ◡

ΘΕ. Κόσμος γ' ἕτοιμος, ᾧ σφε συνθάψει πόσις.　150　| - - | ◡ - || ◡ - | ◡ - || - - | ◡ ◡

ΧΟ. Ἴστω νυν εὐκλεής τε κατθανουμένη,　　　| - - | ◡ - | ' ◡ - | ◡ - || ◡ - | ◡ -

γυνή τ' ἀρίστη τῶν ὑφ' ἡλίῳ μακρῷ.　　　　| ◡ - | ◡ - || - - | ◡ - || ◡ - | ◡ -

---

THE ORDER, AND ENGLISH ACCENTUATION.

Πένθειν μεν, ει τι τύγχανει δεσποταίσι, ξυγγνώστον· δε ει γύνη έστι έτι εμψύχος, είτε ουν ολώλε, αν βουλοίμεθα ειδέναι. ΘΕ. Έστι σοι ειπειν και ζώσαν και θανούσαν. ΧΟ. Και πως αν ὁ αύτος τε κάτθανοι και βλέποι. ΘΕ. Έστι ήδη προνώπης, και ψυχόρραγει. ΧΟ. Ω τλήμον, ων ὁιος ὁιας ἁμάρτανε.ς. ΘΕ. Δέσποτης ούπω οιδε τόδε, πριν αν πάθη. ΧΟ. Έστι μεν ουκετι ελπις σωσάσθαι βίον; ΘΕ. Γαρ πεπρώμενη ημερα βιάζεται. ΧΟ. Ούκουν τα πρόσφορα πράσσεται επι αύτη; ΘΕ. Κόσμος γε ετοίμος, ὦ πόσις συνθάψει σφε. ΧΟ. Ίστω νυν κατθανούμενη τε εύκλεης, τε μάκρω αρίστη γύνη των ύπο ήλιω.

TRANSLATION.

[Feelingly.] To weep in troth, if aught happens to our lords, is pardonable : but whether the lady be still alive, or whether indeed she has perished, we could wish to know!

FEMALE ΛTTENDANT. *[Entering—dejected and very sad.]* Thou mayest call her both living and dead!

CHORUS. And how can the same person be both dead and living?

FEMALE ATTENDANT. She is already at the very point of death,—and breathing her life away!

CHORUS. *[With pathos, in allusion to Admétus.]* Oh wretched man, being what sort thyself of what a wife art thou bereft!

FEMALE ATTENDANT. My master is not as yet sensible of that,—until he suffer! CHORUS. Is there indeed no longer any hope of preserving her life? FEMALE ATTENDANT. *[Denyingly.]* For the fated day assails her!

CHORUS. Are not then suitable preparations made for the event?

FEMALE ATTENDANT. Yes, the pomp is ready, wherewith her husband will inter her!

CHORUS. Let her know then that she will die both glorious, and by far the best woman of all under the sun!

---

143. Aldus and all the earliei editio s have αὐτός. Ελπειν, as Monk rightly observes, is here used for ζῆν, being in contrast with κατθανεῖν. So in the Troades, ὃν ταυτὸν, ὦ παῖ, τῷ βλέπειν τὸ κατθανεῖν.

144 πρ:νωπής, *mórti propínqua:*—yet in its strictest sense, this word would signify, " *mói tua jàm ex interióre aédium párte prodúcta, et in vestíbulo collocáta.*" Kuinoel gives the interpretation to be "*mo-*

ribúnda *vírium défectu, jàm córpore próno ad térram fértur.*"

147. Cùm displicéret σώσασθαι in hâc sententiâ, conjiciébam σάζεσθαι:—ídem fécit Blomfiéldius:—σώσεσθαι Marklándus:—hódiè támen vulgátum defendéndum árbitror. MONK.

149. For ούκουν, several MSS. and editions have ουκοὺν, badly.

152. τῶν ὑφ' ἡλίῳ, *of those under the sun.*

ΘΕ. Πῶς δ᾽ οὐκ ἀρίστη; Τίς δ᾽ ἐναντιώσεται;
Τί χρὴ γενέσθαι τὴν ὑπερθεθλημένην
γυναῖκα; Πῶς δ᾽ ἂν μᾶλλον ἐνδείξαιτό τις   155
πόσιν προτιμῶσ᾽, ἢ θέλουσ᾽ ὑπερθανεῖν;
Καὶ ταῦτα μὲν δὴ πᾶσ᾽ ἐπίσταται πόλις·
ἃ δ᾽ ἐν δόμοις ἔδρασε, θαυμάσει κλύων.
Ἐπεὶ γὰρ ᾔσθεθ᾽ ἡμέραν τὴν κυρίαν
ἥκουσαν, ὕδασι ποταμίοις λευκὸν χρόα   160
ἐλούσατ᾽, ἐκ δ᾽ ἑλοῦσα κεδρίνων δόμων
ἐσθῆτα κόσμον τ᾽, εὐπρεπῶς ἠσκήσατο·
καὶ στᾶσα πρόσθεν ἑστίας, κατηύξατο·
Δέσποιν᾽, ἐγὼ γὰρ ἔρχομαι κατὰ χθονὸς,
παινύστατόν σε προσπίτνουσ᾽ αἰτήσομαι,   165
τέκν᾽ ὀρφανεῦσαι τἀμά· καὶ τῷ μὲν φίλην
ξύζευξον ἄλοχον, τῇ δὲ γενναῖον πόσιν·

THE ORDER, AND ENGLISH ACCENTUATION.

ΘΕ. Δε πως ουκ αρίστη; Δε τις εναντιώσεται; Τι χρη την γυναικα γενέσθαι ὑπερθεθλήμενην; Δε πως αν τις μάλλον ενδειξαίτο προτιμώσα πόσιν, η θελούσα ὑπέρθανειν; Και ταύτα μεν δη πάσα πόλις επίσταται· δε α εδράσε εν δόμοις, θαυμασει κλύων. Γαρ επει ήσθετο την κύριαν ἡμεραν ήκουσαν, ελούσατο λευκον χρόα ποτάμιοις ὕδασι, δε ελούσα εκ κεδρινων δόμων εσθήτα τε κόσμον, ησκήσατο εύπρεπως· και στάσα πρόσθεν έστιας, κατηύξατο· Δεσποίνα, γαρ εγω έρχομαι κάτα χθόνος, προσπιτνούσα σε παινύστατον, αιτήσομαι ορφανεύσαι τά εμα τέκνα· και τω μεν ξυζεύ-ξον φίλην άλοχον, δε τη γενναίον πόσιν·

TRANSLATION.

FEMALE ATTENDANT. [*Sighing.*] And how not the best? But who will dispute it? What must the woman be who has excelled her? For how can any one give more ample proof of esteeming her husband, than by being willing to die for him? And these things, indeed, the whole city knoweth: but what she did in the house, thou wilt marvel on hearing.

For when she perceived that the destined day was come, she washed her delicate skin with water from the river; and having taken from her wardrobes of cedar a vesture and embellishment, she attired herself becomingly; and taking her station before the altar, she prayed thus:—

" *O Mistress, (for I am going below the Earth,) falling prostrate before thee for the last time of all, I will beseech thee to protect my orphan children; and to the one indeed join a loving wife, and unto the other a noble husband:*

---

153. τίς ἐναντιώσεται; *Who will contest or dispute it? Who will maintain the contrary? Who will oppose or gainsay it.*

154. Hæc vérba, lícet mínimè obscúra, némo intérpretum rectè cépit. Vértas, *What must the woman be who has surpassed her?* Virórum doctórum conjectúras síleo. MONK.

158. For θαυμάσει several copies have θαυμάσῃς, or else θαυμάσεις. "Sed," says Monk, "θαυμάζω futúrum hábet θαυμάσομαι, non θαυμάσω.—Múlta sunt vérba, quæ futúra formæ médiæ, núsquàm aútèm actívæ, ápud Atticos sáltèni, adscíscunt." Of this class he instances the following: ἀκούω, σιγῶ, σιωπῶ, ᾄδω, βοῶ, ἁμαρτάνω, θνήσκω, πίπτω, κλάω, πλέω, πνέω.

160—1. ὕδασι ποταμίοις λευκὸν χρόα ἐλούσατο, literally,—*she washed her white skin with river waters.* It is mentioned of Sócratès that just before he drank the poisonous juice of the hemlock, he washed himself: and this custom, as well as that of appearing in full dress, was, on the approach of sure death, extremely prevalent among the ancients.—Ἐκ κεδρίνων δόμων, *from cedar chests or closets.*

164. δέσποινα, *mistress,* viz. *the Goddess* Ἑστία or *Vésta,*—whose altar was in the innermost part of the house.

166. The Scholiast explains ὀρφανεῦσαι by ὀρφανοτροφήσαι.—The two children alluded to in this verse are, Eumélus and Perimédë, called also Perimélë.

μὴδ', ὥσπερ αὐτῶν ἡ τεκοῦσ' ἀπόλλυμαι,
θανεῖν ἀώρους παῖδας, ἀλλ' εὐδαίμονας
ἐκ γῆ πατρώᾳ τερπνὸν ἐκπλῆσαι βίον. 170
Πάντας δὲ βωμοὺς, οἳ κατ' Ἀδμήτου δόμους,
προσῆλθε, κἀξέστεψε, καὶ προσηύξατο,
πτόρθων ἀποσχίζουσα μυρσίνης φόβην,
ἄκλαυστος, ἀστένακτος, οὐδὲ τοὐπιὸν
κακὸν μεθίστη χρωτὸς εὐειδῆ φύσιν. 175
Κᾄπειτα θάλαμον εἰσπεσοῦσα, καὶ λέχος,
ἐνταῦθα δὴ 'δάκρυσε, καὶ λέγει τάδε·
Ὦ λέκτρον, ἔνθα παρθένει' ἔλυσ' ἐγὼ
κορεύματ' ἐκ τοῦδ' ἀνδρὸς, οὗ θνήσκω πέρι,
χαῖρ'· οὐ γὰρ ἐχθαίρω σ'· ἀπώλεσας δ' ἐμὲ 180
μόνην· προδοῦναι γάρ σ' ὀκνοῦσα, καὶ πόσιν,
θνήσκω· σὲ δ' ἄλλη τις γυνὴ κεκτήσεται,
σώφρων μὲν οὐχὶ μᾶλλον, εὐτυχὴς δ' ἴσως.

THE ORDER, AND ENGLISH ACCENTUATION.

μὴδε, ὥσπερ ἡ τεκοῦσα αὐτων ἀπόλλυμαι, παῖδας ἀώρους θανεῖν, ἀλλα εὐδαίμονας εν πατρώᾳ γῃ ἐκπλῆσαι τέρπνον βίον. Δε πάντας βώμους, οἱ κάτα δόμους Ἀδμήτου, προσῆλθε, καὶ ἐξεστέψε, καὶ προσηύξατο, ἀποσχιζούσα φόβην πτόρθων μύρσινης, ακλαύστος, αστένακτος, οὐδε το ἐπιον κάμον μεθίστη εὐειδη φύσιν χρώτος. Και ἐπείτα εἰσπεσοῦσα θάλαμον, καὶ λέχος, ἐνταῦθα δη ἐδάκρευσε, καὶ λέγει τάδε· Ὦ λέκτρον, ἔνθα ἐγὼ ἐλύσα παρθενέια κορεύματα ἐκ τοῦδε ἀνδρὸς, πέρι οὗ θνήσκω, χαῖρε· γὰρ οὐκ ἐχθαίρω σε· δε ἐμε μόνην ἀπώλεσας· γαρ οκνοῦσα προδοῦναι σε, καὶ πόσιν, θνήσκω· δε σε τις ἀλλη γύνη κεκτήσεται, μᾶλλον σώφρων μεν οὐχι, δε ἰσως εὐτύχης.

TRANSLATION.

nor, like as I their mother perish, let my children untimely die; but happy in their paternal land enable them to complete a joyous life."

And all the altars, which are in the house of Admétus, did she go unto and crown; and she prayed, tearing the leaves off from the boughs of myrtle, without-shedding-a-tear, without-uttering-a-groan; nor did the approaching calamity alter the beautiful complexion of her skin!

And afterwards having sped to her chamber, and her bed, she there at length wept, and speaks thus:—

" O bridal bed, whereon I loosed my virgin zone with this man for whom I die, farewell: for I hate thee not! but me alone hast thou undone: for loth to betray thee, and my husband, I die:—but thee will some other female possess,—more chaste indeed not, but peradventure more fortunate."

168. τεκοῦσα seems here usurped substantively, for μήτηρ,—else αὐτῶν should be αὐτοὺς,—the proper regimen of τίκτω being the accusative. In lieu of ἀπόλλυμαι, which Musgrave gives us on the authority of three MSS., the common lection is ἀπόλλυται.

170. For τερπνὸν ἐκπλῆσαι βίον, Wakefield edited τέρμιον' ἐκπλῆσαι βίον, badly.

173. All MSS. have μυρσινῶν φόβην, and yet too the Scholiast seems to have read μυρσίνης φόβην. In sacrificing to the dead it was customary to strip off leaves from boughs of myrtle, and to strew them about as a conciliatory offering.

174. ἄκλαυστος, ἀστένακτος, Monk renders, "flétibus et suspíriis cárens," and he adds, "álibi ἄκλαυστος est 'indeflétus': nótum est pléraque hújus géneris adjectíva dúplicem significatiónem admíttere.

177. Some contend for κἄλεγε in lieu of καὶ λέγει, disliking an aorist and a present tense coupled together, as ἐδάκρευσε and λέγει are in the verse before us:—yet many similar passages occur.

181. For μόνην Blomfield espouses μόνος, tu, thálame, sólus me perdidísti.—Elmsley understood ὀκνῶ here in the sense of αἰσχύνομαι. Monk, however, explains it by "invita sum—ánimus refúgit.

Κυνεῖ δὲ προσπίτνουσα· πᾶν δὲ δέμνιον
ὀφθαλμοτέγκτῳ δεύεται πλημμυρίδι.   185
Ἐπεὶ δὲ πολλῶν δακρύων εἶχεν κόρον,
στείχει προνωπὴς ἐκπεσοῦσα δεμνίων.
Καὶ πολλὰ θάλαμον ἐξιοῦσ᾽ ἐπεστράφη,
κἄῤῥιψεν αὑτὴν αὖθις ἐς κοίτην πάλιν.
Παῖδες δὲ, πέπλων μητρὸς ἐξηρτημένοι,   190
ἔκλαιον· ἡ δὲ, λαμβάνουσ᾽ ἐν ἀγκάλαις,
ἠσπάζετ᾽ ἄλλοτ᾽ ἄλλον, ὡς θανουμένη.
Πάντες δ᾽ ἔκλαιον οἰκέται κατὰ στέγας,
δέσποιναν οἰκτείροντες· ἡ δὲ δεξιὰν
προὔτειν᾽ ἑκάστῳ, κοὔτις ἦν οὕτω κακὸς,   195
ὃν οὐ προσεῖπε, καὶ προσεῤῥήθη πάλιν.
Τοιαῦτ᾽ ἐν οἴκοις ἐστὶν Ἀδμήτου κακά.
Καὶ κατθανών τ᾽ ἂν ὤλετ᾽· ἐκφυγὼν δ᾽ ἔχει
τοσοῦτον ἄλγος, οὗ ποτ᾽ οὐ λελήσεται.

THE ORDER, AND ENGLISH ACCENTUATION.

Δε προσπιτνουσα κυνει· δε παν δέμνιον δεύεται οφθαλμοτεγκτω πλημμυρίδι. Δε έπει είχε κόρον πόλλων δάκρυων στείχει προνωπης εκπεσούσα δέμνιων. Και πόλλα εξιούσα θάλαμον επέστραφη, και αύθις πάλιν εερίψε άυτην εις κοίτην. Δε παίδες, εξηρτήμενοι πέπλων μήτρος, εκλαίον· δε ή, λαμβανούσα εν αγκαλαις, ησπάζετο άλλον άλλοτε, ώς θανουμενη. Δε πάντες οικεται εκλαίον κάτα στέγας, οικτειρόντες δεσποίναν· δε ή προ-ετείνε δέξιαν εκάστω, και ουτις ην ούτω κάκος, ον ου προσείπε, και προσερρήθη πάλιν. Τοιαύτα έστι κάκα εν οίκοις Αδμήτου. Και κάτθανων τοι αν ώ-λετο· δε έκφυγων έχει τοσούτον άλγος, ου ούποτε λελήσεται.

TRANSLATION.

And falling upon it she kisses it: and the whole bed was soaked with the tide that flowed from her eyes. But when she had satiety of many tears, she proceeds hastily-forward, making-off from the couch.

And often after quitting the chamber did she return; and again and again she threw herself upon the bed.

And her children, clinging unto the garments of their mother, wept: and she, taking them in her arms, embraced them—first one, and then another, as being about to die!

And all the servants were weeping about the house, commiserating their mistress: and she to each one outstretched her hand,—and there was none so abject, whom she addressed not, and was answered in turn.

[*Sighing and sobbing.*] Such are the distresses in the house of Admétus! And had he died he would indeed have perished: but having escaped death, he has grief to that degree which he will never forget!

184. Wakefield suggested κυνεῖ for the κύνει of editions,—and δεύεται in the next verse for δεύετο. Porson quotes κυνεῖ and δεύεται, at verse 1138 of the Medéa.

185. ὀφθαλμοτέγκτῳ πλημμυρίδι, by inundation issuing from the eyes.

187. προνωπὴς, praéceps. This word was noticed at verse 144 above.

188. πολλὰ ἐπεστράφη—many a time returned she—often went she back.

189. In several MSS. and editions the reading is αὑτὴν, but most faultily:—αὖθις πάλιν, I have rendered " again and a-

gain," although simply "again" may be the strict meaning, πάλιν being added to strengthen αὖθις. Indeed we sometimes meet with αὖθις αὖ πάλιν or αὖ πάλιν αὖθις, where "often again" is implied.

191. Monk has ἔκλαον here, as well as in verse 193,—and he is consistent elsewhere, following Porson's newer Attic form. For my own part, whatever may be the derivation of κλαίω, I do like not to confound it with κλάω, frángo, mútilo.

199. Aldus here edited ὄυποτ᾽ ἐκλελήσεται, where ὄυποτε stands for οὗ ὄυποτε.

24 200. ΕΥΡΙΠΙΔΟΥ

ΧΟ. Ἦπου στενάζει τοῖσιδ᾽ Ἄδμητος κακοῖς, 200

ἐσθλῆς γυναικὸς εἰ στερηθῆναί σφε χρή;

ΘΕ. Κλαίει γ᾽, ἄκοιτιν ἐν χεροῖν φίλην ἔχων,

καὶ μὴ προδοῦναι λίσσεται, τἀμήχανα

ζητῶν· φθίνει γὰρ, καὶ μαραίνεται νόσῳ.

Παρειμένη δὲ χειρὸς ἄθλιον βάρος, 205

ὅμως δὲ, καίπερ σμικρὸν ἐμπνέουσ᾽ ἔτι,

βλέψαι πρὸς αὐγὰς βούλεται τὰς ἡλίου,

ὡς οὔποτ᾽ αὖθις, ἀλλὰ νῦν πανύστατον

ἀκτῖνα, κύκλον θ᾽ ἡλίου προσόψεται.

Ἀλλ᾽ εἶμι, καὶ σὴν ἀγγελῶ παρουσίαν· 210

οὐ γάρ τι πάντες εὖ φρονοῦσι κοιράνοις,

ὥστ᾽ ἐν κακοῖσιν εὐμενεῖς παρεστάναι·

σὺ δ᾽ εἶ παλαιὸς δεσπόταις ἐμοῖς φίλος.

THE ORDER, AND ENGLISH ACCENTUATION.

ΧΟ. Ἦπου Ἄδμητος στενάζει τοῖσιδε κάκοις, εἰ χρη σφε στερηθῆναι ἐσθλης γυναικος; ΘΕ. Κλαίει γε, ἔχων φίλην ἄκοιτιν εν χέροιν, και λίσσεται μη προδοῦναι, ζητων τα αμήχανα· γαρ φθίνει, και μαραίνεται νόσῳ. Δε παρειμενη ἄθλιον βάρος χείρος, δε ὅμως, καίπερ εμπνευουσα ἔτι σμίκρον, βούλεται βλέψαι προς τας αὐγας ἡλιου, ὡς οὔποτε αὖθις, ἀλλα νυν πανύστατον προσόψεται αντίνα τε κύκλον ἡλιου. Ἀλλα εἰμι, και ἄγγελω σην παρούσιαν· γαρ ου τι πάντες φρονοῦσι εὐ κοίρανοις, ὥστε εν κακοῖσι παρέστανα εὐμενεῖς· συ δε εἰ παλαιος φίλος ἐμοις δέσποταις.

TRANSLATION.

Chorus. Surely Admétus groans at these ills, if that he must be bereft of his excellent wife?

Female Attendant. Yes, he weeps,—holding his dear spouse in his arms; and he implores her not to leave him, asking impossibilities: for she droops, and is wasted away by sickness!

But fainting, a wretched burden on his arm, yet still, though breathing only feebly, she is fain to look upon the rays of the orb of day,—as never again, but now for the last time, about to behold the beam and face of the sun!

But I will go, and announce thy presence: for it is in nowise all who wish well to their lords,—so as in their afflictions to come kindly unto them :—thou, however, art of old a friend to my master. [*Exit Attendant, repairing into the palace.*]

200. Lascar, Aldus, and some others have τοῖσιν, and Musgrave, whom Monk has followed, τοῖσιδ᾽. I have always regarded this word as wrongly accented in editions,—forasmuch as the antepenult of no Greek word whatever can carry a circumflex. Barnes, from mere conjecture, gives us στενάξει᾽ οἶσιν.

202. For χεροῖν φίλην, Wakefield edited χεροῖν φίλαιν, but on no authority.

203. προδοῦναι, simpliciter "*deserere;*" úsu raríssimo, si crédimus Wakefiéldio : sed ídem plánè signíficat infrà, ver. 258, μὴ προδῷς:—et versu 285, μὴ τλῇς με προδοῦναι. Saepíssimè verténdum est, "*to be faithless to* or *to abandon,*"—ut iu hâc fábulâ, vv. 181, 301, 675, 1078. Monk.

204. Matthiæ's reading and punctua-

tion of this line and the next, are, ζητῶν· φθίνει γὰρ καὶ μαραίνεται νόσῳ παρειμένη γε, χειρὸς ἄθλιον βάρος. Elmsley was of opinion that a verse is wanting after βάρος, and in this sentiment Monk indeed appears to accord with him.

207. Instead of βλέψαι πρὸς αὐγὰς ἡλίου, we meet in several editions with κλέψαι προσαυγὰς ἡλίου, *to steal glances of the sun,* if προσαυγὴ be (which is questionable) a legitimate word. I have translated ἡλίου in this line, "*orb of day,*"—because the word "*sun*" occurs again so near.

208-9. These two lines, with προσόψομαι for προσόψεται, occur in the Hécuba, being of that play verses 411 and 412.

213. παλαιὸς φίλος, literally, *an olden* or *a veteran friend*—*a friend of long standing.*

ΧΟ. Ἰὼ Ζεῦ· τίς ἂν πᾶ πόρος κακῶν   [Στροφὴ α'.] ⏑ - - ⏑ -‖- ⏑ - ⏑ -   α'
γένοιτο, καὶ λύσις τύχας,   215 ⏑ -|⏑ -‖⏑ -|⏑ -   β'
ἃ πάρεστι κοιράνοις; Ἔξ-   -⏑|- ⏑‖- ⏑|- - -   γ'
εισί τις; Ἤ τεμῶ τρίχα,   - ⏑ ⏑ -‖⏑ -|⏑ ⏑   δ'
καὶ μέλανα στολμὸν πέπλων   - ⏑ ⏑ -‖- -|⏑ -   ε'
ἀμφιβαλώμεθ' ἤδη;   - ⏑ ⏑ -‖⏑ -|- -   ζ'
Δῆλα μὲν, φίλοι, δῆλά γ'· ἀλλ' ὅμως   220 - ⏑ - ⏑ -‖- ⏑ - ⏑ -   η'
θεοῖσιν εὐχώμεσθα, θεῶν   ⏑ -|⏑ -‖- -|⏑ -   θ'
γὰρ δύναμις μεγίστα.   - ⏑ ⏑ -‖⏑ -|-   ι'
Ὦ 'ναξ Παιὰν,   - - - -   κ'
ἐξεῦρε μηχανάν τιν' Ἀδμήτῳ κακῶν·   - -|⏑ -‖⏑ -|⏑ -‖- -|⏑ - λ'
πόριζε δὴ, πόριζε,   225 ⏑ -|⏑ -‖⏑ -|⏑   μ'
καὶ πάρος γὰρ τοῦδ' ἐφεῦρες·   - ⏑|- -|- ⏑|- ⏑   ν'
λυτήριος ἐκ θανάτου γενοῦ,   ⏑ -|⏑ ⏑ -‖⏑ ⏑ -|⏑ -   ξ'
φόνιόν τ' ἀπόπαυσον Ἀίδαν.   ⏑ ⏑ -|⏑ ⏑ -‖⏑ -|-   ο'

Παπαὶ φεῦ, παπαὶ φεῦ· ἰώ· ἰώ·   [Ἀντιστρ. α'.] ⏑ - - ⏑ -‖- ⏑ - ⏑ -   α'
ὦ παῖ Φέρητος, οἷ' ἔπρα-   230 - -|⏑ -‖⏑ -|⏑ -   β'
ξας δάμαρτος σᾶς στερηθείς.   - ⏑|- ⏑‖- ⏑|- - -   γ'

THE ORDER, AND ENGLISH ACCENTUATION.

ΧΟ. Ἰω Ζευ· τις πόρος κάκων, και λύσις τύχας, ἁ παρέστι κοίρανοις αν πα γενοίτο; Τις εξείσι; Η τέμω τρίχα, και αμφιβαλώμεθα ήδη μέλανα στόλμον πέπλων; Μεν δήλα, φίλοι, γε δήλα· αλλα ομως ευχωμέσθα θεοίσι, γαρ δύναμις θέων μεγίστα. Ωαναξ Παίαν, εξεύρε τίνα μήχαναν κάκων Αδμήτω· πορίζε δη, πορίζε, γαρ και πάρος εφεύρες τουδε· γένου λυτήριος εκ θάνατου, τε αποπαύσον φόνιον Αίδαν. Πάπαι φευ, πάπαι φευ· ιω· ιω· ω παι Φερητος, οία επράξας στερήθεις σας δαμάρτος.

TRANSLATION.

CHORUS. O Júpiter! what means of escape from these evils, and deliv⸗ erance from the fortune that attends my master, can there in any way be? Will any arise? Or must I shear my locks, and clothe me ere long in the sable array of garments? It is indeed plain, my friends; yes it is plain! but nevertheless let us pray unto the Gods—for the power of the Gods is most mighty! [*Kneeling.*] O! king Apollo, devise some remedy for the afflictions of Admétus:—administer it even now, administer it, seeing-that aforetime thou devisedest this: become our deliverer from death, and stay the murderous Plúto. [*Rising up.*] Hey! alas! hey! alas! wo! wo! O son of Phérës, how thou hast fared—being reft of thy wife!

---

214. In Aldus and in many later editions we find πῶς for πᾶ. Matthiæ's lection is ἇ Ζεῦ, πῶς ἂν πόρος κακῶν—

216. Musgrave (and with the concurrence of two MSS.) edited πάρεστιν and κοιράνοισιν. Although I have given "*mastet*" in the singular as the translation of κοιράνοις, yet both "*master and mistress*" are in the original word, implied.

217. In most editions, (nay I believe, in all—with the exception of Erfurdt's and Matthiæ's,) the reading is ἐξεισίν τις.

218. *The sable array of garments* for the *array of sable garments.*

219. Matthiæ has here ἀμφιβαλώμεθα δὴ, contrary to the metre: Lascar, ἀμφιβαλλώμεθα, equally bad.

220. In several editions this verse and the remainder of the strophë are assigned to the Female Attendant,—who is at this time in the palace.

226. Monk says, "*fortásse legéndum* τοῦτ' pro τοῦδ'." At the end of this line, he, in unison with the bulk of MSS. has καὶ νῦν, an addition he justly censures.

229. Several different readings of this verse occur.

230. παῖ Φέρητος, namely, *Admétus.*

D

Ἀῖ, ἀῖ· ἄξια καὶ σφαγᾶς τάδε,   -- ‖ - ◡ ◡ - ‖ ◡ - | ◡ ◡   δ'

καὶ πλέον ἢ βρόχῳ δέραν   - ◡ ◡ - ‖ ◡ - | ◡ -   ε'

οὐρανίῳ πελάσσαι·   - ◡ ◡ - ‖ ◡ - | -   ζ'

τὰν γὰρ οὐ φίλαν, ἀλλὰ φιλτάταν   235   - ◡ - ◡ - ‖ - ◡ ◡ -   η'

γυναῖκα κατθανοῦσαν ἐν   ◡ - | ◡ - ‖ ◡ - | ◡ ◡   θ'

ἄματι τῷδ' ἐσόψει.   - ◡ ◡ - ‖ ◡ - | -   ι'

ἰδού· ἰδού·   ◡ - ◡ -   κ'

ἅδ' ἐκ δόμων δὴ καὶ πόσις πορεύεται.   - - | ◡ - ‖ - - | ◡ - ‖ ◡ - | ◡ ◡   λ'

Βόασον, ὦ στέναξον,   240   ◡ - | ◡ - ‖ ◡ - | ◡   μ'

ὦ Φεραία χθὼν, ἀρίσταν   - ◡ | - - ‖ - ◡ | - -   ν'

γυναῖκα μαραινομέναν νόσῳ   ◡ - | ◡ ◡ - ‖ ◡ ◡ - | ◡ -   ξ'

κατὰ γᾶν, χθόνιον παρ' Ἀΐδαν.   ◡ ◡ - | ◡ ◡ - ‖ ◡ - | -   ο'

Οὔποτε φήσω γάμον εὐφραίνειν   - ◡ ◡ | - - ‖ ◡ ◡ - | - -

πλέον ἢ λυπεῖν, τοῖς τε πάροιθεν   245   ◡ ◡ - | - - ‖ - ◡ ◡ | - -

τεκμαιρόμενος, καὶ τάσδε τύχας   - - | ◡ ◡ - ‖ - - | ◡ ◡ -

λεύσσων βασιλέως, ὅστις ἀρίστης   - - | ◡ ◡ - ‖ - ◡ ◡ | - -

ἀπλακὼν ἀλόχου τῆσδ', ἀβίωτον   ◡ ◡ - | ◡ ◡ - ‖ - ◡ ◡ | - -

τὸν ἔπειτα χρόνον βιοτεύσει.   ◡ ◡ - | ◡ ◡ - ‖ ◡ ◡ - | - *

THE ORDER, AND ENGLISH ACCENTUATION.

Αι, αι· τάδε άξια και σφαγᾶς, και πλέον η πελάσσαι δέραν ουρανίω βρόχω· γαρ ου ταν φίλαν, άλλα φίλταταν γυναικα εν τῷδε άματι εσόψει κατθανοῦσαν. Ἰδου· ἰδου· άδε δη πορεύεται και πόσις εκ δόμων. Βόασον, ω στενάξον, ω Φεραία χθων, αρίσταν γυναικα μαραινομέναν νόσω κάτα γαν πάρα χθόνιον Ἀΐδαν. Οὔποτε φήσω γάμον ευφραίνειν πλέον η λύπειν, τεκμαιρόμενος τε τοις παροίθεν, και λεύσσων τάσδε τύχας βασιλέως, όστις απλακὼν τῆσδε αρίστης αλόχου, βιοτεύσει τον χρόνον επείτα αβίωτον.

TRANSLATION.

Alas! alas! These things would be sufficient cause even for self-murder—and there is more than for which to thrust one's neck into the suspending noose: for not a dear, but a most dear wife wilt thou this day see dead! [*Looking opportunely towards the palace.*] Behold,— behold: she is now coming, and her husband, from out the house! Cry out, Oh! bewail, O land of Phérës, the best woman upon Earth, wasted down by sickness for subterranean Plúto.

Never will I aver that marriage brings more joy than grief,—forming my conjectures both from prior events,—and on observing this fortune of the king; who when he has lost his most excellent consort, will live a life thereafter, not worthy to be called life!

---

232. ἄξια καὶ σφαγᾶς τάδε, *worthy these things even of slaughter.*

233. Every edition (I believe) before that of Musgrave, has πλεῖον, against the metre. For δέραν all have δέρην.

234. πελάσαι ὅmnes praéter Gaisfórdium, qui è Musgrávii emendatióne dédit πελάζειν: réctiùs Erfúrdtius πελάσσαι: gemináre σ in mélicis lícuit. Monk.

238. These words are in many copies wanting. Musgrave inserted them from two MSS. in the library at Paris.

239. For ἅδ' MSS. and editions have ἥδ'. Elmsley conjectured καὶ δὴ πόσις, and Blomfield χὼ (χἀ) πόσις.

241. Monk edited [τὰν] ἀρίσταν: Gaisford and Matthiæ, ἀρίσταν τάνδε. I have followed Erfurdt.

243. Contrary to every MS. and edition Monk has given γᾶς for γᾶν. "Dédi," says he, "postulánte senténtiâ, κατὰ γᾶς, sub térram."

247—8. In several editions the reading is ὃς ἀρίστης ἀμπλακὼν ἀλόχου, badly.

248—9. ἀβίωτον τὸν ἔπειτα χρόνον βιοτεύσει, *he will live the time thereafter lifeless.*

ΑΛΚΗΣΤΙΣ.

"Αλιε, καὶ φάος ἀμέρας,   [Στροφὴ β'.] 250   -◡◡|-◡◡||-◡|-   α'
οὐράνιαί τε δῖναι   -◡◡-||◡-|◡   β'
νεφέλας δρομαίου—   ◡◡-|◡-||-   γ'

ΑΔΜΗΤΟΣ.

Ὁρᾷ σὲ κἀμὲ, δύο κακῶς πεπραγότας,   ◡-|◡-||◡◡◡|◡-||◡-|◡◡
οὐδὲν Θεοὺς δράσαντας, ἀνθ' ὅτου θανεῖ.   --|◡-||-◡|◡-||◡-|◡-

ΑΛ. Γαῖά τε, καὶ μελάθρων στέγαι, ['Αντ. β'.] 255   -◡◡|-◡◡||-◡|◡   α'
νυμφίδιαί τε κοῖται   .◡◡-||◡-|◡   β'
πατρίας Ἰωλκοῦ—   ◡◡-|◡-||-   γ'

ΑΔ. Ἔπαιρε σαυτὴν, ὦ τάλαινα, μὴ προδῶς·   ◡-|◡-||-◡|◡-||◡-|◡-
λίσσου δὲ τοὺς κρατοῦντας οἰκτεῖραι Θεούς.   --|◡-||◡-|◡-||--|◡-

ΑΛ. Ὁρῶ, δίκωπον ὁρῶ σκάφος· [Στροφὴ γ'.] 260   ◡-|◡-||◡◡-|◡◡   α'
νεκύων δὲ πορθμεὺς,   ◡◡-|◡-||-   β'
ἔχων χέρ' ἐπὶ κόντῳ· Χάρων μ'   ◡-|◡◡◡◡||--|◡-   γ'
ἤδη καλεῖ· Τί μέλλεις;   --|◡-||◡-|-   δ'

THE ORDER, AND ENGLISH ACCENTUATION.

ΑΛ. "Αλιε, καὶ φάος ἀμέρας, τε οὐράνιαι δῖναι δρομαίου νεφέλας—ΑΔ.—ὁρᾷ σε καὶ ἐμὲ, δύο πε-
πράγοντας κάκως, δρασάντας οὐδὲν Θεούς, ἀντι ὅτου Θάνει. ΑΛ. Τε γαῖα, καὶ στέγαι μέλαθρων, τε
νυμφίδιαι κοῖται πάτριας Ἰωλκου—. ΑΔ. Επαιρε σαυτην, ω ταλαινα, μη πρόδως· δε λίσσου τους
κρατούντας Θεους οικτείραι. ΑΛ. Ὁρω, ὁρω δικώπον σκάφος· δε πόρθμευς νεκύων ἔχων χέρα ἐπι
κόντῳ· Χάρων ἤδη κάλει με' Τι μέλλεις;

TRANSLATION.

ALCESTIS. [*Entering with languid step, attended by her two children, and
leaning on her husband's arm.*] O Sun, and thou light of day, and ye heavenly eddies of the fleeting clouds—ADMETUS. [*Most sorrowfully.*] Be-
holds thee and me, two creatures wretchedly circumstanced,—having
done nought unto the Gods, for which thou shouldest die!
ALCESTIS. [*Piteously.*] O Earth, and ye roofs of the palace, and thou
bridal bed of my native Iólcos—!
ADMETUS. Cheer thyself up, O hapless one, leave me not : but entreat
the powerful Gods to have pity! ALCESTIS. [*Deliriously.*] I see, I see the
two-oared boat : and the ferryman of the dead, holding his hand upon
the boat-hook:—Cháron even now calls to me:—"*Why dost thou delay?*

253. The nominative to ὁρᾷ, (as Monk
observes,) is ἥλιος, being the substantive
first mentioned by Alcéstis.—Δύο κακῶς
πεπραγότας, *two wretchedly circumstanced
creatures—two persons in woful plight.*

257. Musgrave from MSS. edited πα-
τρῷας. Aldus has πατρίας, which the metre requires.—Monk, with reference as
well to this verse as to the two before it,
says:—" si cui tánti vísum érit, alitèr hi
vérsus distríbui póterunt:—

Γαῖά τε, καὶ μελάθρων |-◡◡-||◡-|-
στέγαι, νυμφίδιαί τε κοῖ- |◡-||-◡◡-||◡-
ται πατρίας Ἰωλκοῦ. |-◡◡-||◡-|-

260. Several MSS. have ἐν λίμνα after
σκάφος. Lascar omitting the second ὁρῶ,
edited simply : ὁρῶ δίκωπον σκάφος ἐν λίμνα.

262. Charon was ferryman upon the
Stýgian lake, and transported the souls
of the dead across the sable rivers Styx
and Acheron. His boat, which was ever
a favorite subject with the poets, is three
times mentioned in this play : viz. here,
and in verses 371 and 451, below. Matthiæ encloses Χάρων in brackets, intima-
ting that he thought, as Monk seems also
to have thought, that this word did not
originally belong to the text.

28 · **264. ΕΥΡΙΠΙΔΟΥ**

'Επείγου· σὺ κατείργεις τάδε. Τοῖα
σπερχόμενος ταχύνει. 265

ΑΔ. Οἴμοι· πικράν γε τήνδε μοι ναυκληρίαν
ἔλεξας. Ὦ δύσδαιμον, οἷα πάσχομεν.

ΑΛ. Ἄγει μ', ἄγει μέ τις (οὐχ ὁρᾷς;) ['Αντ. γ'.]
νεκύων ἐς αὐλάν·
ὑπ' ὀφρύσι κυαναυγέσι 270
βλέπων πτερωτὸς Ἀΐδας.
Τί ῥέξεις; Ἄφες. Οἵαν ὁδὸν ἁ δει-
λαιοτάτα προβαίνω.

ΑΔ. Οἰκτρὰν φίλοισιν, ἐκ δὲ τῶν, μάλιστ' ἐμοὶ,
καὶ παισὶν, οἷς δὴ πένθος ἐν κοινῷ τόδε. 275

ΑΛ. Μέθετε, μεθετέ μ' ἤδη· ['Επωδός.]
κλίνατέ μ', οὐ σθένω ποσίν·
πλησίον Ἀΐδας, σκοτία δ'
ἐπ' ὄσσοισι νὺξ ἐφέρπει.

THE ORDER, AND ENGLISH ACCENTUATION.

Επείγου· συ κατείργεις τάδε· τοῖα σπερχόμενος ταχύνει. ΑΔ. Οἴμοι· πίκραν ναυκλήριαν μοι γε τήνδε ελέξας. Ω δυσδαιμον, ὅια πάσχομεν. ΑΛ. Ἄγει με, τις ἄγει με (οὐκ ὅρας;) ἐς αὐλαν νέκυων· πτερώτος Ἀΐδας βλέπων ὕπο κυαναύγεσι ὀφρύσι. Τι ῥέξεις; Ἄφες. Ὅιαν ὁδον ἁ δειλαιότατα προβαίνω. ΑΔ. Οἴκτραν φιλοισι, δε εκ των, μαλιστα εμοι, και παισιν, οἱς δη τοδε πένθος εν κοινῳ. ΑΛ. Μέθετε με, ἤδη μέθετε· κλίνατε με, ου σθένω ποσι· Ἀΐδας πλησιον, δε σκοτια νυξ εφέρπει επι οσσοισι.

TRANSLATION.

Haste! Thou detainest me here."—With such words vehement he accelerates me! ADMETUS. Woes my heart! A bitter voyage unto me at least this thou hast mentioned! Ah! hapless one, what we suffer!

ALCESTIS. He pulls me—some one pulls me (dost thou not see?) to the hall of the dead: the winged Pluto staring from beneath his dusky eyebrows! [*As if speaking either to Plúto or to Cháron.*] What wilt thou do? Loose thine hold! [*To Admétus.*] What a journey am I (most wretched) going!

ADMETUS. A mournful one to thy friends—and of these especially to me, and to thy children, unto whom this grief is now in common!

ALCESTIS. Desist supporting me, even now desist: lay me down,—I have no strength in my feet: death is at hand, and darkling night creeps in upon mine eyes! [*Here Alcéstis sinks down upon a couch in front of the palace, and Admétus continues most attentive to her.*]

269. Wakefield imagined αὐλὰν should be ἱλαν—and he contrasts the remainder of the sentence with Homer, Il. Α'.:528, ῆ, καὶ κυανέησιν ἐπ' ὀφρύσι νεῦσε Κρονίων.

272. The common reading is τί ῥέξεις; on which Monk says: " néscio an praésens ῥέζω násquàm usurpârint Attici."

274. Aldus has ἐκ δὲ τῶνδε, which seve-ral subsequent editors thoughtlessly adopted :—τῶν is here put for τούτων. "Articulum," says Monk, " pro pronómine οὗτος vel ἐκεῖνος sequéntibus μὲν, δὲ, et γὰρ lícuit ómnibus scriptóribus adhibére.

277. Vúlgò πόσι—vértunt támen intérpretes quási scríptum ésset ποσί,— quod prócul dúbio mélius est. MONK.

Τέκνα, τέκν᾽, οὐκέτι δὴ,   280
οὐκέτι δὴ μάτηρ σφῷν ἐστίν.
Χαίροντες, ὦ τέκνα, τόδε φάος ὁρῴτην.

ΑΔ. Οἴμοι· τόδ᾽ ἔπος λυπρὸν ἀκούω,
καὶ παντὸς ἐμοὶ θανάτου μεῖζον.
Μὴ, πρός σε θεῶν, τλῆς με προδοῦναι·   285
μὴ, πρὸς παίδων, οὓς ὀρφανιεῖς·
ἀλλ᾽ ἄνα, τόλμα·
σοῦ γὰρ φθιμένης, οὐκέτ᾽ ἂν εἴην·
ἐν σοὶ δ᾽ ἐσμὲν καὶ ζῆν, καὶ μή·
σὴν γὰρ φιλίαν σεβόμεσθα.   290
ΑΔ. Ἄδμηθ᾽, ὁρᾷς γὰρ τἀμὰ πράγμαθ᾽ ὡς ἔχει,
λέξαι θέλω σοι, πρὶν θανεῖν, ἃ βούλομαι.
Ἐγὼ σὲ πρεσβεύουσα, κἀντὶ τῆς ἐμῆς
ψυχῆς καταστήσασα φῶς τόδ᾽ εἰσορᾷν,
θνήσκω, παρόν μοι μὴ θανεῖν, ὑπὲρ σέθεν·   295

THE ORDER, AND ENGLISH ACCENTUATION.

Τέκνα, τέκνα, οὐκετι δη, οὐκετι δη ἐστι μήτηρ σφων. Χαιρόντες, ω τέκνα, ὁρῴτην τόδε φάος. ΑΔ. Οἴμοι· ἀκούω τόδε λύπρον ἔπος, και μεῖζον ἐμοι πάντος θάνατου. Μη, προς θέων σε, τλης προδοῦναι με· μη, προς παίδων, οὓς ορφάνιεις· ἀλλα ἄνα, τόλμα· γαρ σου φθίμενης, οὐκετι αν εἴην δε εν σοι ἔσμεν και ζην, και μη· γαρ σην φίλιαν σεβομέσθα· ΑΔ. Ἄδμητε, γαρ ὁρᾳς ὡς τα ἔμα πράγματα ἔχει, θέλω λέξαι σοι, πριν θάνειν, ἃ βούλομαι. Ἐγω πρεσβεύουσα σε, και καταστησάσα ἀντι της ἐμης ψύχης εἰσορᾳν τόδε φως, θνήσκω ὕπερ σέθεν, πάρον μοι μη θάνειν·

TRANSLATION.

[*Gazing affectionately on her little son and daughter.*] My children, my children, no longer now,—no longer now have ye a mother. [*Stretching out both her hands.*] Faring happily, O children, may ye view the light! ADMETUS. [*Sighing most deeply.*] Woes my heart! I hear this afflicting speech,—and more to me than any death! [*With entreaty.*] Do not, by the Gods I implore thee, have the cruelty to forsake me: do not, by these children, whom thou wilt render orphans:—but rise, be of good courage,—seeing-that, thee dead, I should no longer be,—for on thee depend we both to live and not:—because thy love we adore! ALCESTIS. [*Seriously and composedly.*] Admétus, (for thou perceivest in what condition my affairs are,) I wish to tell thee, ere I die, what I would have done:—

"*I testifying my regard for thee, and causing thee at the price of my life, to view the light, am about to die for thee, it being in my power not to die:*

282. Vúlgò interpretántur, "*laéti hoc lúmen intueámini:*" debébant, "*vívite et valéte.*" Participium χαίρων hanc habére potestátem jamprídem mónui ad Hippólyti ver. 1438. Hábet φῶς Lascáris : ὁρῶτον ómnes :—sed præcláré osténdit Elmsleíus ad Aristóphanis Acharn. ver. 773, secúndam persónam duálem núnquàm à tértiâ divérsam fuísse. MONK.

285. In lieu of πρός σε θεῶν, Aldus has πρὸς τῶν θεῶν, which Porson condemns.

287. τολμᾶν, nèc áliter aorístus τλῆναι,

(nàm τλῆμι et τλάω non éxstant,) válet 'sustinére,'—quæ quídem significátio làtè se exténdit: est enim "*sustinére, to endure,*" non obstánte vel perículo, vel pudóre, vel supérbiâ, vel dolóre ánimi, vel misericórdiâ. MONK.—For the rest of the learned editor's note, see his own edition. Aldus's reading of this verse is ἀλλ᾽ ἀνατόλμα.

291. In Lascar's text γὰρ is wanting.

293. ἐγὼ σε ómnes :—πρεσβεύουσα ídem válet ac προτιμῶσα, ver. 156. MONK.

ἀλλ' ἄνδρα τε σχεῖν Θεσσαλῶν, ὃν ἤθελον, | - - | ◡ - || - - | ◡ - || ◡ - | ◡ ◡

καὶ δῶμα ναίειν ὄλβιον τυραννίδι, | - - | ◡ - || - - | ◡ - || ◡ - | ◡ ◡

οὐκ ἠθέλησα ζῆν ἀποσπασθεῖσα σοῦ | - - | ◡ - || - - | ◡ - || ◡ - | ◡ ◡

ξὺν παισὶν ὀρφανοῖσιν· οὐδ' ἐφεισάμην, | - - | ◡ - || - - || ◡ - || ◡ - | ◡ ◡

ἥβης ἔχουσα δῶρ', ἐν οἷς ἐτερπόμην.   300 | - - | ◡ - || - - | ◡ - || ◡ - | ◡ ◡

Καίτοι σ' ὁ φύσας χ' ἡ τεκοῦσα προύδοσαν, | - - | ◡ - || ◡ - | ◡ - || ◡ - | ◡ ◡

καλῶς μὲν αὐτοῖς κατθανεῖν ἧκον βίου, | ◡ - | ◡ - || - - | ◡ - || ◡ - | ◡ ◡

καλῶς δὲ σῶσαι παῖδα, κεὐκλεῶς θανεῖν· | ◡ - | ◡ - || - - | ◡ ◡◡ | - - | ◡ ◡

μόνος γὰρ αὐτοῖς ἦσθα· κοὔτις ἐλπὶς ἦν, | ◡ - | ◡ - || - - | ◡ - || ◡ ◡ | ◡ ◡

σοῦ κατθανόντος, ἄλλα φιτύσειν τέκνα.   305 | - - | ◡ - || ◡ ◡ | ◡ - || ◡ - | ◡ ◡

Κἀγώ τ' ἂν ἔζων, καὶ σὺ τὸν λοιπὸν χρόνον, | - - | ◡ - || - - | ◡ - || ◡ - | ◡ ◡

κοὐκ ἂν μονωθεὶς σῆς δάμαρτος ἔστενες, | - - | ◡ - || - - | ◡ - || ◡ - | ◡ ◡

καὶ παῖδας ὠρφάνευες. Ἀλλὰ ταῦτα μὲν | - - | ◡ - || - - || ◡ - || ◡ - | ◡ ◡

θεῶν τις ἐξέπραξεν ὥσθ' οὕτως ἔχειν. | ◡ - | ◡ - || - ◡ | ◡ - || - - | ◡ ◡

Εἶεν· σὺ δή μοι τῶνδ' ἀπόμνησαι χάριν·   310 | - - | ◡ - || - - | ◡ - || ◡ - | ◡ ◡

αἰτήσομαι γάρ σ' ἀξίαν μὲν οὔποτε· | - - | ◡ - || - - | ◡ - || ◡ - | ◡ ◡

THE ORDER, AND ENGLISH ACCENTUATION.

ἀλλὰ τε σχεῖν ἄνδρα Θέσσαλων, ὃν ἤθελον, καὶ ναίειν δῶμα ὄλβιον τυράννιδι, οὐκ ἠθέλησα ζῆν ἀποσπασθεῖσα σου ξὺν ὀρφανοῖσι παῖσι· οὐδὲ ἐφείσαμην, ἐχούσα δῶρα ἥβης, ἐν οἷς ἐτέρπομην. Καίτοι ὁ φύσας καὶ ἡ τεκούσα σε προ-έδοσαν, ἦκον αὐτοῖς βίου μεν κάλως κάτθανειν, δὲ κάλως σῶσαι παῖδα, καὶ θάνειν εὐκλεως· γὰρ ἦσθα μόνος αὐτοῖς· καὶ ἐλπις ἦν οὔτις, σου κατθανόντος, φιτύσειν ἄλλα τέκνα. Καὶ τε ἐγω ἂν ἔζων, καὶ σὺ τὸν λοίπον χρόνον, καὶ οὐκ ἂν ἔστενες μονωθεις σῆς δαμάρτος, καὶ ωρφανεύες παῖδας. Ἀλλὰ ταύτα μεν τις θέων ἐξεπράξε ὥστε ἔχειν οὕτως. Εἶεν· σὺ δη ἀπομνήσαι χάριν μοι τώνδε· γὰρ οὔποτε μεν αἰτήσομαι σε ἀξίαν·

TRANSLATION.

but, although I might have married a husband from among the Thessálians, (whom I would,) and have inhabited a palace blest with regal-sway, yet was I not willing to live bereft of thee, with my orphan children: neither spared I myself, though possessing the gifts of youth, in which I had delight.

And yet he that begat thee, and she who bare thee, forsook thee; although they had arrived at a time of life, indeed, when they might well have died, and have nobly delivered their son—and have expired with glory: for thou wast their only child,—and hope was there none that, when thou wert dead, they could have other children!

And then I could have lived, and thou,—the remainder of our days; and thou wouldest not be groaning deprived of thy wife,—and have had to rear thine orphan children! But these things, troth, hath some one of the Gods brought about, that it should be thus!

[With great resignation.] *Be it so: do thou, however, remember to make me a return for this,—seeing I shall never, indeed, ask thee for an equal one,*

---

296. ἄνδρα τε σχεῖν,—understand παρόν μοι, repeated from the foregoing verse, it was in my power (or rather, it is in my power) to have a husband, that is, after thy decease, by suffering thee to die if I choose to retract my consent to die for thee.

300. ἥβης δῶρα, the gifts of youth, namely, sprightliness, beauty, grace, bloom, activity, liveliness, wit, &c. For ἥβης Aldus has ἡοῦς, most likely by an error at press.

302. αὐτοῖς ἧκον βίου, literally, it being

come to them of life, i. e., they being arrived at that advanced age.

305. φυτεύσειν editiónes ánte Musgrávium,—reclamánte métro: némo, énim, hódiè Barnésium aúdiet—docéntem φυτεύειν prímam prodúcere. Vérbum φιτύειν in vulgárius φυτεύειν fèrè sémpèr mutábant librárii. MONK.

306. The vulgate lection here, is, ἔζην, bad in the extreme: τὸν λοιπὸν χρόνον, the remaining time—the rest of our lives.

ψυχῆς. γὰρ οὐδέν ἐστι τιμιώτερον·   --|ᴗ-‖ᴗ-|ᴗ-‖ᴗ-|ᴗ ᴗ

δίκαια δ', ὡς φήσεις σύ· τούσδε γὰρ φιλεῖς   ᴗ-|ᴗ-‖-ᴗᴗ|ᴗ-‖ᴗ-|ᴗ-

ὀυχ ἧσσον ἢ 'γὼ παῖδας, εἴπερ εὖ φρονεῖς·   --|ᴗ-‖-ᴗ|ᴗ-‖ᴗ-|ᴗ-

τούτους ἀνάσχου δεσπότας ἐμῶν δόμων,   315   --|ᴗ-‖--|ᴗ-‖ᴗ-|ᴗ-

καὶ μὴ 'πιγήμης τοῖσδε μητρυιὰν τέκνοις,   --|ᴗ-‖-ᴗ|ᴗ-‖-|ᴗ-

ἥτις, κακίων οὖσ' ἐμοῦ γυνή, φθόνῳ   --|ᴗ-‖-ᴗ|ᴗ-‖ᴗ-|ᴗ ᴗ

τοῖς σοῖσι κἀμοῖς παισὶ χεῖρα προσβαλεῖ.   --|ᴗ-‖--|ᴗ-‖ᴗ-|ᴗ-

Μὴ δῆτα δράσῃς ταῦτά γ', αἰτοῦμαί σ' ἐγώ·   --|ᴗ-‖ -‖ᴗ-‖--|ᴗ-

ἐχθρὰ γὰρ ἡ 'πιοῦσα μητρυιὰ τέκνοις   320   --|ᴗ-‖ᴗᴗ|ᴗ-‖--|ᴗ-

τοῖς πρόσθ', ἐχίδνης οὐδὲν ἠπιωτέρα.   --|ᴗ-‖-ᴗ|ᴗ-‖ᴗ-|ᴗ-

Καὶ παῖς μὲν ἄρσην πατέρ' ἔχει πύργον μέγαν·   --|ᴗ-‖-ᴗᴗ|ᴗ-‖--|ᴗ ᴗ

σὺ δ', ὦ τέκνον μοι, πῶς κορευθήσει καλῶς;   ᴗ-|ᴗ-‖-ᴗ|ᴗ-‖-|ᴗ-

Ποίας τυχοῦσα συζύγου τῷ σῷ πατρί;   --|ᴗ-‖ᴗ|ᴗ-‖ᴗ-|ᴗ-

Μή σοι τιν' αἰσχρὰν προσβαλοῦσα κληδόνα,   325   --|ᴗ-‖--|ᴗ-‖ᴗ-|ᴗ ᴗ

ἥβης ἐν ἀκμῇ σοὺς διαφθείρῃ γάμους.   --|ᴗ-‖--|ᴗ-‖-|ᴗ-

Ου γάρ σε μήτηρ οὔτε νυμφεύσει ποτὲ,   --|ᴗ-‖--|ᴗ-‖ᴗ-|ᴗ ᴗ

THE ORDER, AND ENGLISH ACCENTUATION.

γαρ οὐδὲν ἐστι τιμιώτερον ψύχης· δὲ δικαία, ὡς συ φήσεις· γαρ φίλεις τούσδε παῖδας οὐκ ἧσσον η ἐγω, εἴπερ φρόνεις εὐ· τούτους ἀνάσχου δέσποτας ἐμων δόμων, καὶ μη ἐπιγήμης μητρυίαν τοῖσδε τέκνοις, ἥτις, οὐσα κακίων γύνη ἐμου, φθόνῳ πρόσβαλει χείρα τοις σοῖσι παῖσι καὶ ἐμοις. Μη δράσῃς δῆτα ταύτα γε, ἐγω αἰτουμαι σε· γαρ μητρυία η ἐπιουσα ἐχθρα τέκνοις τοις πρόσθε, οὐδεν ἠπιώτερα ἐχίδνης. Καὶ ἄρσην παις μεν ἔχει πάτερα μέγαν πύργον· δε συ, ω τέκνον μοι, πως καλως κορευθήσει; Τυχούσα ποίας σύζυγου τω σω πάτερ; Μη προσβαλούσα τίνα αἰσχραν κλήδονα σοι, διαφθείρῃ σους γάμους εν ἀκμη ἥβης. Γαρ οὔτε οὔποτε μήτηρ νυμφεύσει σε,

TRANSLATION.

(for nothing is more precious than life,) but a just one,—as thou wilt confess:—for thou lovest these children not less than I do, if thou employest thy mind aright:—them bring thou up lords of my house, and introduce not by a second marriage a stepmother over these youngsters,—who, being a less-kindly woman than I, will through envy stretch forth her hand against thy children and mine. Do not then this at least, I beseech thee: for a stepmother supervening by a second marriage is an enemy to the children of the former one,—in nowise milder than a viper! [Reconciledly to her little son.] *And my manly boy in troth has his father, a mighty tower of defence: but* [Embracing her little daughter most affectionately.] *thou, O my child, how wilt thou be happily trained during thy virgin years? Chancing to meet with what sort of woman for consort to thy father?* [Sighing heavily.] *Oh! may she not, by casting some evil obloquy upon thee, destroy thy nuptials in the bloom of youth! For neither will thy mother ever attend thee at thy wedding,*

---

316. καὶ μὴ 'πιγήμης τοῖσδε μητρυιὰν τέκνοις, *and bring not in by another marriage a stepmother over these children.* Monk remarks :—" eâdem potestáte adhibétur ἐπὶ, vérsu 383, μὴ γαμεῖν ἄλλην ποτὲ γυναῖκ' ἐφ' ὑμῖν: nec dissímili in Oréste, 582, ὀυ γὰρ ἐπεγάμει πόσει πόσιν. Med. 692, γυναῖκ' ἐφ' ἡμῖν δεσπότιν δόμων ἔχει."

317. ἥτις, κακίων οὖσ' ἐμοῦ γυνὴ, *verbally, who, (which stepmother) being a worse woman than myself,—being less humane and affectionate than I have been.*

322. In most if not in all editions we find after this verse the following, being a repetition (with very slight alteration) of verse 196, above :—ὃν καὶ προσεῖπε καὶ προσερρήθη πάλιν. Matthiæ put it betwixt brackets, as being suspicious if not spurious, and Monk has cancelled it.

323. Monk says, " fortásse legéndum sit, ὦ τέκνον, πῶς μοι κορευθήσει καλῶς ;"

324. Reiske gives ποίας for ποίας, and in the next verse ἢ σοι for μή σοι. Kninoel has no point of interrogation until after γάμους. The Attics, Monk tells us, used σύζυξ and σύζυγος indiscriminately.

οὔτ' ἐν τόκοισι σοῖσι θαρσυνεῖ, τέκνον,

παροῦσ', ἵν' οὐδὲν μητρὸς εὐμενέστερον.

Δεῖ γὰρ θανεῖν με· καὶ τόδ' οὐκ εἰς αὔριον,   330

οὐδ' εἰς τρίτην μοι μηνὸς ἔρχεται κακὸν,

ἀλλ' αὐτίκ' ἐν τοῖς οὐκέτ' οὖσι λέξομαι.

Χαίροντες εὐφραίνοισθε· καὶ σοὶ μὲν, πόσι,

γυναῖκ' ἀρίστην ἐστί κομπάσαι λαβεῖν,

ὑμῖν δὲ, παῖδες, μητρὸς ἐκπεφυκέναι.   335

ΧΟ. Θάρσει· πρὸ τούτου γὰρ λέγειν οὐχ ἅζομαι·

δράσει τάδ', ἥπερ μὴ φρενῶν ἁμαρτάνη.

ΑΔ. Ἔσται τάδ', ἔσται, μὴ τρέσῃς· ἐπεί σ' ἐγὼ

καὶ ζῶσαν εἶχον, καὶ θανοῦσ' ἐμὴ γυνὴ

μόνη κεκλήσει, κοὔτις ἀντὶ σοῦ ποτὲ   340

τόνδ' ἄνδρα νύμφη Θεσσαλὶς προσφθέγξεται·

οὐκ ἐστὶν οὕτως οὔτε πατρὸς εὐγενοῦς,

οὔτ' εἶδος ἄλλως ἐκπρεπεστάτη γυνή.

THE ORDER, AND ENGLISH ACCENTUATION.

οὔτε θάρςυνει, τέκνον, παροῦσα ἐν σοῖσι τοκοίσι, ἵνα οὐδὲν εὐμενέστερον μήτρος. Γαρ δει με θά-
νειν· και τόδε κάκον ουκ ἐρχεται μοι εις αὔριον, οὐδὲ εις τρίτην μηνος, ἀλλα αὐτικα λέξομαι εν τοις
οὔκετι οὐσι. Χαιρόντες εὐφραινοίσθε· και σοι μεν ἐστι, πόσι, κόμπασαι λαβειν ἀρίστην γυναικα,
δε ὑμιν, παιδες, ἐκπεφύκεναι μήτρος. ΧΟ. Θάρσει· γαρ ουκ ἅζομαι λέγειν προ τούτου· δράσει
τάδε, ἥνπερ μη ἁμάρταιη φρένων. ΑΔ. Τάδε ἐσται, ἐσται, μη τρέσῃς· ἐπει ἐγω εἰχον σε και ζώσαν, και θανούσα κεκλήσει ἐμη μόνη γύνη, και οὕτις Θεσσαλις νύμφη πότε προσφθέγξεται τόνδε
ἄνδρα ἀντι σου· ουκ ἐστι γύνη οὔτε οὕτως εὐγενους πάτρος, οὔτε ἄλλως ἐκπρεπέστατη εἰδος.

TRANSLATION.

nor strengthen thee, my daughter, being present at thy accouchements, where
nothing is more kind than a mother. Because I must die:—and this calamity
comes not upon me to-morrow, nor on the third day of the month, but forth-
with shall I be numbered among those who are no more! [Taking the children by the hand.] Faring happily may ye have joy: [To Admétus.] and
thine indeed it is, my husband, to boast having had a most excellent wife, and
yours, my children, that ye were born of a most excellent mother."

CHORUS. [To Alcéstis exhortingly.] Be of courage: for I fear not to an-
swer for him:—he will do these-things if he be not reft of his senses.

ADMETUS. [Greatly affected.] It shall be so, it shall,—be not afraid:
for-since I possessed thee when alive, so when thou art dead thou shalt
be my only wife,—and no Thessálian bride shall ever address this man
[Pointing to himself.] in the place of thee:—there is not [With an air of
the most fixed determination.] a woman who shall,—either of so noble a
sire, or otherwise most exquisite in beauty.

---

331. εἰς τρίτην μηνὸς,—with allusion to
persons capitally condemned, who were
obliged to drink of the poisonous juice of
the hemlock within three days, at most,
after sentence was passed on them. The
Attics, indeed, more frequently joined ἡ-
μέραν with τρίτην, but yet in the common
language of Greece it was customary to
say εἰς τρίτην,—ἡμέραν being understood.

333. χαίροντες εὐφραίνοισθε, freely, fare
ye well and be happy. See v. 282, above.

336. οὐχ ἅζομαι, for the οὐ χάζομαι of

MSS. and editions, is the emendation of
Barnes. From the Scholiast's interpretation οὐκ εὐλαβοῦμαι, it is probable that
οὐχ ἅζομαι was the reading in his time.

341. τόνδ' ἄνδρα pro ἐμέ: notíssimæ cir-
cumlocutiónis exémpla hábes in hâc tra-
goédiâ, vv. 706, 735, 1103, 1113.—Sim-
plícitèr τᾷδε pro ἐμοί, 752, 1109. MONK.

343. For ἐκπρεπεστάτη some few MSS.
have εὐπρεπεστάτη. See Porson's note at
verse 564 of the Hécuba. Instead of ἄλλως Wakefield edited ἄλλων.

῞Αλις δὲ παίδων· τῶνδ᾽ ὄνησιν εὔχομαι
Θεοῖς γενέσθαι· σοῦ γὰρ οὐκ ὠνήμεθα.   345
᾿Οίσω δὲ πένθος οὐκ ἐτήσιον τὸ σὸν,
ἀλλ᾽ ἔς τ᾽ ἂν αἰὼν οὑμὸς ἀντέχῃ, γύναι,
στυγῶν μὲν ἥ μ᾽ ἔτικτεν, ἐχθαίρων δ᾽ ἐμὸν
πατέρα· λόγῳ γὰρ ἦσαν, οὐκ ἔργῳ, φίλοι.
Σὺ δ᾽, ἀντιδοῦσα τῆς ἐμῆς τὰ φίλτατα   350
ψυχῆς, ἔσωσας. ᾿Αρά μοι στένειν πάρα,
τοιᾶσδ᾽ ἁμαρτάνοντι συζύγου σέθεν;
Παύσω δὲ κώμους, ξυμποτῶν θ᾽ ὁμιλίας,
στεφάνους τε, μοῦσάν θ᾽, ἣ κατεῖχ᾽ ἐμοὺς δόμους.
᾿Ου γάρ ποτ᾽ οὔτ᾽ ἂν βαρβίτου θίγοιμ᾽ ἔτι,   355
οὔτ᾽ ἂν φρέν᾽ ἐξαίροιμι πρὸς Λίβυν λακεῖν
αὐλόν· σὺ γάρ μου τέρψιν ἐξείλου βίου.
Σοφῇ δὲ χειρὶ τεκτόνων δέμας τὸ σὸν
εἰκασθὲν ἐν λέκτροισιν ἐκταθήσεται·

THE ORDER, AND ENGLISH ACCENTUATION.

Δε παίδων ἅλις· τώνδε εὔχομαι Θέοις γενέσθαι ονήσιν· γαρ σου ουκ ωνήμεθα. Δε το σον πένθος οίσω ουκ ετήσιον, ἀλλα ες τε, γυναι, ὁ ἐμος αίων αν άντεχη, στύγων μεν ἡ ετικτε με, δε εχθαίρων ἐμον πάτεϱα· γαρ ησαν λόγῳ, ουκ έργῳ, φίλοι. Δε συ, αντιδούσα τα φίλτατα της ἐμης ψύχης, ε-σώσας. ῾Αρα πάρα μοι στένειν, ἁμαρτανόντι σέθεν τοιᾶσδε σύζυγου· Δε παύσω κώμους, τε ὁμιλίας ξύμποτων, τε στέφανους, τε μούσαν, ἡ κατείχε ἐμους δόμους. Γαρ ούτε αν ούποτε έτι θιγοίμι βάρβιτου, ούτε αν εξαίροίμι φρένα λάκειν προς Λίβυν αύλον· γαρ συ εξείλου μου τέρ-ψιν βίου. Δε σόφη χείρι τέκτονων εικάσθεν το σον δέμας εκταθήσεται εν λέκτροίσι·

TRANSLATION.

For of children I have enow:—of them I pray the Gods there may be enjoyment to me: because thee we enjoy not. [*Weeps with bitterness.*]

But this sorrow for thee [*Wringing his hands distressedly.*] shall I feel, not for a year, but as long, O lady, as my life endures,—detesting her for troth who brought me forth, and hating my father:—for they were in word, not in deed, my friends! But thou, by giving what was dearest to thee for my life, hast rescued me!

[*Sobbing very deeply.*] Have I not reason, then, to groan at being in thee deprived of such a spouse?

But I will put an end to the feasts, and to the meetings of those-who-drink-together, and to the garlands,—and the song, which was wont to dwell in mine house! For neither can I, ever any more, touch the lyre; nor lift up my heart to sing to the Líbyan lute:—for [*Shedding a flood of tears.*] thou hast taken away from me the joy of life. But, by the skilful hand of artists imaged, shall thy figure be extended on the bridal bed:

---

346. *οίσω δὲ πένθος οὐκ ἐτήσιον τὸ σὸν*, literally, *but I will endure the thy grief not annual*, that is, *I will not lament for thee during the short space of a single year.* For τὸ σὸν, most editors (Láscar and one or two others, indeed, excepted) have τόδε. The ancients generally set apart a greater or less number of months to mourn for deceased relatives, according to the proximity of relationship.

347. αἰὼν, *life* or *life-time—the period of human existence:*—so again in verse 490,

below. Hesýchius rightly explains it by, ὁ βίος τῶν ἀνθρώπων· ὁ τῆς ζωῆς χρόνος.

349. Monk notices how very similar in meaning this passage is to verse 281 of the Oréstes.

356. Wakefield conjectured ἐξάραιμι, which Elmsley greatly approved. Most editions, before Musgrave's, have ἐξάροιμι, faultily. On λακεῖν, Monk says : "hoc vérbum, quod ápud Trágicos frequéntiùs dícitur de canéntibus vaticínia, nunc signíficat *cantáre ad tíbium.*"

E

ᾧ προσπεσοῦμαι, καὶ περιπτύσσων χέρας,   360   --|◡-||--|◡-||--|◡◡

ὄνομα καλῶν σὸν, τὴν φίλην ἐν ἀγκάλαις   ◡◡◡|◡-||--|◡-||◡-|◡-

δόξω γυναῖκα, καίπερ οὐκ ἔχων, ἔχειν·   --|◡-||◡-|◡-||◡-|◡-

ψυχρὰν μὲν, οἶμαι, τέρψιν· ἀλλ᾽ ὅμως βάρος   --|◡-||◡-|◡-||◡-|◡-

ψυχῆς ἀπαντλοίην ἄν· ἐν δ᾽ ὀνείρασι   --|◡-||◡-|◡-||--|◡◡

φοιτῶσά μ᾽ εὐφραίνοις ἄν· ἡδὺ γὰρ φίλος   365   --|◡-||--|◡-||◡-|◡◡

κἂν νυκτὶ λεύσσειν, ὅντιν᾽ ἂν παρῇ χρόνον.   --|◡-||◡-|◡-||◡-|◡◡

Εἰ δ᾽ Ὀρφέως μοι γλῶσσα καὶ μέλος παρῆν,   --|◡-||◡-|◡-||◡-|◡-

ὡς τὴν κόρην Δήμητρος, ἢ κείνης πόσιν   --|◡-||◡-|◡-||--|◡-

ὕμνοισι κηλήσαντά σ᾽ ἐξ Ἅιδου λαβεῖν,   --|◡-||◡-|◡-||--|◡-

κατῆλθον ἂν· καί μ᾽ οὔθ᾽ ὁ Πλούτωνος κύων,   370   ◡-|◡-||◡-|◡-||--|◡-

οὔθ᾽ οὑπὶ κώπῃ ψυχοπομπὸς ἂν Χάρων   --|◡-||◡-|◡-||◡-|◡-

ἔσχον, πρὶν εἰς φῶς σὸν καταστῆσαι βίον.   --|◡-||◡-|◡-||--|◡-

Ἀλλ᾽ οὖν ἐκεῖσε προσδόκα μ᾽, ὅταν θάνω,   --|◡-||◡-|◡-||◡-|◡-

καὶ δῶμ᾽ ἑτοίμαζ᾽, ὡς ξυνοικήσουσά μοι.   --|◡-||◡-|◡-||--|◡-

---

THE ORDER, AND ENGLISH ACCENTUATION.

ᾧ προσπεσούμαι, καὶ περιπτύσσων χέρας, κάλων σον ὄνομα, δόξω ἔχειν τὴν φίλην γυναῖκα ἐν ἀγκάλαις, καίπερ οὐκ ἔχων· ψύχραν τέρψιν μεν, οἶμαι· ἀλλὰ ὅμως αν ἀπαντλοίην βάρος ψύχης· δε φοιτῶσα με ἐν ὀνείρασι αν εὐφραίνοις· γὰρ φίλος ἡδὺ λεύσσειν και ἐν νύκτι, ὅντινα χρόνον αν πάρῃ. Δε εἰ γλώσσα καὶ μέλος Ὀρφέως πάρην μοι, ὡς κηλήσαντα ὑμνοίσι τὴν κόρην Δημήτρος, η πόσιν κείνης, λάβειν σε ἐξ Ἅιδου, αν κατῆλθον· και οὔτε ὁ κύων Πλουτώνος, οὔτε Χάρων ὁ ψυχοπόμπος ἐπι κώπη αν ἔσχον με, πριν καταστῆσαι σον βίον εἰς φως. Ἀλλα ἐκείσε οὖν πρόσδοκα με, ὅταν θάνω, και ἑτοιμάζε δώμα, ὡς ξυνοικησούσά μοι.

TRANSLATION.

on which I will fall, and clasping mine arms around it, calling upon thy name, I shall fancy I have my dear wife in my embraces,—though having her not:—a cold enjoyment indeed, I ween: but still I may draw off the weight from my soul:—and by visiting me in my dréams thou mayest delight me; for a friend is sweet to behold even in the night, at whatever hour he may come! [*Gazing wistfully on Alcéstis.*] But if the tongue and music of Orpheus were mine, so as that, by invoking with hymns the daughter of Cérës, or her husband, I could receive thee back from the shades, I would descend; and neither the dog of Plúto, nor Cháron (the ferryman of departed spirits) at his oar, should stop me,—before I had restored thy life to the light!

[*Sighing and pointing downwards.*] But yonder then expect me when I die, and prepare a mansion for me, that thou mayest dwell with me.

---

363. ψυχρὰν τέρψιν, *a frigid delight,* the accusative—in apposition with δέμας of verse 358, to which the whole sentence has allusion. Monk rightly observes that this passage bears resemblance to καὶ δοκεῖ μ᾽ ἔχειν, κενὴν δόκησιν, οὐκ ἔχων: Hélena, 35. He considers the force of οἶμαι here, he says, to be that of an interjection, in the sense of ' *no doubt* or *I suppose:*'—"*I wot*—*I ween.*" For οἶμαι, however, some contend for οἶδα, but without reason.

364. ψυχῆς ἀπαντλοίην ἂν, *I may drain off from the soul* the load of grief or sorrow which oppresses it. Hesýchius explains ἀπαντλοίην by ἐπικουφίσαιμι.

365. For εὐφραίνοις, Lascar gives εὐφρέ-

νοις. In MSS. and most editions the reading is ἡδὺ γὰρ φίλοις. Musgrave from conjecture edited φίλος, which has been adopted by Gaisford, Matthiæ, and others. Elmsley proposes φίλους,—and in one edition we find φίλον.

367. γλῶττα dedère editóres ómnes ánte Wakefiéldium. Huic germánus est lócus Iphigeníæ in Aúlide, 1211. Cónferas quóque Medéæ, 543. Monk.

368. κόρην Δήμητρος, viz. *Próserpine.*

369. κηλήσαντα, the accusative for the dative. Aldus has κηλήσαντ᾽ ἄν.

372. ἔσχον—in the plural number, and having for nominative two nouns singular disjoined: which Porson defends.

Ἐν ταῖσιν αὐταῖς γάρ μ᾽ ἐπισκήψω κέδροις   375   `--|◡-|·|--|◡-||--|◡-`
σοὶ τούσδε θεῖναι, πλευρά τ᾽ ἐκτεῖναι πέλας   `--|◡-||--|◡-||--|◡◡`
πλευροῖσι τοῖς σοῖς· μηδὲ γὰρ θανών ποτε   `--|◡-||--|◡-||◡-|◡◡`
σοῦ χωρὶς εἴην τῆς μόνης πιστῆς ἐμοί.   `--|◡-||--|◡-||--|◡-`
ΧΟ. Καὶ μὴν ἐγώ σοι πένθος, ὡς φίλος φίλῳ.   `--|◡-||--|◡-||◡-|◡-`
λυπρὸν ξυνοίσω τῆσδε· καὶ γὰρ ἀξία.   380   `--|◡-||--|◡-||◡-|◡-`
ΑΛ. Ὦ παῖδες, αὐτοὶ δὴ τάδ᾽ εἰσηκούσατε   `--|◡-||--|◡-||--|◡◡`
πατρὸς λέγοντος, μὴ γαμεῖν ἄλλην ποτὲ   `◡-|◡-||--|◡-||--|◡◡`
γυναῖκ᾽ ἐφ᾽ ὑμῖν, μηδ᾽ ἀτιμάσειν ἐμέ.   `◡-|◡-||--|◡-||--|◡◡`
ΑΔ. Καὶ νῦν γέ φημι, καὶ τελευτήσω τάδε.   `--|◡-||◡◡|◡-|◡-|◡◡`
ΑΛ. Ἐπὶ τοῖσδε παῖδας χειρὸς ἐξ ἐμῆς δέχου. 385   `◡◡-|◡-||--|◡-||◡-|◡-`
ΑΔ. Δέχομαι φίλον γε δῶρον ἐκ φίλης χερός.   `◡◡-|◡-||◡-|◡-||◡-|◡◡`
ΑΛ. Σύ νυν γένου τοῖσδ᾽ ἀντ᾽ ἐμοῦ μήτηρ τέκνοις.   `◡-|◡-||--|◡-||--|◡-`
ΑΔ. Πολλή μ᾽ ἀνάγκη, σοῦ γ᾽ ἀπεστερημένοις.   `--|◡-||--|◡-||--|◡-`
ΑΛ. Ὦ τέκν᾽, ὅτε ζῆν χρῆν μ᾽, ἀπέρχομαι κάτω.   `--|◡-||--|◡-||◡-|◡-`

THE ORDER, AND ENGLISH ACCENTUATION.

Γαρ επισκήψω τούσδε θεῖναι με εν ταῖσι αὐταις κέδροις σοι, τε εκτεῖναι πλευρα πέλας τοῖς σοις πλευροῖσι· γαρ θανον μηδε ποτε εἰην χωρις σου της μόνης πιστης εμοι. ΧΟ. Και εγω μην ξυνοίσω σοι, ὡς φίλος φίλῳ; λύπρον πένθος τῆσδε· γαρ και ἀξία. ΑΛ. Ω παῖδες, αὐτοι εἰσηκούσατε τάδε πατρος λεγόντος, μη ποτε γάμειν ἀλλην γυναικα επι ὑμιν, μηδε ἀτιμάσειν εμε. ΑΔ. Και νυν γε φημι τάδε, και τελευτήσω. ΑΛ. Επι τοῖσδε δέχου παῖδας εξ εμης χειρος. ΑΔ. Δέχομαι φίλον δωρα γε εκ φίλης χειρος. ΑΛ. Γενου συ νυν μήτηρ τοῖσδε τέκνοις ἀντι εμου. ΑΔ. Πόλλη ἀναγκη με, ἀπεστερήμενος γε σου. ΑΛ. Ω τέκνα, ἀπέρχομαι κάτω, ὁτε χρην με ζην.

TRANSLATION.

For I will enjoin these [*Looking at his children.*] to deposit me in the same cedar with thee—and to lay my side near to thy side:—for when dead may I never be separate from thee, the only one faithful to me!

CHORUS. [*Admiringly and most sympathizingly.*] And I, troth, will bear in common with thee, as a friend with a friend, this sorrowful grief for her,—because that [*Shedding tears.*] she is worthy!

ALCESTIS. [*To her little son and daughter.*] O! children,—ye just now heard those words of your father—saying that he will never marry another woman to be over you,—nor dishonor me!

ADMETUS. And now too I say this, and I will perform it!

ALCESTIS. [*With an air of satisfaction.*] For this receive these children from my hand. [*She consigns the children over to their father.*]

ADMETUS. [*Deeply affected.*] I receive a dear gift in sooth from a dear hand! ALCESTIS. Be thou then a mother to these children in my stead.

ADMETUS. There is much need for me *to be so,*—deprived, at least, as they are of thee! ALCESTIS. [*Looking wistfully upon her little ones.*] O my children, I am going away below, at a time when I ought to live!

375. ἐν κέδροις, *in cedars,* that is, *in cedar coffin* or *tomb.* Cedar, it was affirmed, had the property of preserving dead bodies from putrefaction for many years. The Scholiast explained κέδροις by σόροις, *lóculis—sepúlchro.* Wakefield compares this passage with verse 1051 of the Oréstes.

376. For τούσδε θεῖναι, πλευρά τ᾽, Aldus printed τάσδε θεῖναι πλευράς, to the utter destruction of the metre. Barnes, part-

ly from conjecture, edited σοὶ τἀμὰ θεῖναι, συνθεῖναι πέλας.

377–8. μηδὲ γὰρ θανών ποτε σοῦ χωρὶς εἴην τῆς μόνης πιστῆς ἐμοί, is, as Brunck justly notices, a parody on μηδὲ γὰρ θανών ποτε σοῦ χωρὶς εἴην ἐντετευτλανωμένος of Aristóphanes, Acharn. 893—4.

385. ἐπὶ τοῖσδε, *upon these conditions.*

388. πολλή γ᾽ ἀνάγκη ómnes editiónes: sed invenúste repetítur γε. MONK.

ΑΔ. Οἴμοι, τί δράσω δῆτα σοῦ μονούμενος; 390 | - - | ◡ - || - - | ◡ - || ◡ - | ◡ ◡

ΑΛ. Χρόνος μαλάξει σ'· οὐδέν ἐσθ' ὁ κατθανών. | ◡ - | ◡ - || - - | ◡ - || ◡ - | ◡ -

ΑΔ. Ἄγου με σύν σοι, πρὸς θεῶν, ἄγου κάτω. | ◡ - | ◡ - || - - | ◡ - || ◡ - | ◡ -

ΑΛ. Ἀρκοῦμεν ἡμεῖς οἱ προθνήσκοντες σέθεν. | - - | ◡ - || - - | ◡ - || - - | ◡ ◡

ΑΔ. Ὦ δαῖμον, οἵας ξυζύγου μ' ἀποστερεῖς. | - - | ◡ - || - - | ◡ - || ◡ - | ◡ -

ΑΛ. Καὶ μὴν σκοτεινὸν ὄμμα μου βαρύνεται, 395 | - - | ◡ - || ◡ - | ◡ - || ◡ - | ◡ ◡

ΑΔ. Ἀπωλόμην ἄρ', εἴ με δὴ λείψεις, γύναι. | ◡ - | ◡ - || ◡ - | ◡ - | ◡ - | ◡ ◡

ΑΛ. Ὡς οὐκ ἔτ' οὖσαν, οὐδὲν ἂν λέγοις ἐμέ. | - - | ◡ - || ◡ - | ◡ - || ◡ - | ◡ ◡

ΑΔ. Ὄρθου πρόσωπον· μὴ λίπῃς παῖδας σέθεν. | - - | ◡ - || - - | ◡ - || - - | ◡ ◡

ΑΛ. Οὐ δῆθ' ἑκοῦσά γ'· ἀλλὰ χαίρετ', ὦ τέκνα. | - - | ◡ - || ◡ - | ◡ - || ◡ - | ◡ ◡

ΑΔ. Βλέψον πρὸς αὐτούς, βλέψον. ΑΛ. Οὐδὲν εἰμ' ἔτι. | - - | ◡ - || - - | ◡ - || ◡ - | ◡ ◡

ΑΔ. Τί δρᾷς; Προλείπεις; ΑΛ. Χαῖρ'. 401 | ◡ - | ◡ - || - - |

ΑΔ. Ἀπωλόμην τάλας. | ◡ - || ◡ - | ◡ -

ΧΟ. Βέβηκεν, οὐκ ἔτ' ἐστὶν Ἀδμήτου γυνή. | ◡ - | ◡ - || ◡ - | ◡ - || - - | ◡ -

ΕΥΜΗΛΟΣ.

Ἰώ μοι τύχας· μαῖα δὴ κάτω [Στροφὴ.] | ◡ - - ◡ - || - ◡ - ◡ - α'

βέβακεν· οὐκέτ' ἐστὶν, ὦ | ◡ - | ◡ - || ◡ - | - β'

THE ORDER, AND ENGLISH ACCENTUATION.

ΑΔ. Οἴμοι, τι δράσω δῆτα, σου μονούμενος; ΑΛ. Χρόνος μαλάξει σε· ὁ κάτθανων ἐστι οὐδεν. ΑΔ. Ἄγου με συν σοι, προς θεῶν, ἄγου κάτω. ΑΛ. Ἀρκούμεν ἡμεις οἱ προθνησκόντες σέθεν. ΑΔ. Ὦ δαίμον, οἵας ξύζυγου ἀπόστερεις με. ΑΛ. Και μην σκοτεινον ὄμμα μου βαρύνεται. ΑΔ. Ἀπώλομην ἄρα, ει δη λείψεις με, γύναι. ΑΛ. Ὡς οὔσαν οὔκετι, αν λέγοις ἐμε οὐδεν. ΑΔ. Ὄρθου προσώπον· μη λιπῃς παιδας σέθεν. ΑΛ. Ου δῆτα ἑκούσα γε· ἀλλα χαίρετε, ω τέκνα. ΑΔ. Βλέψον προς αὐτους, βλέψον. ΑΛ. Εἰμι οὐδεν ἔτι. ΑΔ. Τι δρᾳς; Προλείπεις; ΑΛ. Χαίρε. ΑΔ. Ἀπώλομην τάλας. ΧΟ. Βεβήκε γύνη Ἀδμήτου ἐστι οὔκετι. ΕΥ. Ἰω μοι τύχας· μαῖα δη βεβάκε κάτω· ἐστι οὔκετι, ω

TRANSLATION.

ADMETUS. [*Sorrowing.*] Woes my heart! what shall I do then, of thee bereft? ALCESTIS. Time will assuage thee:—he who is dead is nothing! ADMETUS. [*Inconsolably.*] Take me with thee, by the Gods,—take me below! ALCESTIS. Enow are we who die for thee! ADMETUS. [*Clasping his hands.*] O fate, of what a wife thou bereavest me! ALCESTIS. [*Heavily.*] And lo! my darkening eye is weighed down! ADMETUS. [*Embracing his spouse tenderly.*] I am undone then, if thou really leave me, my wife! ALCESTIS. [*Reclining her head.*] As being no more, thou mayest speak of me as nought. ADMETUS. [*With tears.*] Raise up thy face: desert not thy children! ALCESTIS. Not indeed willingly, at least!—but, farewell, O children! ADMETUS. [*Sobbing.*] Look upon them,—O look! ALCESTIS. [*Heaving a sigh.*] I am no more! ADMETUS. [*Weeping.*] What doest thou?—Dost thou leave us? ALCESTIS. [*Faintly.*] Farewell. [*Alcéstis dies.*] ADMETUS. [*Groaning.*] I am undone, wretched man! CHORUS. She is gone,—Admetus's wife is no more! EUMELUS.Ah! me my state: ma is now gone down: she is no longer, O

---

391. χρόνος μαλάξει, *time will emolliate* or *soften*, that is, *time will assuage thy sorrow.* The same expression occurs again below, verse 1104.

396. Barnes (most likely by an error at press) has λείψει: Lascar, from a similar cause, ἀπολόμην and λείψης.

399. In lieu of χαίρετ', ὦ τέκνα, Lascar,

Aldus, and indeed most editors before Musgrave, have χαιρέτω, τέκνα.

403. Lascar's reading is, ἰώ μοι μοι τύχας, μαῖα δέ. Elmsley conjectured ἰὼ ἰὼ τύχας. I have given "ma," as the translation of μαῖα, and which I believe to be its meaning here, though it strictly implies "*nurse*" rather than "*mother.*"

πάτερ, ὑφ᾽ ἁλίῳ·   405   ‿‿‿–‿–   γ´
προλιποῦσα δ᾽ ἁμὸν   ‿‿–|‿‿–   δ´
βίον ὠρφάνισεν τλάμων.   ‿‿–|‿‿–‖--   ε´
῍Ιδε γάρ, ἴδε βλέφαρον, καὶ   ‿‿‿‿–‖‿‿--   ζ´
παρατόνους χέρας.   ‿‿‿–‿‿   η´
῾Υπάκουσον, ἄκουσον, ὦ   410   ‿‿–|‿‿–‖‿–   ϑ´
μᾶτερ, ἀντιάζω σ᾽·   –‿|–‿‖--   ι´
ἐγώ σ᾽, ἐγὼ, μᾶτερ,   ‿–|‿–‖–‿   κ´
νῦν γε καλοῦμαι, ὁ σὸς ποτὶ σοῖσι πί-   –‿‿|–‿‿|–‿‿|–‿‿ λ´
τνων στόμασιν νεοσσός—   –‿‿‖–‿|–‿   μ´

ΑΔ. Τὴν οὐ κλύουσαν, οὐδ᾽ ὁρῶσαν· ὥστ᾽ ἐγὼ   415   --|‿–‖‿–|‿–‖‿–|‿–
καὶ σφὼ βαρείᾳ ξυμφορᾷ πεπλήγμεθα.   --|‿–‖--|‿–‖‿–|‿‿

ΕΥ. Νέος ἐγώ, πάτερ, λείπομαι φίλας [᾽Αντιστρ.] ‿‿‿–‿–‖‿–‿–   α´
μονόστολός τε ματρός· ὦ   ‿–|‿–‖‿–|‿–   β´
σχέτλια δὴ παθὼν   ‿‿‿–‿‿   γ´
ἐγὼ ἔργα * *   420   ‿‿–|‿**   δ´
* * * * * * *   ***|***‖**   ε´
σύ τε μοι, ξύγκασι κούρα,   ‿‿–‖‿‿--   ζ´
ξυνέτλας. ῏Ω πάτερ,   ‿‿‿–‿‿   η´

THE ORDER, AND ENGLISH ACCENTUATION.

πάτερ, ὑπο ἁλιω· δε προλιποῦσα τλάμων ωρφάνισε ἁμον βίον. Γαρ ἰδε, ἰδε βλέφαρον, και παρά-
τονους χέρας. ῾Υπακουσον, ακουσον, ω μάτερ, αντιάζω σε· ἐγω καλουμαι σε, ἐγω γε νυν, μάτερ,
ὁ σος νεόσσος πιτνων πότι σοῖσι στόμασι. ΑΔ. Την ου κλυουσαν, οὐδε ὁρῶσαν· ὥστε ἐγω και σφω
πεπλήγμεθα βαρείᾳ ξύμφορᾳ. ΕΥ. Νέος ἐγω λείπομαι, πάτερ, τε φίλας μάτρος μονόστολος· ω ἐ-
γω δη πάθων σχέτλια ἔργα· τε συ, ξύγκασι κούρα, ξύνετλας μοι. Ω πάτερ,

TRANSLATION.

father, under the sun: and having left me, the unhappy woman, she has
rendered my life an orphan's! For look, look thou at her eyelid, and her
nerveless arms. [*Calling impassionately.*] List, listen, O mother, I entreat
thee: I call thee, I, verily, call thee now, mother,—thy little son falling
upon thy mouth. [*He kisses her lips affectionately.*]

ADMETUS. Upon her's who hears not, nor sees :—so that [*Taking his
children in his arms.*] I and you-two are struck with a heavy calamity!

EUMELUS. [*With much pathos.*] Young am I left, O father, and by my
dear mother deserted: Oh! me who have already experienced dreadful
doings: [*Taking his sister kindly by the hand.*] and thou, O youthful-maid
my sister, hast suffered with me! [*Sorrowfully to Admétus.*] Oh! father,

408. For ἴδε γάρ, ἴδε, Musgrave proposed ἴδε γὰρ δὴ, as answering better to the
Iónic à minóre, in the antistrophë, viz., σύ
τε μοι ξύγ-: Monk, however, defends the
vulgate—two short syllables being ever
equivalent to a long one.

411. Addidi σ᾽, ut vitétur hiátus, quo
cáret vérsus antistróphicus. MONK.

413. Lascar omitted νῦν γε. Aldus has
προσπίτνων,—Musgrave, πιτνῶν,—Gaisford, πιτνῶν. Monk says, "non displicéret πρτὶ σοῖς προπίτνων."

414. νεοσσὸς, very literally, *a little nest-
ling* or *an unfledged bird.* This term was
(particularly by the Tragic writers) en-
dearingly applied to children.

415. The Scholiast fills up the ellipsis
in the construction here, by reading ταύτην δὴ καλεῖς before τὴν οὐ κλύουσαν.

420. Hiátum hîc primus detéxit Can-
térus:—ex ingénio supplevérunt Barnésius et Wakefiéldius. MONK.

423. Most editions have ἀνόνητ᾽ ἀνόνητ᾽.
Matthiæ restored the Doric form.

ἀνόνατ᾽, ἀνόνατ᾽ ἐνύμ-   ‿‿-|‿‿-‖‿-   θ'
φευσας, οὐδὲ γήρως   -‿|-‿‖--   ι'
ἕβας τέλος ξὺν τᾷδ᾽,   425   ‿-|‿-‖--   κ'
ἔφθιτο γὰρ πάρος· οἰχομένας δὲ σοῦ,   -‿‿|-‿‿|-‿‿|-‿-   λ'
μᾶτερ, ὄλωλεν οἶκος.   -‿‿‖-‿|-‿   μ'

XO. Ἄδμητ᾽, ἀνάγκη τάσδε συμφορὰς φέρειν·   --|‿-‖--|‿-‖·-|‿-
οὐ γάρ τι πρῶτος, οὐδὲ λοίσθιος βροτῶν,   --|‿-‖·‿-|‿-‖‿-|‿-
γυναικὸς ἐσθλῆς ἤπλακες· γίγνωσκε δὲ,   430   ‿-|‿-‖--|‿-‖-‿‿
ὡς πᾶσιν ἡμῖν κατθανεῖν ὀφείλεται.   --|‿-·|··--|‿-‖‿-|‿-
ΑΔ. Ἐπίσταμαί γε, κοὐκ ἄφνω κακὸν τόδε   ‿-|‿-‖|‿-‖‿-|‿-‿
προσέπτατ᾽· εἰδὼς δ᾽ αὔτ᾽ ἐτειρόμην πάλαι.   ‿-|‿-‖·-|‿-‿·‿-|‿-
Ἀλλ᾽, ἐκφορὰν γὰρ τοῦδε θήσομαι νεκροῦ,   --|‿-‖·‿-|‿-‖·-|‿-
πάρεστε, καὶ μένοντες, ἀντηχήσατε   435   ‿-|‿-‖·‿-|‿-‖·-|‿‿
παιᾶνα τῷ κάτωθεν ἀσπόνδῳ θεῷ.   -|‿-‖‿-|‿-|·-|‿-
Πᾶσιν δὲ Θεσσαλοῖσιν, ὧν ἐγὼ κρατῶ,   --|‿-‖‿-|‿-‖‿-|‿-
πένθους γυναικὸς τῆσδε κοινοῦσθαι λέγω,   --|‿-‖--|·‿-‖-|‿-

THE ORDER, AND ENGLISH ACCENTUATION.

ανονάτα, ανονάτα ενυμφεύσας, οὐδὲ ξὺν τᾷδε ἕβας τέλος γήρως, γὰρ ἔφθιτο πάρος· δε συ οιχό-
μενας, μάτερ, οἶκος ολώλε. XO. Ἀδμήτε, ανάγκη φέρειν τάσδε σύμφορας· γαρ ου τι πρῶτος, ουδὲ
λοίσθιος βρότων, ἤπλακες ἐσθλῆς γυναίκος· δε γιγνώσκε, ὡς κάτθανειν οφείλεται ἡμιν πᾶσι. ΑΔ.
Ἐπίσταμαι γε, και οὐκ ἄφνω τόδε κάκον προσέπτατο· δε πάλαι εἰδὼς αὐτο ετείρομην. Ἀλλα, γαρ
θήσομαι τοῦδε νέκρου εκφοραν, παρέστε, και μενόντες, αντηχήσατε παιάνα τω θέω κατάθεν ασ-
πόνδω. Δε πᾶσι Θεσσαλοῖσι, ὧν εγω κρᾶτω, λέγω κοινούσθαι πένθους τῆσδε γυναίκος,

TRANSLATION.

in vain, in vain didst thou marry, nor [*Looking at his mother.*] with her
arrivedst thou at the term of senility,—for [*Sobbing.*] she has perished
beforehand :—but [*Shedding tears on his mother.*] thou being gone, mother, the house is undone!

CHORUS. [*Consolingly to the king.*] Admétus,—it is requisite that thou
bear-with this disaster: for thou (in nowise the first, nor the last of mortals) hast lost an amiable wife:—but know, that to die is a debt incumbent on us all.

ADMETUS. [*With lamentation and many sobs.*] I know it indeed,—and
not of a sudden is this calamity come upon me : but long since aware
of it have I been afflicted!

[*With earnest entreaty.*] But, for I will have the corse borne forth, be
present,—and, while ye stay, chant a hymn to the God below who-ac-
cepteth-not-libations!

[*With the commanding air of princely authority.*] And all the Thessa-
lians, over whom I reign, I enjoin to participate-in grief for this lady,

425. τέλος, end: freely, *period* or *stage*.
429. Monk notices that the Chorus u-
ses words much to the same effect again,
below, verse 916: τλᾶθ᾽, ὅν σὺ πρῶτος ὤ-
λεσας γυναῖκα: and verse 954, τί νέον τόδε;
Πολλοὺς ἤδη παρέλυσεν θάνατος δάμαρτος.
430. Lascar, Aldus, and most other e-
ditors, except Gaisford, have ἤμπλακες.
431. ὡς πᾶσιν ἡμῖν κατθανεῖν ὀφείλεται, literally, *that it is due for us all to die*:—so
again in verse 798, βροτοῖς ἅπασι κατθανεῖν

ὀφείλεται, *it is owing for all mortals to die,*
that is, *all mankind must die.*
434. ἐκφορὰν τοῦδε θήσομαι νεκροῦ, *I will
put the corpse forth* or *out of doors—I will
lay the dead body out,* literally, *beyond the
gates:* but, as Alcéstis is represented as
having died outside the palace, we may
by ἐκφορὰν understand simply, "*out*" or
"*out of this place.*"
438. In most copies we find πένθος, but
πένθους is unquestionably preferable.

κουρᾷ ξυρῆκεῖ, καὶ μελαμπέπλῳ στολῇ.

Τέθριππά τε ζεύγνυσθε, καὶ μονάμπυκας   440

πώλους σιδήρῳ τέμνετ᾽ αὐχένων φόϐην.

᾽Αυλῶν δὲ μὴ κατ᾽ ἄστυ, μὴ λύρας κτύπος

ἔστω, σελήνας δώδεκ᾽ ἐκπληρουμένας.

᾽Ου γάρ τιν᾽ ἄλλον φίλτερον θάψω νεκρὸν

τοῦδ᾽, οὐδ᾽ ἀμείνον᾽ εἰς ἔμ᾽. ᾽Αξία δέ μοι   445

τιμῆς, ἐπεὶ τέθνηκεν ἀντ᾽ ἐμοῦ μόνη.

ΧΟ.῏Ω Πελία θύγατερ, χαί-   [Στροφὴ α᾽.]   α᾽

ρουσά μοι ἐν ᾽Αΐδα δόμοισιν   β᾽

τὸν ἀνάλιον οἶκον οἰκετεύοις.   γ᾽

῎Ιστω δ᾽ ᾽Αΐδας ὁ μελαγχαίτας   450   δ᾽

θεός, ὅς τ᾽ ἐπὶ κώπᾳ   ε᾽

πηδαλίῳ τε γέρων   ζ᾽

νεκροπομπὸς ἴζει,   η᾽

THE ORDER, AND ENGLISH ACCENTUATION.

ξυρῆκει κούρᾳ, καὶ μελάμπέπλῳ στολῇ. Τε ζευγνύσθε τεθρίππα, καὶ τέμνετε σιδήρῳ μονάμπυκας πώλους φόϐην αὐχένων. Δε μὴ ἔστω κτύπος αὐλῶν κάτα ἄστυ, μὴ λύρας, δῶδεκα ἐκπληρούμενας σελήνας. Γαρ οὕτινα ἄλλον νέκρον φίλτερον τοῦδε θάψω, οὐδε ἀμείνονα εἰς ἐμε. Δε ἄξια τίμης μοι, ἐπεὶ μόνη τεθνήκε ἀντὶ ἐμοῦ. ΧΟ. Ω θύγατερ Πελία, χαιρούσα μοι οικετεύοις τον οἶκον ἀνάλιον εἰν δομοῖσι ᾽Αΐδα. Δε ᾽Αΐδας, ὁ μελαγχαίτας θέος, ἴστω, τε γέρων νεκροπόμπος ὁς ἴζει ἐπι κώπᾳ τε πηδάλιῳ,

TRANSLATION.

with shorn locks, and in sable garb! And yoke your four-horse-teams, and crop with the shears your single-bridled steeds as to the manes on their necks!

And let there not be the noise of pipes throughout the city,—nor of the lyre, for twelve completed moons.

⁚ For no other corpse more dear than this shall I inter, or [*Greatly affected.*] more kind towards me.

Yea [*Making sign for the procession to move onward.*] she is worthy of honor from me, seeing-that she alone hath died for me! [*Exit Admétus followed by mourners bearing the dead body of Alcéstis.*]

CHORUS. [*In a strain solemn and impressive.*] O daughter of Pélias, faring blessedly to me may thou dwell in that dwelling which sun never visiteth,—within the mansions of Plúto.

[*Firmly.*] And let Plúto, the God with ebon hair, know,—and the old man the ferryman of the dead who sits intent upon his oar and rudder,

---

439. κουρᾷ ξυρῆκεῖ, *with rasile tonsure* or *with shorn pate:*—μελαμπέπλῳ στολῇ, *in black-robed cloak* or *clothing.*

440. Another reading is, τέθριππά θ᾽ οἱ ζεύγνυσθε. Reiske proposed "τέθριππα δὲ ζεύγη τε καὶ, &c.," *and both from your chariot teams and single horses cut the manes.*

445. Libénter (observes Monk) reposúerim τῆσδ᾽ pro τοῦδ᾽. Deinde ἀξία δέ μοι τιμῆς verténdum, "*digna quæ à me honórem accípiat,*" ad méntem Porsóni, Hec. ver.313: úbi ádvocat hunc lócum, et Aristoph. Acharn. 633. Pac. 918.

447. The common reading here is Πελίου. Monk says,—" prímus restítui Dóricam fórmam quæ éxtat in Píndari Pýthiis, iv. 239."

448. Láscar, Aldus, and most editors have ἐν ᾽Αΐδα δόμοισι. In Músgrave's text however the preposition is wanting. To Wakefield we are indebted for the restoratiou of εἰν, which the metre evidently demands, and which beyond doùbt is the original and correct lection.

449. For οἰκετεύοις, Aldus has ἱκετεύοις, and Láscar, οἰκετεύεις.

πολὺ δὴ, πολὺ δὴ γυναῖκ᾿ ἀρίσταν   ⏑⏑–|⏑⏑–‖⏑–|⏑–‖– ϑ´

λίμναν Ἀχεροντίαν πο-   455   ––|⏑⏑–‖⏑–|⏑   ι´

ρεύσας ἐλάτᾳ δικώπῳ.   ––|⏑⏑–‖⏑–|–   κ´

Πολλά σε μουσοπόλοι μέλ-   [Ἀντιστροφὴ α´.]   –⏑⏑|–⏑⏑‖––   α´

ψουσι καθ᾿ ἑπτάτονόν τ᾿ ὀρείαν   –⏑⏑|–⏑⏑‖–⏑|––   β´

χέλυν, ἐν τ᾿ ἀλύροις κλέοντες ὕμνοις,   ⏑⏑–|⏑⏑–‖⏑–|⏑–‖–   γ´

Σπάρτᾳ, κύκλος ἀνίκα Καρνείου   460   ––|⏑⏑–‖⏑⏑–|––   δ´

περινίσσεται ὥρᾳ   ⏑⏑–|⏑⏑–‖–   ε´

μηνός, ἀειρομένας   –⏑⏑|–⏑⏑|–   ϛ´

παννύχου σελάνας,   –⏑|–⏑‖––   η´

λιπαραῖσί τ᾿ ἐν ὀλβίαις Ἀθάναις·   ⏑⏑–|⏑⏑–‖⏑–|⏑–‖–   ϑ´

τοίαν ἔλιπες θανοῦσα   465   ––|⏑⏑–‖⏑–|⏑   ι´

μολπὰν μελέων ἀοιδοῖς.   ––|⏑⏑–‖⏑–|–   κ´

Εἴθ᾿ ἐπ᾿ ἐμοὶ μὲν εἴη,   [Στροφὴ β´.]   –⏑⏑|–‖⏑–|–   α´

δυναίμαν δέ σε πέμψαι   ⏑–‖–⏑⏑–‖–   β´

φάος ἐξ Ἀΐδα τερέμνων,   ⏑⏑–|⏑⏑–‖⏑–|–   γ´

Κωκυτοῦ τε ῥείθρων,   470   ––‖–⏑⏑–‖–   δ´

ποταμίᾳ νερτέρᾳ τε κώπᾳ.   ⏑⏑⏑–‖–⏑–‖⏑––   ε´

THE ORDER, AND ENGLISH ACCENTUATION.

πορεύσας γυναῖκα πόλυ δη, δη πόλυ ἀρίσταν, δικώπῳ ἐλάτᾳ Ἀχερόντιαν λίμναν. Πόλλα μουσόπολοι κλεόντες σε τε κάτα ἑπτάτοτον ὀρείαν χέλυν, τε εν ἀλυροις ὕμνοις, μελψοῦσι Σπάρτᾳ, ἄνικα κύκλος περινίσσεται ὥρα Καρνείου μηνός, σελάνας αειρόμενας πάννυχου, τε εν λιπαραῖσι ὀλβίαις Ἀθάναις· τοίαν μόλπαν ἔλιπες, θανοῦσα, ἀοιδοῖς μέλεων. Εἴθε μεν εἴη επί ἐμοι, δε δυναίμαν πέμψαι σε φάος εκ τερέμνων Ἀΐδα, τε ῥείθρων Κωκύτου, ποτάμια τε νέρτερα κώπα.

TRANSLATION.

that he is conducting a woman, by far now, ay by far, the best,—in his two-oared boat across the Stýgian lake.

Often shall the servants of the Muses, celebrating thee, both on the seven-stringed mountain lute, and in hymns unaccompanied by the lyre, sing of thee in Sparta, when the anniversary comes round in the season of the Carnéan month, the moon being up the whole night long; and in splendid, happy Athens: such a song hast thou left by thy death to the minstrels of melodies. [*Feelingly.*] Would, indeed, it rested with me, and that I could waft thee into the light from the mansions of Hádēs, and the streams of Cocýtus, by the fluvial and subterraneous oar!

---

455. Ἀχεροντίαν, *Stýgian* or (more properly) *Acheróntian*. The Scholiast seems to have read Ἀχερουσίαν: Láscar, contrary to all others, has Ἀχεροντείαν.

457. μουσοπόλοι, *the servants of the Muses*, namely, *the poets or bards.*

458. ὀρείαν, *belonging to the hills :* more freely, *on the mountains.* The Scholiast has οὐρείαν, and he explains ἑπτάτονος χέλυς by ἑπτάχορδος.

459. For κλέοντες, MSS. have κλείοντες.

460. All the early editors give Σπάρτα κύκλος. Barnes, on the recommendation of Scáliger, adopted, Σπάρτᾳ κυκλὰς ἀνίκα

Καρνείου περινίσσεται ὥρα—a reading Musgrave and some others have greatly approved: Matthiæ and Monk, however, object to the phrase κυκλὰς ὥρα, as being unlike the style of Enrípidès.

461. Musgrave and Matthiæ give περινείσεται,—and in lieu of ὥρᾳ or ὥρα, some contend for ὥρας.

463. ὅτε γὰρ πανσέληνός ἐστι, δι᾿ ὅλης τῆς νυκτὸς φέγγει. SCHOLIAST.

469. Láscar has Ἄδου,—Aldus, Ἀΐδου. Editions have τεράμνων. Hesýchius gives δικήματα as the sense of τέρεμνα.

470. Many different readings occur.

Σὺ γὰρ, ὦ μόνα, ὦ φίλα γυ-   ◡◡-|◡◡-‖◡-|◡   ζ΄

ναικῶν, σὺ τὸν αὑτᾶς   - - ◡‖- -   η΄

ἔτλας πόσιν ἀντὶ σᾶς ἀμεῖψαι   ◡- ◡◡‖- ◡|- ◡‖- ◡   ϑ΄

ψυχᾶς ἐξ Ἅιδα. Κούφα σοι   475   -|- -|- -|- -   ι΄

χθὼν ἐπάνωθε πέσοι, γύναι· εἰ δέ τι   -◡◡|-◡◡|-◡◡|-◡◡   κ΄

καινὸν ἕλοιτο πόσις λέχος, ἦ μάλ᾿ ἐ-   -◡◡|-◡◡|-◡◡|-◡◡   λ΄

μοί γ᾿ ἂν εἴη στυγη-   -◡-‖-◡-   μ΄

θεὶς τέκνοις τε τοῖς σοῖς.   -◡|-◡‖--   ν΄

———

Μάτερος οὐ θελούσας   [Ἀντιστρ. β΄.] 480   -◡◡-‖◡-|-   α΄

πρὸ παιδὸς χθονὶ κρύψαι   ◡-‖-◡◡-‖-   β΄

δέμας, οὐδὲ πατρὸς γεραιοῦ   ◡◡-|◡◡-‖◡-|-   γ΄

* * * * * *   ***‖***   δ΄

ὃν ἔτεκον δ᾿, οὐκ ἔτλαν ῥύσασθαι   ◡◡◡-‖-◡-‖---   ε΄

σχετλίω, πολιὰν ἔχοντε   ◡◡-|◡◡-‖◡-|◡   ζ΄

χαίταν· σὺ δ᾿ ἐν ἥβᾳ   485   --◡◡‖--   η΄

νέᾳ προθανοῦσα φωτὸς οἴχει.   ◡-◡◡‖-◡|-◡‖-   ϑ΄

Τοιαύτας εἴη μοι κύρσαι   -··|- -|- -|- -   ι΄

ξυνδυάδος φιλίας ἀλόχου· τὸ γὰρ   -◡◡|-◡◡|-◡◡|-◡◡   κ΄

ἐν βιότῳ σπάνιον μέρος· ἦ γὰρ ἐ- |-◡◡|-◡◡|-◡◡|-◡◡ λ΄

THE ORDER, AND ENGLISH ACCENTUATION.

Γαρ συ, ω μόνα, ω φίλα γυναίκων, συ ετλας αμείψαι αντι σας ψύχας αύτας τον πόσιν εξ Ἅιδα. Κούφα χθων πέσοι επανώθε σοι, γύναι· δε ει πόσις ελοίτο τι καινόν λέχος, η εμοί γε τε τοις σοις τέκνοις αν είη μάλα στυγηθεις. Μάτερος ου θελούσας κρύψαι δέμας χθόνι προ παιδος, ουδέ γεραίου πάτρος, * * * * *, δε σχέτλιω εχοντε πόλιαν χαίταν ουκ ετλαν ρυσάσθαι ον ετεκον· δε συ εν νέα ήβα οίχει προθανούσα φωτός. Είη μοι κύρσαι ξυνδυάδος τοιαύτας φίλιας αλόχου· γαρ σπάνιον εν βιότω το μέρος· γαρ η

TRANSLATION.

For thou, O unexampled, O dear among women, thou hadst the courage to receive in exchange for thine own life thy husband from the realms below.

Light may the earth fall upon thee, lady:—and if thy husband seeks any new alliance, assuredly by me at least and by thy children will he be greatly detested!

When his mother was not willing to hide her body in the ground for her son, nor his aged father, * * * *, but those two wretches both of them having hoary locks, had not the heart to rescue him whom they begat:—yet didst thou in blooming youth depart,—dying in thy husband's stead. [Admiringly and emphatically.] Be it mine to meet with the like of such a dear consort, (but rare in life is such a portion,) for surely

---

472. ὦ μόνα, *O thou alone, O thou the only one*: ὦ φίλα γυναικῶν for ὦ φιλτάτα γυναικῶν, *O dear among women* for *O thou dearest of women*. Schaefer's reading is, σὺ γὰρ, ὦ φίλα, ὦ φίλα γυναικῶν.

473. Vulgò σύ γε τὸν σαυτᾶς, invito métro. Delévi γε, quod omittunt MSS. dúo Parisiénses, et édidi αὑτᾶς. Μονκ.

476. In most editions we find ἐπάνω πέσοις,—faultily. Matthiæ has ἐπάνωθεν πέ-

σοι,—and Erfurdt, whom Monk has followed, ἐπάνωθε πέσοι.

482-3. A verse to complete the metre as well as the sense seems here wanting.

483. Suspéctum hábeo ῥύσασθαι,—cújus príma prodúcta métro stróphico málè respóndet. Μονκ.

487. For εἴη μοι κύρσαι, many MSS. and editions have εἴη με κυρῆσαι,—and, in the next line, φίλας for φιλίας.

μοί γ' ἄλυπος δι' αἰ-   490 |- ◡ -||- ◡ -   μ'

ῶνος ἂν ξυνείη. |- ◡|- ◡||- -   ν'

ΗΡΑΚΛΗΣ.

Ξένοι, Φεραίας τῆσδε κωμῆται χθονός, |◡ -|◡ -||- -|◡ -||- -|◡ ◡

Ἄδμητον ἐν δόμοισιν ἆρα κιγχάνω; |- -|◡ -||◡ -|◡ -||◡ -|◡ -

ΧΟ. Ἔστ' ἐν δόμοισι παῖς Φέρητος, Ἡράκλεις. |- -|◡ -||◡ -|◡ -||◡ -|◡ -

Ἀλλ' εἰπὲ, χρεία τίς σε Θεσσαλῶν χθόνα   495 |- -|◡ -||◡ -|◡ -||◡ -|◡ ◡

πέμπει, Φεραῖον ἄστυ προσβῆναι τόδε; |- -|◡ -||◡ -|◡ -||- -|◡ ◡

ΗΡ. Τιρυνθίῳ πράσσω τιν' Εὐρυσθεῖ πόνον. |- -|◡ -||◡ -|◡ -||- -|◡ ◡

ΧΟ. Ποῖ καὶ πορεύει; Τῷ ξυνέζευξαι πλάνῳ; |- -|◡ -||◡ -|◡ -||- -|◡ -

ΗΡ. Θρηκὸς τέτρωρον ἅρμα Διομήδους μέτα. |- -|◡ -||◡ -|◡ ◡ ◡||- -|◡ ◡

ΧΟ. Πῶς οὖν δυνήσει; Μῶν ἄπειρος εἶ ξένου;   500 |- ◡|◡ -||◡ -|◡ -||◡ -|◡ -

ΗΡ. Ἄπειρος· οὔπω Βιστόνων ἦλθον χθόνα. |◡ -|◡ -||◡ -|◡ -||- -|◡ -

ΧΟ. Οὐκ ἔστιν ἵππων δεσπόσαι σ' ἄνευ μάχης· |- -|◡ -||◡ -|◡ -||◡ -|◡ -

ΗΡ. Ἀλλ' οὐδ' ἀπειπεῖν τοὺς πόνους οἷόν τε μοι. |- -|◡ -||◡ -|◡ -||- -|◡ -

ΧΟ. Κτανὼν ἄρ' ἥξεις, ἢ θανὼν αὐτοῦ μενεῖς. |◡ -|◡ -||◡ -|◡ -||- -|◡ - ◠

THE ORDER, AND ENGLISH ACCENTUATION.

γε ἂν ξυνείη ἐμοὶ δία αἰώνος ἀλύπος. ΗΡ. Ξένοι, κωμῆται τῆσδε Φεραίας χθόνος, ἆρα κιγχάνω Ἄδμητον ἐν δόμοῖσι; ΧΟ. Παῖς Φερῆτος ἐστι ἐν δομοῖσι, Ἡράκλεις. Ἀλλα εἶπε, τις χρεία πέμπει σε χθόνα Θεσσαλων, προσβῆναι τόδε Φεραῖον ἄστυ; ΗΡ. Πράσσω τίνα πόνον Τιρυνθίω Εὐρυσθει. ΧΟ. Καὶ ποι πορεύει; Τῷ πλάνω ξυνεζεύξαι; ΗΡ. Μέτα τετρώρον ἅρμα Διομήδους Θρῆκος. ΧΟ. Πως οὖν δυνήσει; Μων εἰ ἀπείρος ξένου; ΗΡ. Ἀπείρος· οὔπω ἦλθον χθόνα Βιστόνων. ΧΟ. Οὐκ ἐστι σε δέσποσαι ἵππων ἄνευ μάχης. ΗΡ. Ἀλλα οὐδὲ οἷον τε μοι ἀπείπειν τοὺς πόνους. ΧΟ. Κτάνων ἆρα ἥξεις, ἢ θάνων μένεις αὐτου.

TRANSLATION.

at least she would be [*Smiling joyously, and seeming delighted.*] with me for ever without once causing pain!

HERCULES. [*Entering.*] Ye strangers, inhabitants of this land of Phérës, can I find Admétus in the palace?

CHORUS. The son of Phérës is in the palace, Hérculës. But inform me what business sends thee to the country of the Thessálians, occasioning thee to come to this city of Phéræ?

HERCULES. I am performing a certain labor for the Tirýnthian Eurýstheus. CHORUS. [*Inquisitively.*] And whither goest thou? Upon what roving-expedition art thou bound?

HERCULES. After the four-horse chariot of Díomede the Thracian.

CHORUS. How then wilt thou be able? Art thou ignorant of this lord?

HERCULES. [*Assentingly.*] Ignorant:—I have never as yet been to the land of the Bistónians. CHORUS. It is not that thou canst make thyself master of these steeds, without battle!

HERCULES. But neither is it possible for me to renounce the labors.

CHORUS. Having slain, then, thou wilt [*Glancing significantly at the hero.*] come back,—or being slain thou wilt remain there!

---

492. κωμῆται· οἱ γείτονες· κώμη γὰρ ἡ γειτονία ἢ γειτνία, *vicinitas*. SUIDAS.

493. κιχάνω, Lascáris, Aldus, &c. quod apértè métrum vítiat: restítuit Atticam fórmam κιγχάνω Gaisfórdius. MONK.

495. Some copies have πόλιν for χθόνα.

497. Eurýstheus was son of Sthénelus king of Argos and Mycénæ: having succeeded his father in the government of those kingdoms, he imposed on Hérculës several most difficult and dangerous enterprizes—known by the name of the twelve labors of that hero.

498. For ποῖ καὶ, all MSS. have καὶ ποῖ;

ΗΡ. Ὁυ τόνδ᾽ ἀγῶνα πρῶτον ἂν δράμοιμ᾽ ἐγώ. 505   --|∪-||∪-|∪-||∪-|∪-

ΧΟ. Τί δ᾽ ἂν κρατήσας δεσπότην πλέον λάβοις;   ∪-|∪-||--|∪-||∪-|∪-

ΗΡ. Πώλους ἀπάξω κοιράνῳ Τιρυνθίῳ.   --|∪-||--|∪-||-|∪-

ΧΟ. Ὀυκ ἐυμαρὲς χαλινὸν ἐμβαλεῖν γνάθοις.   --|∪-||∪-|∪-||∪-|∪-

ΗΡ. Ἐι μή γε πῦρ πνέουσι μυκτήρων ἄπο.   --|∪-||∪-|∪-||-|∪∪

ΧΟ. Ἀλλ᾽ ἄνδρας ἀρταμοῦσι λαιψηραῖς γνάθοις. 510 --|∪-||∪-|∪-||∪-|∪-

ΗΡ. Θηρῶν ὀρείων χόρτον, ὀυχ ἵππων, λέγεις.   --|∪-||-|∪-||∪-|∪-

ΧΟ. Φάτνας ἴδοις ἂν αἵμασιν πεφυρμένας.   --|∪-||∪-|∪-||∪-|∪-

ΗΡ. Τίνος δ᾽ ὁ θρέψας παῖς πατρὸς κομπάζεται;   ∪-|∪-||∪-|-|∪-||--|∪∪

ΧΟ. Ἄρεος, ζαχρύσου Θρηκίας πέλτης ἄναξ.   ∪∪-|∪-||-|∪-||-|∪-

ΗΡ. Καὶ τόνδε τοὐμοῦ δαίμονος πόνον λέγεις, 515 --|∪-||--|∪-||∪-|∪-

(σκληρὸς γὰρ ἀιεὶ, καὶ πρὸς ἀῖπος ἔρχεται,)   --|∪-||--|∪-||∪-|∪∪

ἐι χρή με παισὶν, ὀῖς Ἄρης ἐγείνατο,   --|∪-||∪-|∪-||∪-|∪-

μάχην ξυνάψαι, πρῶτα μὲν Λυκάονι,   ∪-|∪-||--|∪-||∪-|∪∪

ἀῦθις δὲ Κύκνῳ, τόνδε δ᾽ ἔρχομαι τρίτον   --|∪-||∪-|∪-||∪-|∪∪

ἀγῶνα πώλοις δεσπότῃ τε συμβαλῶν. 520   ∪-|∪-||--|∪-||∪-|∪-

THE ORDER, AND ENGLISH ACCENTUATION.

ΗΡ. Ου πρώτον αγῶνα τόνδε ἐγω αν δραμοίμι. ΧΟ. Δε τι πλέον αν λάβοις κρατήσας δέσποτην; ΗΡ. Απάξω πώλους Τιρυνθίω κοίρανω. ΧΟ. Ουκ εύμαρες ἐμβαλειν χαλίνον γνάθοις. ΗΡ. Ει γε μη πνεούσι πυρ απο μυκτήρων. ΧΟ. Ἀλλα αρταμούσι άνδρας λαιψηραις γνάθοις. ΗΡ. Χόρτον ο ρείαν θήρων, ουκ ίππων, λέγεις. ΧΟ. Αν ίδοις φάτνας πεφύρμενας αίμασι. ΗΡ. Δε παις τίνος πά τρος ο θρέψας κομπάζεται; ΧΟ. Ἀρεος, άναξ Θρηκιας πέλτης ζαχρύσου. ΗΡ. Και τόνδε πόνον λέγεις του εμου δαίμονος, (γαρ αίει σκληρος, και έρχεται προς αίπος,) ει χρη με ξυνάψαι μάχην παίσι, ὁις Ἀρης εγείνατο, πρωτα μεν Λυκάονι, δε αύθις Κύκνω, — δε έρχομαι τόνδε τρίτον αγῶνα σύμβαλων πώλοις τε δέσποτη.

TRANSLATION.

HERCULES. Not the first contest this in which I shall have entered the lists! CHORUS. But what more wilt thou accomplish when thou hast sub-dued their owner? HERCULES. I will drive away the horses to the Tirýn-thian king. CHORUS. It will not be an easy matter to put the bit in their chops. HERCULES. [*Smiling.*] If at least they breathe not fire from their nostrils! CHORUS. But they tear men to pieces—with their devouring jaws! HERCULES. [*Laughing.*] The provender of mountain beasts, not of horses, thou discoursest about. CHORUS. Thou mayest see their stalls distained with blood! HERCULES. But son of what sire does their own-er boast himself to be? CHORUS. Of Mars, prince of the Thracian target rich with gold! HERCULES. And this labor thou mentionest is one my fate compels me to, (for it is ever hard, and tends to arduous,) if I must join battle with sons whom Mars begat; first, indeed, with Lycáon, and then with Cýcnus,—and I come to this third combat; about to engage with the horses and their master.

---

505. *Not the first race this I may have run—not the first encounter I may have en-gaged in.* The taking of the mares of Dí-omede was Hércules's eighth labor.

506. τί δ᾽ ἂν πλέον λάβοις, *but what more wilt thou get? What progress or advance wilt thou have made?*

508. Hesýchius explains ἐυμαρὲς by ἐυ-χερὲς—ἀσφαλὲς—ῥάδιον.

510. ἀρταμοῦσι· μαγείρουσι· ἄρταμος γὰρ λέγεται ὁ μάγειρος. SCHOLIAST.

514. The Scholiast, and (on his autho-rity) Lascar and some others have Ἄρε-ως. The former joined ζαχρύσου with Ἄρε-ως or Ἄρεος, not with πέλτης. For Θρηκίας most MSS. and editions have Θρακίας.

515. Verbally, *and thou speakest of this labor of my fate,* that is, *a labor my destiny subjects me to perform.*

516. πρὸς ἀῖπος ἔρχεται, *tends to loftiness* or *steepness.* Hesýchius gives κάματος ἢ ὑψηλὸς τόπος as the signification of ἀῖπος.

44   521. ΕΥΡΙΠΙΔΟΥ

'Αλλ' ούτις εστίν ος τον 'Αλκμήνης γόνον   --|◡-‖◡-|◡-‖--|◡◡
τρέσαντα χείρα πολεμίων ποτ' όψεται.   ◡-|◡-‖◡◡◡|◡-‖◡-|◡◡
ΧΟ. Και μην όδ' αυτός τησδε κοίρανος χθονός   --|◡-‖--|◡-‖◡-|◡◡
"Αδμητος έξω δωμάτων πορεύεται.   --|◡-‖--|◡-‖◡-|◡◡
ΑΔ. Χαῖρ', ω Διός παῖ, Περσέως τ' αφ' αίματος. 525 --|◡-‖--|◡-‖◡-|◡◡
ΗΡ. "Αδμητε, και συ χαῖρε, Θεσσαλων άναξ.   --|◡-‖◡-|◡-‖◡-|◡-
ΑΔ. Θέλοιμ' άν' εύνουν δ' όντα σ' εξεπίσταμαι.   ◡-|◡-‖◡-|◡-‖◡-|◡̈◡
ΗΡ. Τί χρῆμα κουρᾷ τῇδε πενθίμῳ πρέπεις;   ◡-|◡-‖--|◡-‖◡◡-|◡-
ΑΔ. Θάπτειν τιν' εν τῇδ' ημέρᾳ μέλλω νεκρόν.   --|◡-‖--|◡-‖--|◡◡
ΗΡ. 'Απ' ουν τέκνων σων πημονην είργοι θεός. 530   ◡-|◡-‖◡-|◡-‖--|◡◡
ΑΔ. Ζωσιν κατ' οίκους παῖδες, ους έφυσ' εγώ.   --|◡-‖--|◡-‖◡-|◡-
ΗΡ. Πατήρ γε μην ωραῖος, είπερ οίχεται.   ◡-|◡-‖--|◡-‖◡-|◡-
ΑΔ. Κάκεῖνος έστι, χ' η τεκοῦσά μ', 'Ηράκλεις.   --|◡-‖◡-|◡-‖◡-|◡-
ΗΡ. 'Ου μην γυνή γ' όλωλεν "Αλκηστις σέθεν;   --|◡-‖◡-|◡-‖--|◡-
ΑΔ. Διπλοῦς επ' αυτῇ μῦθος έστι μοι λέγειν. 535   ◡-|◡-‖--|◡-‖◡-|◡◡
ΗΡ. Πότερα θανούσης είπας, η ζώσης πέρι;   ◡◡◡|◡-‖--|◡-‖◡-|◡◡

THE ORDER, AND ENGLISH ACCENTUATION.

'Αλλα ούτις έστι ος πότε όψεται τον γόνον Αλκμήνης τρεσάντα χείρα πολέμιων. ΧΟ. Και μην όδε πορεύεται Αδμήτος αύτος κοίρανος τήσδε χθόνος έξω δώματων. ΑΔ. Χαίρε, ω παι Διός, τε άπο αίματος Πέρσεως. ΗΡ. Χαίρε και συ, Αδμήτε, άναξ Θεσσαλων. ΑΔ. Αν Θελοίμι' εξεπίσταμαι δε σε όντα εύνουν. ΗΡ. Τι χρήμα πρέπεις τήδε πένθιμω κούρᾳ; ΑΔ. Μέλλω θάπτειν τίνα νέκρον εν τήδε ήμερα. ΗΡ. Πάτηρ γε, είπερ οίχεται, μην ωραίος. ΑΔ. Και εκείνος έστι, και η τεκούσα με, 'Ηράκλεις. ΗΡ. Μην γε γύνη σέθεν Αλκήστις ουκ ολώλε; ΑΔ. 'Εστι δίπλους μύθος μοι λέγειν επι αύτη. ΗΡ. Πότερα θανούσης είπας πέρι, η ζώσης;

TRANSLATION.

But [*Resolutely.*] none there is who shall ever behold the son of Alcména fearing the hand of his enemies.

Chorus. And lo! here comes Admétus himself, lord of this land, from out of the palace!

Admetus. [*Entering, addresses Hérculës.*] Hail, O son of Jove, and of the blood of Pérseus.

Hercules. Joy thou too, Admétus, king of the Thessálians.

Admetus. Would I could:—I know, however, that thou art well-disposed towards me. Hercules. [*Looking close.*] For what reason art thou trimmed with the tonsure of mourning?

Admetus. [*Sighing.*] I am about this day to bury a certain dead person. Hercules. May heaven then avert the misfortune from thy children! Admetus. The children whom I begat are alive in the palace.

Hercules. [*Conjecturingly.*] Thy father at least, if he be gone, is indeed full-of-years! Admetus. [*Carelessly.*] Both he lives,—and she who bare me, Hérculës. Hercules. [*With mistrust.*] Surely then at least thy wife Alcéstis is not dead? Admetus. [*Sorrowfully.*] There is a twofold account for me to render of her! Hercules. [*Very gravely.*] Whether as dead speakest thou concerning her, or as living?

525. In MSS. and the early editions τ' is wanting. Pérseus was great grandfather to Hérculës on the mother's side.
527. Θέλοιμ' άν, (understand the infinitive χαίρειν,) *I wish I could joy* or *rejoice at meeting an old and a valued friend.*

Monk observes, as follows:—"idem lusus est in vóce χαῖρε, Hec. [426.] 430."
528. τί χρῆμα,—subintéllige διὰ, *quáre.* Sic Hec. 971, &c.: πρέπεις réctè interpretátur "*insígnis es.*" Monk.
535. διπλοῦς μῦθος, freely, *two accounts.*

ΑΔ. Ἔστιν τι, κοὐκ ἔτ᾽ ἔστιν᾽ ἀλγύνει δέ με.　　- -|◡ -||◡ -|◡ -||- -|◡ ◡

ΗΡ. Οὐδέν τι μᾶλλον οἶδ᾽· ἄσημα γὰρ λέγεις.　　- -|◡ -||◡ -|◡ -||◡ -|◡ -

ΑΔ. Οὐκ οἶσθα μοίρας ἧς τυχεῖν αὐτὴν χρεών;　　- -|◡ -||- -|◡ -||- -|◡ -

ΗΡ. Οἶδ᾽ ἀντὶ σοῦ γε κατθανεῖν ὑφειμένην.　　540　　- -|◡ -||◡ -|◡ -||◡ -|◡ -

ΑΔ. Πῶς οὖν ἔτ᾽ ἔστιν, εἴπερ ἤνεσεν τάδε;　　- -|◡ -||◡ -|◡ -||◡ -|◡ ◡

ΗΡ. Ἄ, μὴ πρόκλαι᾽ ἄκοιτιν᾽ εἰς τόδ᾽ ἀναβαλοῦ.　　- -|◡ -||◡ -|◡ -||◡ ◡ ◡ ◡|

ΑΔ. Τέθνηχ᾽ ὁ μέλλων, χ᾽ ὁ θανὼν οὐκ ἔστ᾽ ἔτι.　　◡ -|◡ -||- -|◡ -||- -|◡ ◡

ΗΡ. Χωρὶς τό τ᾽ εἶναι, καὶ τὸ μὴ, νομίζεται.　　- -|◡ -||- -|◡ -||◡ -|◡ ◡

ΑΔ. Σὺ τῇδε κρίνεις, Ἡράκλεις, κείνη δ᾽ ἐγώ.　　545　　◡ -|◡ -||- -|◡ ⋯||- -|◡ -

ΗΡ. Τί δῆτα κλαίεις; Τίς φίλων ὁ κατθανών;　　◡ -|◡ -||- -|◡ -||◡ -|◡ -

ΑΔ. Γυνή· γυναικὸς ἀρτίως μεμνήμεθα.　　◡ -|◡ -||◡ -|◡ -||- -|◡ ◡

ΗΡ. Ὀθνεῖος, ἤ σοι ξυγγενὴς γεγῶσά τις;　　◡ -|◡ -||- -|◡ -||◡ -|◡ ◡

ΑΔ. Ὀθνεῖος· ἄλλως δ᾽ ἦν ἀναγκαία δόμοις.　　◡ -|◡ -||- -|◡ -||◡ -|◡ -

ΗΡ. Πῶς οὖν ἐν οἴκοις σοῖσιν ὤλεσεν βίον;　　550　　- -|◡ -||- -|◡ -||◡ -|◡ -

ΑΔ. Πατρὸς θανόντος, ἐνθάδ᾽ ὠρφανεύετο.　　◡ -|◡ -||◡ -|◡ -||◡ -|◡ ◡

ΗΡ. Φεῦ. Εἴθ᾽ εὕρομέν σ᾽, Ἄδμητε, μὴ λυπούμενον.　　-||- -|◡ -||- -|◡ -||- -|◡ ◡

THE ORDER, AND ENGLISH ACCENTUATION.

ΑΔ. Τε ἐστι, και ἐστι ουκ ἐτι· δε αλγύνει με. ΗΡ. Οιδα οὐδεν τι μᾶλλον᾽ γαρ λέγεις αςήμα. ΑΔ. Ουκ οἰσθα μοίρας ἡς χρέων αὐτην τύχειν; ΗΡ. Οιδα γε ὑφειμενην κάτθανειν ἀντι σου. ΑΔ. Πως ουν ἐστι ἐτι, εἰπερ ἡνεσε τάδε; ΗΡ. Α, μη προκλαιε ἀκοιτιν᾽ ἀναβαλου εις τόδε. ΑΔ. Ὁ μέλλων τεθνηκε, και ὁ θάνων ἐστι ουκ ἐτι. ΗΡ. Τε το ειναι, και το μη, νομίζεται χωρις. ΑΔ. Συ κρίνεις τήδε, Ἡρακλεις, δε ἐγω κείνη. ΗΡ. Τι δήτα κλαίεις; Τις φίλων ὁ κάτθανων; ΑΔ. Γύνη᾽ γυναικος ἀρτιως μεμνήμεθα. ΗΡ. Οθνειος, η τις γεγωσα ξύγγενης σοι; ΑΔ. Οθνειος᾽ δε ἀλλως αναγκαία ην δόμοις. ΗΡ. Πως ουν ὠλεσε βίον εν σοίσι οἰκοις; ΑΔ. Πάτρος θανόντος, ωρφανευετο ἐνθαδε. ΗΡ. Φευ. Ειθε, Αδμήτε, εὑρομεν σε μη λυπούμενον.

TRANSLATION.

ADMETUS. [*Wringing his hands.*] She both is, and is no more: and she grieves me!

HERCULES. I am not one whit the wiser:—for thou talkest obscurely. ADMETUS. Knowest thou not the fate which it was incumbent on her to meet with? HERCULES. I know indeed that she undertook to die in lieu of thee! ADMETUS. How then is she any more, if that she consented [*Shedding tears.*] to this? HERCULES. Ah, do not weep aforehand for thy wife: wait till the event. ADMETUS. [*Sobbing.*] He that is about to die is dead, and he that is dead is no more. HERCULES. To be, and not to be, are considered quite-different. ADMETUS. Thou judgest in this way, Hérculës, but I in that. HERCULES. Why then weepest thou? What one of thy friends is dead? ADMETUS. [*Sighing.*] A woman:—a woman we lately mentioned. HERCULES. Unconnected-by-birth, or some one born akin to thee? ADMETUS. By-birth-unconnected,—but in other respects dear was she to the family! HERCULES. How, then, departed she life in thy house? ADMETUS. Her father being dead, she lived an orphan here. HERCULES. Alas! I would, Admétus, we had found thee not mourning!

538. οὐδέν τι μᾶλλον οἶδα, *I know nothing in anywise more— I am not one tittle wiser on this subject than at first.*

540. ὑφειμένην, *se summisisse:* —mínùs accuráte vértunt "pollícitam." MONK.

542. For εἰς τόδ᾽, Wakefield learnedly conjectured εἰς τότ᾽: Elmsley, however, ridiculed τότ᾽, and defends τόδ᾽.

544. Literally, *the to be, and the not, is regarded separate,* that is, *to be alive, and not to be alive, are accounted two distinctly different things.*

548-9. ὀθνεῖος, *foreign — extrinsic—not of the same nation* or *kindred.*

549. ἄλλως válet *áliam ob caúsam:* cónjicit Blomfiéldius ἀλλ᾽ ὥς. MONK.

46   553. ΕΥΡΙΠΙΔΟΥ

ΑΔ. Ὡς δὴ τί δράσων τόνδ᾽ ὑπορράπτεις λόγον;

ΗΡ. Ξένων πρὸς ἄλλην ἑστίαν πορεύσομαι.

ΑΔ. Οὐκ ἔστιν, ὦ ᾽ναξ· μὴ τοσόνδ᾽ ἔλθοι κακόν. 555

ΗΡ. Λυπουμένοις ὀχληρὸς, εἰ μόλοι, ξένος.

ΑΔ. Τεθνᾶσιν οἱ θανόντες· ἀλλ᾽ ἴθ᾽ εἰς δόμους.

ΗΡ. Αἰσχρὸν δὲ παρὰ κλαίουσι θοινᾶσθαι φίλοις.

ΑΔ. Χωρὶς ξενῶνές εἰσιν, οἷ σ᾽ εἰσάξομεν.

ΗΡ. Μέθες με, καί σοι μυρίαν ἕξω χάριν. 560

ΑΔ. Οὐκ ἔστιν ἄλλου σ᾽ ἀνδρὸς ἑστίαν μολεῖν.

Ἡγοῦ σὺ, τῶνδε δωμάτων ἐξωπίους

ξενῶνας οἴξας· τοῖς τ᾽ ἐφεστῶσιν φράσον,

σίτων παρεῖναι πλῆθος· ἐν δὲ κλείσατε

θύρας μεσαύλους· οὐ πρέπει θοινωμένους 565

κλύειν στεναγμῶν, οὐδὲ λυπεῖσθαι ξένους.

ΧΟ. Τί δρᾷς; Τοσαύτης ξυμφορᾶς προσκειμένης,

Ἄδμητε, τολμᾷς ξενοδοχεῖν; Τί μῶρος εἶ;

THE ORDER, AND ENGLISH ACCENTUATION.

ΑΔ. Ὡς δη δράσων τι ὑπορράπτεις τόνδε λόγον; ΗΡ. Πορεύσομαι προς ἄλλην ἑστιαν ξένων. ΑΔ. Οὐκ ἐστι, ω ἀναξ· μη τοσόνδε κάκον ἐλθοι. ΗΡ. Ὀχληρος ξένος, ει μόλοι, λυπουμένοις. ΑΔ. Ὁι θανόντες τεθνάσι· ἀλλα ἰθι εις δόμους. ΗΡ. Δε αἰσχρον θοινᾶσθαι παρα κλαιούσι φίλοις. ΑΔ. Ξενώνες, ὁι εισάξομεν σε, εἰσι χώρις. ΗΡ. Μέθες με, και ἐξω σοι μύριαν χάριν. ΑΔ. Οὐκ ἐστι σε μόλειν ἑστιαν ἀλλου ἀνδρος. Ἡγου συ, οἰξας ξενώνας εξωπίους τώνδε δώματων· τε φράσον τοις ε-φεστώσι, παρεῖναι πλήθος σίτων· δε εννκλείσατε μεσαύλους θύρας· ου πρέπει θοινώμενους ξένους κλύειν στενάγμων, οὐδε λυπεῖσθαι. ΧΟ. Τι δρᾳς; Τοσαύτης ξύμφορας προσκείμενης, τόλμᾳς, Ἄδμητε, ξενόδοχειν; Τι ει μώρος;

TRANSLATION.

ADMETUS. As about then to do what, makest thou use of these words? HERCULES. I will go to some other fireside of those who receive guests! ADMETUS. It must not be, O king:—let not so great an ill befal! HERCULES. Molestful is a guest, if he come, to mourners! ADMETUS. The dead are dead; wherefore, go into the house. HERCULES. But it is a shameful thing to feast with weeping friends! ADMETUS. The guest-chambers, (to which we will conduct thee,) are apart! HERCULES. [*Urgently.*] Let me go away, and I shall owe thee ten thousand thanks! ADMETUS. [*Pressingly.*] It must not be that thou go to another man's hearth.

[*To the chief Page.*] Lead-on thou,—throwing open the guest-rooms that are detached from the house: and tell those who have the management, to let there be plenty of refreshments,—and shut ye the mid-hall doors: it is not fit that feasting guests should hear groans, nor that they should be made sad! [*Exit Hércules, conducted into the palace.*]

CHORUS. [*To Admétus, rebukingly.*] What doest thou? When so great a calamity is present before thee, hast thou the hardihood, Admétus, to receive guests? Wherefore art thou unwise?

---

553. In place of τόνδ᾽ ὑπορράπτεις λόγον, a few editions have τούσδ᾽ ὑπορράπτεις λόγους, a reading Porson justly censured.

554. ξένων πρὸς ἄλλην ἑστίαν, *unto another hearth of guest-receivers*, for ξένων πρὸς ἄλλων ἑστίαν, *to the hearth of other hosts.*

558. In all MSS. δὲ is wanting. The fi-

nal syllable of παρὰ, it is asserted, cannot (see Porson at verse 64 of the Oréstës) be lengthened before initial κλ, and consequently without δὲ, for which Elmsley has given τι, the second foot would be a pyrrhic instead of a tribrach.

559. For οἷ in this verse, Aldus has οἷς.

'ΑΔ. 'Αλλ' εἰ δόμων σφε καὶ πόλεως ἀπήλασα
ξένον μολόντα, μᾶλλον ἄν μ' ἐπήνεσας;   570
'Ου δῆτ', ἐπεί μοι ξυμφορὰ μὲν οὐδὲν ἂν
μείων ἐγίγνετ', ἀξενώτερος δ' ἐγώ·
καὶ πρὸς κακοῖσιν, ἄλλο τοῦτ' ἂν ἦν κακὸν,
δόμους καλεῖσθαι τοὺς ἐμοὺς ἐχθροξένους.
'Αυτὸς δ' ἀρίστου τοῦδε τυγχάνω ξένου,   575
ὅταν περ Ἄργους διψίαν ἔλθω χθόνα.
ΧΟ. Πῶς οὖν ἔκρυπτες τὸν παρόντα δαίμονα,
φίλου μολόντος ἀνδρὸς, ὡς αὐτὸς λέγεις;
ΑΔ. 'Ουκ ἄν ποτ' ἠθέλησεν εἰσελθεῖν δόμους,
εἰ τῶν ἐμῶν τι πημάτων ἐγνώρισε.   580
Καὶ τῷ μὲν, οἶμαι, δρῶν τάδ', οὐ φρονεῖν δοκῶ,
οὐδ' αἰνέσει με· τἀμὰ δ' οὐκ ἐπίσταται
μέλαθρ' ἀπωθεῖν, οὐδ' ἀτιμάζειν ξένους.

ΧΟ. Ὦ πολύξεινος, καὶ ἐλεύθερος   [Στροφὴ α'.]   α'
ἀνδρὸς ἀεί ποτ' οἶκος,   585   β'

THE ORDER, AND ENGLISH ACCENTUATION.

ΑΔ. 'Αλλα ει απήλασα δόμων και πόλεως σφε μολόντα ξένον, αν επήνεσας με μάλλον; Ου δῆτα, ἐπεί ξύμφορα μοι μεν αν εγίγνετο ουδεν μείων, δε εγω αξενώτερος· και προς κακοῖσι, αν ην τοῦτο άλλο κάκον, τους εμους δόμους καλεῖσθαι εχθρόξενους. Δε αυτος τύγχανω τοῦδε αρίστου ξένου, ὅταν περ έλθω δίψιαν χθόνα Αργους. ΧΟ. Πως ουν εκρύπτες τον παρόντα δαίμονα, φίλου ανδρος, ως αυτος λέγεις, μολόντος; ΑΔ. Ουκ αν ποτε ηθελήσε εισελθειν δόμους, ει εγνώρισε τι των εμων πημάτων. Και τω μεν, οίμαι, δόκω, δρων τάδε, ου φρόνειν, ουδε αίνεσει με· δε τα εμα μελάθρα ουκ επίσταται απώθειν, ουδε ατιμάζειν ξένους. ΧΟ. Ω πολυξεινος, και αει πότε ελεύθερος οίκος ανδρος,

TRANSLATION.

ADMETUS. But if I had driven from my house, and the city, him who had come my guest, wouldest thou have praised me rather? No in sooth,—since my calamity indeed would have been nothing the less, and I the more inhospitable: and in addition to my evils, there would have been this other calamity,—that my house would have been called the stranger-hating mansion. [*Pleasedly.*] But I myself find this man a most excellent host, whensoever I visit the thirsty land of Argos! CHORUS. Why then didst thou conceal thy present fate, when a man thy friend, as thou thyself sayest, came? ADMETUS. He never would have been willing to enter the house, if he had known aught of my sufferings. And to him indeed, I wot, do I appear, acting thus, to have judged unwisely, nor will he praise me: but my roof knows not to drive away, nor to dishonor visitors. [*Exit Admetus, repairing into the palace.*] CHORUS. O greatly-hospitable, and ever liberal mansion of this man,

573. Similia dícit ìnfrà, ver. 1058, ἀλλ' ἄλγος ἄλγει τοῦτ' ἂν ἦν προσκείμενον,—εἴπερ πρὸς ἄλλου δώμαθ' ὡρμήθης ξένου. MONK.
574. For καλεῖσθαι, Lascar has κεκλῆσθαι, nor badly.
581. Monk says: " τῷ pro τινὶ accipiunt Heáthius et Marklándus." Had the reading been καί τῳ, then indeed would τῳ have stood for τινὶ—whereas τῷ with an accent can stand only for itself,—or for τίνι, with interrogation.
584. Barnes, contrary to every authority, as well as to the metre, edited πολύξενος, induced no doubt by the words φιλόξενος, ἐχθρόξενος, and the like. But it is well known that in the choruses the Ionic dialect was admissible, and that ξεῖνος for ξένος occurs even in iambic verse.

σέ τοι καὶ ὁ Πύθιος   ∪ – ∪ ∪‖– ∪ ∪   γ´
εὐλύρας Ἀπόλλων   – ∪|– ∪‖– –   δ´
ἠξίωσε ναίειν·   – ∪|– ∪‖– –   ε´
ἔτλα δὲ σοῖσι μηλονόμας   ∪ –|∪ –‖∪ –‖∪ ∪ –   ζ´
ἐν δόμοις γενέσθαι,   590   – ∪|– ∪‖– –   η´
δοχμιᾶν διὰ κλιτύων   – ∪‖– ∪ ∪ –‖∪ –   θ´
βοσκήμασι σοῖσι συρίζων   – – ∪ ∪‖– ∪ –‖– –   ι´
ποιμνίτας ὑμεναίους.   – –|– ∪ ∪|– –   κ´

Ξὺν δ᾽ ἐποιμαίνοντο, χαρᾷ μελέ-   [Ἀντιστρ. α´.]   – ∪|– –‖– ∪ ∪ –‖∪ ∪   α´
ων, βαλιαί τε λύγκες,   595   – ∪ ∪ –‖∪ –|∪   β´
ἔβα τε λιποῦσ᾽ Ὄθρυ-   ∪ – ∪ ∪‖– ∪ ∪   γ´
ος νάπαν λεόντων   – ∪|– ∪‖– –   δ´
ἁ δαφοινὸς ἴλα.   – ∪|– ∪‖– –   ε´
Χόρευσε δ᾽ ἀμφὶ σὰν κιθάραν,   ∪ –|∪ –‖∪ –|∪ ∪ –   ζ´
Φοῖβε, ποικιλόθριξ   600   – ∪|– ∪‖– –   η´
νεβρὸς, ὑψικόμων πέραν   – ∪‖– ∪ ∪ –‖∪ –   θ´
βαίνουσ᾽ ἐλατᾶν σφυρῷ κούφῳ,   – – ∪ ∪‖– ∪ –‖– –   ι´·
χαίρουσ᾽ εὔφρονι μολπᾷ.   – –|– ∪ ∪|– –   κ´

Τοιγὰρ πολυμηλοτάταν   [Στροφὴ β´.]   – – ∪ ∪‖– ∪ ∪ –   α´
ἑστίαν οἰκεῖ, παρὰ καλλίναον   605   – ∪ – –‖– ∪ ∪ –‖∪ ∪ –   β´

THE ORDER, AND ENGLISH ACCENTUATION.

σὲ τοι καὶ ὁ Πύθιος εὐλύρας Ἀπόλλων ἠξίωσε ναίειν· δὲ ἔτλα γενέσθαι μηλόνομας ἐν σοῖσι δόμοις, συρίζων σοῖσι βοσκήμασι διὰ δόχμιαν κλιτύων ποιμνίτας ὑμεναίους. Δὲ ξυνεποιμαίνοντο, χάρᾳ μέλεων, τε βάλιαι λύγκες, τε ἁ δαφοίνος ἴλα λεόντων, λιποῦσα νάπαν Ὄθρυος, ἔβα. Ἀμφὶ σὰν κιθάραν δὲ, Φοῖβε, χορεῦσε ποικιλόθριξ νέβρος, βαινοῦσα κούφῳ σφύρῳ πέραν ὑψικόμων ἐλάταν, χαιροῦσα εὔφρονι μόλπᾳ. Τοίγαρ οἰκεις πολυμηλότατον ἔστιαν, πάρα καλλίναον

TRANSLATION.

thee troth did even the Pýthian Apóllo, master of the lyre, deign to inhabit: and he endured to become a shepherd in thine abodes,—piping to thy flocks across the slanting hills, his pastoral lays!

And there were wont to feed with him, through delight of his minstrelsy, the spotted lynxes,—and the tawny troop of lions, having left the forest of Othrys, came.

Around thy harp too, O Phoébus, frisked the dappled fawn, advancing with light step beyond the lofty-crested pines, joying in the gladdening strain! [Looking round exultingly towards the palace.] Wherefore thou dwellest in a home most rich in flocks, and beside the fair-flowing

---

586. For καὶ ὁ, Lascar here edited χ᾽ὡ.

587. εὐλύρας, good-lyrist, that is, master of the lyre or harp.

588. ἠξίωσε ναίειν, dignátus est habitáre, he vouchsafed or condescended to inhabit.– Monk bids the reader compare this passage with verse 659 of the Andrómachë, and likewise with καὶ ξυντράπεζον ἀξιοῖς ἔχειν βίον, Æschyli Prom. Vinct. 223.

591. κλυτείων Scholiástes mendósè scilicet pro κλειτύων. Scholiástæ explicátio in editióne Barnésii sic légitur: κλυτείων·

τῶν ἀνακεκλιμένων καὶ πλαγίων ὀργάδων: sed Arsénius dédit ὀργῶν: lége ígitur, uníus litérulæ mutatióne, ὀρέων. MONK.

593. ποιμνίτας: íta MS. únum Pariénse, et edítio Lascáris,—eâdem analógiâ quâ ὁπλίτης, ὀρίτης, χωρίτης, δεκδρίτης. Editióne Aldinâ, ποιμνήτας:. MUSGRAVE.

598. δαφοινὸς, blood-coloured—tawny.

605. Monk has οἰκεῖ contrary to every authority, and (in my opinion) to the intention of the author—as well as to the action of the drama, and the sense.

Βοιβίαν λίμναν· ἀρότοις δὲ γυᾶν, |-ᴗᴗ-‖-ᴗᴗ-‖ᴗᴗ-   γ'
καὶ πεδίων δαπέδοις ὅρον, |-ᴗᴗ|-ᴗᴗ|-ᴗᴗ   δ'
ἀμφὶ μὲν ἀελίου κνεφαίαν |-ᴗᴗ|-ᴗᴗ‖|-ᴗ|--   ε'
ἱππόστασιν, αἰθέρα |--ᴗᴗ‖|-ᴗᴗ   ζ'
τὰν Μολοσσῶν τίθεται,   610 |-ᴗ-‖|-ᴗᴗ-   η'
πόντιον δ' Αἰγαῖον ἐπ' ἀκτὰν |-ᴗᴗ-‖|-ᴗᴗ-‖|-   ϑ'
ἀλίμενον Πηλίου κρατύνει. |-ᴗᴗ-‖|-ᴗ|-ᴗ|--   ι'

Καὶ νῦν δόμον ἀμπετάσας,   ['Αντιστρ. β'.] |--ᴗᴗ‖|-ᴗᴗ-   α'
δέξατο ξεῖνον νοτερῷ βλεφάρῳ, |-ᴗ--‖|-ᴗᴗ-‖ᴗᴗ-   β'
τᾶς φίλας κλαίων ἀλόχου νέκυν ἐν   615 |-ᴗ--‖|-ᴗᴗ-‖ᴗᴗ-   γ'
δώμασιν ἀρτιθανῆ· τὸ γὰρ |-ᴗᴗ|-ᴗᴗ|-ᴗᴗ   δ'
εὐγενὲς ἐκφέρεται πρὸς αἰδῶ. |-ᴗᴗ|-ᴗᴗ‖|-ᴗ|--   ε'
'Εν τοῖς ἀγαθοῖσι δὲ |--ᴗᴗ‖|-ᴗᴗ   ζ'
πάντ' ἔνεστιν σοφίας. |-ᴗ-‖|-ᴗᴗ-   η'
Πρὸς δ' ἐμᾷ ψυχᾷ θράσος ἦσται,   620 |-ᴗᴗ-‖|-ᴗᴗ-‖ᴗ   ϑ'
Θεοσεβῆ φῶτα κεδνὰ πράξειν. |-ᴗᴗ-‖|-ᴗ|-ᴗ‖|--   ι'

THE ORDER, AND ENGLISH ACCENTUATION.

Βοίβιαν λίμναν· δε ἀρότοις γυᾶν, καὶ δάπεδοις πέδιων, ἀμφι κνεφαίαν ἱππόστασιν μεν ἀελίου, τίθεται ταν αἰθέρα Μολόσσων ὅρον, δε κρατύνει ἐπι ἀλίμενον ἀκταν Αιγαίον πόντιον Πήλιου. Και νυν ἀμπέτασας δόμον, νότερῳ βλέφαρῳ δέξατο ξείνον, κλαίων νέκυν τας φίλας ἀλόχου, ἀρτίθανη εν δώμασι· γαρ το εὔγενες ἐκφέρεται προς αἰδω. Δε εν τοις ἀγαθοίσι ἐνέστι πάντα σόφιας. Δε Θράσος ἦσται προς ἐμα ψύχα, Θεόσεβη φῶτα πράξειν κέδνα.

TRANSLATION.

lake of Boébë : and to the tillage of his fields, and the extent of his plains, towards the dusky setting indeed of the sun, he makes the clime of the Molóssians the limit,—and holds-dominion as far as the portless shore of the Ægéan sea at Pélion.

And now, having thrown-open his mansion, he hath with humid eyelid received his guest,—weeping over the corse of his beloved consort just-now-dead in the palace :—for a noble disposition is prone to acts of respect.

[*With placidness and an air expressive of hope.*] But in the good there is inherent all manner of wisdom! And confidence sits on my soul that the man who reveres the Gods will fare prosperously!

606. γυᾶν Lascáris : γυιὰν Aldus, et sic vúlgò :—γυᾶν corréxit Barnésius. Hic lócus víros dóctos miserè exércuit. Alii contórtis verbórum inversiónibus strúere labórant ; álii ut corrúpta et desperáta relínquunt. Sólus intérpretum Wakefiéldius, quod miréris, rectè cépit : *aratiónibus júgerum, et campórum plánis spátiis fines círca sólis occiduam statiónem, áxem Molossórum síbi státuit* : ne pósthac in hís vérbis hæreátur, sénsus in língua vernáculâ exhibéndus est : *he makes the clime of the Molossians the limit to his domain (to his tillage and to his plains) on the west.* Γύη ápud véteres de *árvo*, seù ágro ad aráudum ápto díctum est. MONK.

608-9. The Scholiast interpreted κνεφαίαν ἱππόστασιν, rightly by—"τὴν δύσιν, ὅπου ὁ ἥλιος κατὰ κνέφας ἵστησι τοὺς ἵππους καὶ καταλύει."

610. Wakefield (forgetting that αἰθὴρ was sometimes feminine) changed τὰν to τὸν, contrary to every authority.

611. For δ', several MSS. and editions have τ', but badly—on account of μὲν in verse 608, above. Wakefield and Gaisford, on the conjecture of Musgrave, edited 'Αγαῖων' in place of 'Αιγαῖον.'

614. For δέξατο, Aldus printed δέξεται : and for ξεῖνον, Lascar has ξένον.

621. Θεοσεβῆ φῶτα κεδνὰ πράξειν, *that the pious man will fare deservedly.*

G

50   622. ΕΥΡΙΠΙΔΟΥ

ΑΔ. Ἀνδρῶν Φεραίων εὐμενὴς παρουσία,
νέκυν μὲν ἤδη πάντ᾽ ἔχοντα πρόσπολοι
φέρουσιν ἄρδην εἰς τάφον τε, καὶ πυράν.
Ὑμεῖς δὲ τὴν θανοῦσαν, ὡς νομίζεται,   625
προσείπατ᾽ ἐξιοῦσαν ὑστάτην ὁδόν.
ΧΟ. Καὶ μὴν ὁρῶ σὸν πατέρα γηραιῷ ποδὶ
στείχοντ᾽, ὀπαδούς τ᾽ ἐν χεροῖν δάμαρτι σῇ
κόσμον φέροντας, νερτέρων ἀγάλματα.

ΦΕΡΗΣ.

Ἥκω κακοῖσι σοῖσι συγκάμνων, τέκνον·   630
ἐσθλῆς γὰρ (οὐδεὶς ἀντερεῖ) καὶ σώφρονος
γυναικὸς ἡμάρτηκας· ἀλλὰ ταῦτα μὲν
φέρειν ἀνάγκη, καίπερ ὄντα δύσφορα.
Δέχου δὲ κόσμον τόνδε, καὶ κατὰ χθονὸς
ἴτω· τὸ ταύτης σῶμα τιμᾶσθαι χρεών,   635
ἥτις γε τῆς σῆς πρόύθανε ψυχῆς, τέκνον,
καί μ᾽ οὐκ ἄπαιδ᾽ ἔθηκεν, οὐδ᾽ εἴασε σοῦ
στερέντα γήρᾳ πενθίμῳ καταφθίνειν.

THE ORDER, AND ENGLISH ACCENTUATION.

ΑΔ. Εὐμενὴς παρουσία Φεραίων ἀνδρῶν, πρόσπολοι ἤδη φέρουσι ἄρδην νέκυν ἐχόντα πάντα μὲν εἰς τε τάφον, καὶ πυράν. Δὲ ὑμεῖς, ὡς νομίζεται, προσείπατε τὴν θανοῦσαν ἐξιοῦσαν ὑστάτην ὁδόν. ΧΟ. Καὶ μὴν ὁρῶ σον πατέρα γηραιῷ ποδὶ στειχόντα, τε ὀπαδοὺς φερόντας ἐν χέροιν κόσμον σῇ δαμάρτι, ἀγάλματα νέρτερων. ΦΕ. Ἥκω, τέκνον, συγκάμνων σοῖσι κακοῖσι· γὰρ ἡμάρτηκας, οὐδεὶς ἀντερεῖ, ἐσθλῆς καὶ σώφρονος γυναικὸς· ἀλλὰ ταῦτα μὲν ἀνάγκη φέρειν, καίπερ ὄντα δύσφορα. Δέχου δὲ τόνδε κόσμον, καὶ ἴτω κάτα χθονός· τὸ σῶμα ταύτης χρεῶν τιμᾶσθαι, ἥτις γε προέθανε τῆς σῆς ψύχης, τέκνον, καὶ ἔθηκε με οὐκ ἄπαιδα, οὐδὲ εἴασε καταφθίνειν στερέντα σοῦ πένθιμῳ γήρᾳ.

TRANSLATION.

ADMETUS. [*Entering from out of the palace, followed by the funeral procession of his beloved queen.*] O kindly presence of you men of Phéræ, my servants are already bearing aloft the corse, with all due honor indeed, to the tomb, and to the pyre. But do ye, as is the custom, salute the deceased going forth on her last journey! [*The Chorus cheers.*]

CHORUS. And behold! I see thy father with aged foot advancing, and pages bearing in their hands decoration for thy consort, due honors of those below! [*The procession halts.*]

PHERES. [*Entering, followed by attendants bearing presents.*] I am come, my son, sympathizing with thy misfortunes: for thou hast lost (no one will deny it) a good and a chaste wife: but these things indeed it is requisite for thee to bear, though they are hard to be borne. Accept however [*Pointing to the gifts.*] this decoration,—and let it go with her beneath the earth: her body it is right to honor, who in sooth died a ransom for thy life, my son, and rendered me not childless, neither suffered me to pine away bereft of thee, in an old age doomed to sorrow!

---

624. The reading of most, if not of all MSS. and editions, is, πρὸς τάφον. On this reading Monk says, 'álteram lectiónem ἐς τάφον, quam pórrigit Eustáthius ad Il. Θ. p. 707, 37, praéfert Blomfíeldius glóssâ Æschyli Prometh.Vinct. 1087, réctè, méâ quídem senténtiâ. Confer vérsum

844, — λέγων θυραῖον κῆδος εἰς τάφον φέρειν.'
629. Wakefield wished to insert τ᾽ before ἀγάλματα. The construction here is that of verse 1051 of the Oréstës.
638. Omnes, praéter Matthiaéum, καταφθινεῖν, quae vox níhili est. Lascáris πενθίμῳ, et vérsu 642, κὴν ᾄδου. MONK.

ΑΛΚΗΣΤΙΣ. 639.   51

Πάσαις δ' ἔθηκεν εὐκλεέστατον βίον
γυναιξὶν, ἔργον τλᾶσα γενναῖον τόδε.   640
Ὦ τόνδ' ἐμὸν σώσασ', ἀναστήσασα δὲ
ἡμᾶς; πίτνοντας, χαῖρε, κἀν Ἅιδου δόμοις
εὖ σοι γένοιτο. Φημὶ τοιούτους γάμους
λύειν βροτοῖσιν, ἢ γαμεῖν οὐκ ἄξιον.
ΑΔ. Οὔτ' ἦλθες εἰς τόνδ' ἐξ ἐμοῦ κληθεὶς τάφον, 645
οὔτ' ἐν φίλοισι σὴν παρουσίαν λέγω.
Κόσμον δὲ τὸν σὸν οὔποθ' ἥδ' ἐνδύσεται·
οὐ γάρ τι τῶν σῶν ἐνδεὴς ταφήσεται.
Τότε ξυναλγεῖν χρῆν σ', ὅτ' ὠλλύμην ἐγώ.
Σὺ δ' ἐκποδὼν στὰς, καὶ παρεὶς ἄλλῳ θανεῖν 650
νέῳ γέρων ὢν, τόνδ' ἀποιμώζεις νεκρόν;
Οὐκ ἦσθ' ἄρ' ὀρθῶς τοῦδε σώματος πατὴρ,
οὐδ' ἡ τεκεῖν φάσκουσα, καὶ κεκλημένη
μήτηρ μ' ἔτικτε· δουλίου δ' ἀφ' αἵματος,
μαστῷ γυναικὸς σῆς ὑπεβλήθην λάθρα.   655

THE ORDER, AND ENGLISH ACCENTUATION.

Δε εθήκε βίον πάσαις γυναίξι ευκλεέστατον, τλάσα τόδε γενναίον έργον. Ω σωσάσα τόνδε έμον, δε αναστησάσα ήμας πιτνόντας, χαίρε, και εν δόμοις Ἅιδου γενοίτο ευ σοι. Φήμι τοιούτους γάμους λύειν βροτοίσι, η ουκ άξιον γάμειν. ΑΔ. Ούτε κλήθεις εξ έμου ήλθες εις τόνδε τάφον, ούτε λέγω σην παρούσιαν εν φιλοίσι. Δε τον σον κόσμον ήδε ούποτε ενδύσεται· γαρ ου τι ένδεης των σων ταφήσεται. Τότε χρην σε ξυνάλγειν, ότε εγω ωλλυμην. Δε συ στας έκποδων, και ων γέρων πάρεις άλλω νέω θάνειν, αποιμώζεις τόνδε νέκρον; Ουκ ήσθα άρα ορθως πάτηρ τούδε σώματος, ουδε η φασκούσα τέκειν, και κεκλημένη μήτηρ ετίκτε με· δε απο δουλίου αίματος λάθρα υπεβλήθην μάστω σης γυναίκος.

TRANSLATION.

But she has made the life of all women most illustrious, by daring this noble deed! [*Addressing the corpse.*] O thou that hast preserved this my son, and hast upraised us who were falling, farewell,—and in the mansions of Plúto may it be well with thee! [*With great gladness.*] I affirm that such marriages are profitable to men, else it is not meet to marry!

ADMETUS. [*Scornfully.*] Neither bidden of me hast thou come to this funeral, nor do I count thy presence among things pleasing! But thine ornaments she shall never put on: for in nowise indebted to thy bounties shall she be interred! At that time oughtest thou to have sorrowed with me, when I was perishing. [*Sneeringly.*] But dost thou, who stoodest aloof, and, being thyself old, permittedst another, a young person, to die, dost thou lament over this dead body? Thou wast not, then, really the father of this body of mine,—neither did she who says she bare me (and is called my mother) bring me forth: but sprung from slavish blood I was secretly placed under the breast of thy wife!

641. For τόνδ' ἐμὸν, Matthiæ has τόνδε μὲν,—nor badly.
642. In all MSS. and editions prior to Monk's, the reading is πιτνοῦντας. Wakefield places no comma after χαῖρε, but a full stop after δόμοις,—and this punctuation has been adopted, and very plausibly defended by several of the learned.
644. λύει pro λυσιτελεῖ, (interpretánte Hesýchio,) ut in Medéâ, 566:—vel quod plénè dictum Sóphoclis Œdip. Tyrann. 316, τέλη λύει. MONK.
651. Lascar edited ἀποιμώζη consentingly with MSS.—Aldus has ἀποιμώξεις, and Matthiæ ἀποιμμάξει.
652. Dícitur ' τόδε σῶμα' δεικτικῶς pro ἐγὼ, ut saépe álias, et Heraclid. ver. 90, et íterùm ver. 529. BARNES.

Ἔδειξας εἰς ἔλεγχον ἐξελθὼν, ὃς εἶ·
καί μ᾿ οὐ νομίζω παῖδα σὸν πεφυκέναι.
Ἦτ᾿ ἄρα πάντων διαπρέπεις ἀψυχίᾳ,
ὃς, τηλίκοσθ᾿ ὢν, κἀπὶ τέρμ᾿ ἥκων βίου,
οὐκ ἠθέλησας, οὐδ᾿ ἐτόλμησας θανεῖν   660
τοῦ σοῦ πρὸ παιδός· ἀλλὰ τήνδ᾿ εἰάσατε
γυναῖκ᾿ ὀθνείαν, ἣν ἐγὼ καὶ μητέρα
πατέρα τ᾿ ἂν ἐνδίκως ἂν ἡγοίμην μόνην.
Καίτοι καλόν γ᾿ ἂν τόνδ᾿ ἀγῶν᾿ ἠγωνίσω,
τοῦ σοῦ πρὸ παιδὸς κατθανών· βραχὺς δέ σοι   665
πάντως ὁ λοιπὸς ἦν βιώσιμος χρόνος·
κἀγώ τ᾿ ἂν ἔζων, χ᾿ ἥδε τὸν λοιπὸν χρόνον,
κοὐκ ἂν μονωθεὶς ἔστενον κακοῖς ἐμοῖς.
Καὶ μὴν ὅσ᾿ ἄνδρα χρὴ παθεῖν εὐδαίμονα,
πέπονθας· ἥβησας μὲν ἐν τυραννίδι,   670
παῖς δ᾿ ἦν ἐγώ σοι τῶνδε διάδοχος δόμων,
ὥστ᾿ οὐκ ἄτεκνος κατθανὼν ἄλλοις δόμον
λείψειν ἔμελλες ὀρφανὸν διαρπάσαι.

Ἔδειξας ἐξέλθων εἰς ἐλέγχον, ὃς εἶ· καὶ νομίζω με οὐ πεφύκεναι σου παῖδα. Ἤτοι ἄρα διάπρεπεις πάντων αψύχιᾳ, ὃς, ἂν τηλίκοσδε, καὶ ἥκων ἐπὶ τέρμα βίου, οὐκ ηθέλησας, οὐδὲ ετολμήσας θάνειν προ του σου παιδός· ἀλλα εἰάσατε τήνδε οθνείαν γυναικα, ἣν μόνην ἐγω αν ενδίκως αν ηγοίμην και μήτερα τε πάτερα. Καίτοι γε αν ηγώνισω τόνδε αγώνα κάλον, κάτθανων προ του σου παιδός· δε ὁ λοίπος χρόνος βιώσιμος σοι ην πάντως βράχυς· και τε ἐγω αν ἔζων, και ἥδε τον λοίπον χρόνον, και ουκ αν μονώθεις ἐστενον εμοις κάκοις. Και μην πεπένθας ὅσα χρη ευδαίμονα ἄνδρα πάθειν· ηβήσας μεν εν τυράννιδι, δε ἐγω αν παις σοι διάδοχος τώνδε δόμων, ὥστε ουκ εμέλλες, κάτθανων ατέκνος, λείψειν δόμον ορφανον άλλοις διάρπασαι.

Thou shewedst when thou camest to the test, who thou art: and I am of opinion that I am not thy son. Else assuredly dost thou exceed all in nothingness of soul, who, being of the age thou art, and having arrived at the very goal of life, neither hadst the will nor the courage to die for thy son: but sufferedst this alien lady *to die,* whom alone I might justly have considered both mother and father. And yet mightest thou have run this race with glory—expiring for thy son: for thy residual lifetime was at all events short:—and I should have lived; and she, the rest of our days; and I should not, bereft of her, be groaning at my miseries. And in sooth thou hadst enjoyed as much as it is requisite for a happy man to enjoy: thou passedst-the-vigor-of-thy-life indeed in sovereign rule, and I was thy son thy successor in the palace, so that thou wast not, by dying childless, about to leave thy house desolate for others to plunder.

658. ἦτ᾿ ἄρα πάντων Lascáris, Aldus, et sic vulgò. Réctiùs ἦτ᾿ ἄρ᾿, scilicet ἦτοι ἄ-ρα,—non elísâ diphthóngo ánte lóngam vocálem, (quod putávit Heáthius,) sed crási fáctâ cum a brévi. Monk.

659. Aldus's lection is ὅθ᾿ ἥλικος τ᾿ ὤν: Duport's, ὁ τηλίκοσθ᾿ ὤν: Valckenaer's, ἐ τηλίκοσθ᾿ ὤν. Musgrave, from Lascar and MSS., restored the genuine text.

663. τέ γ᾿ ἐνδίκως editiónes ómnes; sed

γέ τε núnquàm conjúngere Atticos mó-net Porsónus ad Med. 863. Monk.

667. This line is, with only one altera-tion, a repetition of line 306 above. In both instances some of the best editions have ἔζην faultily for ἔζων.

671. Both Lascar and Aldus edited δό-μον here, and δόμων in the next verse, to the entire destruction of the sense.

673. MSS. and Lascar have διαρπάσειν.

ΑΛΚΗΣΤΙΣ. 674.   53

'Ου μὴν ἐρεῖς γέ μ', ὡς ἀτιμάζων τὸ σὸν
γῆρας θανεῖν προύδωκά σ', ὅστις αἰδόφρων   675
πρός σ' ἦν μάλιστα· κἀντὶ τῶνδέ μοι χάριν
τοιάνδε καὶ σὺ χ' ἡ τεκοῦσ' ἠλλαξάτην·
τοιγὰρ φυτεύων παῖδας οὐκ ἔτ' ἂν φθάνοις,
οἳ γηροβοσκήσουσι, καὶ θανόντα σε
περιστελοῦσι, καὶ προθήσονται νεκρόν·   680
οὐ γάρ σ' ἔγωγε τῇδ' ἐμῇ θάψω χερί·
τέθνηκα γὰρ δὴ τοὐπί σ'· εἰ δ' ἄλλου τυχὼν
σωτῆρος αὐγὰς εἰσορῶ, κείνου λέγω
καὶ παῖδά μ' εἶναι, καὶ φίλον γηροτρόφον.
Μάτην ἄρ' οἱ γέροντες εὔχονται θανεῖν,   685
γῆρας ψέγοντες, καὶ μακρὸν χρόνον βίου·
ἦν δ' ἐγγὺς ἔλθῃ θάνατος, οὐδ' εἷς βούλεται
θνήσκειν, τὸ γῆρας δ' οὐκέτ' ἔστ' αὐτοῖς βαρύ.
ΧΟ. Παύσασθ'· ἅλις γὰρ ἡ παροῦσα συμφορά·
ὦ παῖ, πατρὸς δὲ μὴ παροξύνῃς φρένα.   690

TRANSLATION.

Thou canst not, however, say of me at least, that dishonouring thine old age I gave thee up to die, I who have been particularly respectful towards thee :—and for this both thou and she who bare me have made me such return : wherefore thou hast no longer to defer begetting children, who will succour thee in thine old age, and deck thee when dead, and lay out thy corse : for I will not bury thee with this mine hand ; for ere now died I as far as in thee lay—and if, having met with another deliverer, I view the light, I say that I am both his child, and the friendly supporter of his age.

Preposterously then do old folks pray to be dead, complaining of advanced age, and the weary hours of life ; for if death draw near, not one is willing to die, and [*With a smile of ridicule and contempt.*] old age is no longer burdensome to them.

CHORUS. Desist ye,—for the present calamity is enough : and [*To Admétus.*] do not, O my son, exasperate the mind of thy father !

674–5. The reading in all editions prior to Monk's is ἀτιμάζοντα σὸν γῆρας θανεῖν προύδωκας: yet Monk is borne out by the Florentine and two Parisian MSS. Our editor thinks the discrepancy first arose from some copyist writing προύδωκας instead of προύδωκά σ'.

678. Elmsley explained οὐκ ἂν φθάνοις, (joined with a present participle,) most correctly indeed by '*non prævénies occasiónem.*' Monk has rendered the phrase into English, " *you have no time to lose,* or *you cannot make too much haste.*"

686. μακρὸν χρόνον βίου, strictly, *the long time of life,* meaning " *the tedious time* or *wearisome hours of frail old age.*"

687. For οὐδ' εἷς, MSS. and editions in general have οὐδείς, but less elegantly.

ΦΕ. Ὦ παῖ, τίν' αὐχεῖς, πότερα Λυδὸν ἢ Φρύγα,   --|∪-||-∪∪|∪-||∪-|∪∪

κακοῖς ἐλαύνειν, ἀργυρώνητον σέθεν;   ∪-|∪-||--|∪-||--|∪∪

Οὐκ οἶσθα Θεσσαλόν με, κἀπὸ Θεσσαλοῦ   --|∪-||∪-|∪-||∪-|∪-

πατρὸς γεγῶτα, γνησίως ἐλεύθερον;   ∪-|∪-||∪-|∪-||∪-|∪∪

"Αγαν ὑβρίζεις, καὶ νεανίας λόγους   695   ∪-|∪-||--|∪-||∪-|-∪-

ῥίπτων ἐς ἡμᾶς, ὃν βαλὼν οὕτως ἄπει.   --|∪-||-∪-|∪-||∪-|∪-

Ἐγὼ δέ σ' οἴκων δεσπότην ἐγεινάμην,   ∪-|∪-||--|∪-||∪-|∪-

κἄθρεψ', ὀφείλων οὐχ ὑπερθνήσκειν σέθεν·   --|∪-||--|∪-||--|∪∪

οὐ γὰρ πατρῷον τόιδ' ἐδεξάμην νόμον,   --|∪-||--|∪-||∪-|∪∪

παίδων προθνήσκειν πατέρας, οὐδ' Ἑλληνικόν·   700   --|∪-⁎||-∪∪|∪-||--|∪∪

σαυτῷ γὰρ, εἴτε δυστυχὴς εἴτ' εὐτυχής,   --|∪-||--|∪-||--|∪-

ἔφυς· ἃ δ' ἡμῶν χρῆν σε τυγχάνειν, ἔχεις.   ∪-|∪-||--|∪-||∪-|∪-

Πολλῶν μὲν ἄρχεις, πολυπλέθρους δέ σοι γύας   --|∪-||-∪∪|∪-||∪-|∪-

λείψω· πατρὸς γὰρ ταῦτ' ἐδεξάμην πάρα.   --|∪-||--|∪-||∪-|∪∪

Τί δῆτά σ' ἠδίκηκα; Τοῦ σ' ἀποστερῶ;   705   ∪-|∪-||∪-|∪-||∪-|∪-

Μὴ θνῆσχ' ὑπὲρ τοῦδ' ἀνδρὸς, οὐδ' ἐγὼ πρὸ σοῦ.   --|∪-||--|∪-||∪-|∪-

---

THE ORDER, AND ENGLISH ACCENTUATION.

ΦΕ. Τίνα, ω παι, αὐχεις ελαύνειν κάκοις, πότερα Λύδον η Φρύγα, αργυρωνητον σέθεν; Ουκ οίσθα με Θέσσαλον, και γεγώτα απο Θεσσαλου πάτρος, γνήσιως ελεύθερον; Ὑβρίζεις άγαν, και ρίπτων ες ήμας λόγους νεάνιας, βάλων ουκ ούτως άπει. Δε εγω εγείναμην σε δεσπότην οίκων, και εθρέψα, ουκ οφείλων ὑπερθνήσκειν σέθεν· γαρ ουκ εδεξάμην τόνδε πατρώον, ουδε Ἑλληνικον νόμον, πάτερας προθνήσκειν παίδων· γαρ εφυς σαυτω, είτε δύστυχης είτε εὐτυχης· δε ά ήμων χρην σε τύγχανειν, εχεις. Άρχεις μεν πόλλων, δε λείψω σοι πολύπλεθρους γύας· γαρ ταυτα εδεξάμην πάρα πάτρος. Τι δήτα ηδικηκα σε; Του αποστέρω σε; Μη Θνήσκε ὑπερ τούδε άνδρος, ουδε εγω προ σου.

TRANSLATION.

PHERES. [*To Admétus.*] Whom, O son, dost thou presume thou art gibing with thy reproaches, whether a Lýdian or a Phrýgian, purchased by thee with money?

Knowest thou not that I am a Thessálian, and sprung from a Thessálian father, truly free? Thou art over insolent,—and casting at us the words of youthful-age, shalt not, having cast them, thus depart!

But I begat thee lord of my house, and I brought thee up,—not thy debtor to die for thee:—seeing I received not this patriarchal, nor yet Grecian law, " *That fathers should die for their children:*" for thou wast born for thyself—whether unfortunate or fortunate: and what from us it behoved thee to have, thou hast.

Thou rulest indeed over many, and I will leave thee extensive territories—for these I received from my father.

In what then have I wronged thee? Of what do I defraud thee? Die not thou for me, neither will I for thee!

691. αὐχεῖς seems here usurped in the sense of "*presumest thou*" rather than of "*gloriest thou:*" so in verse 95, above, οὐκ αὐχῶ, *I presume not.*

695. ἄγαν μ' ὑβρίζεις éditi: solébant aútèm librárii líteram post ἄγαν interpoláre, nesciéntes scílicet últimam hújus vócis prodúci:—νεανία hîc válet *audax, fórtis, véhemens.* MONK.

698. For ὀφείλων, in this verse, Lascar has ὀφείλω, badly: and for ὑπερθνήσκειν Al-

dus and most of the early editions have ὑπερθνήσκων. Markland conjectured ὀφείλειν and ὑπερθνήσκειν.

701. Elmsley thought that Eurípidës may have written δυστυχεῖς and εὐτυχεῖς, not δυστυχὴς and εὐτυχής.

703. Wakefield, but certainly without any reason whatever, conjectured ἀρχάς. Aldus and his followers give γυίας, viz. a spondee for the last foot: Barnes tacitly restored the genuine lection.

Χαίρεις ὁρῶν φῶς, πατέρα δ᾽ οὐ χαίρειν δοκεῖς;

Ἦ μὴν πολύν γε τὸν κάτω λογίζομαι

χρόνον, τὸ δὲ ζῆν σμικρὸν, ἀλλ᾽ ὅμως γλυκύ.

Σύ γ᾽ οὖν ἀναιδῶς διεμάχου τὸ μὴ θανεῖν,   710

καὶ ζῆς παρελθὼν τὴν πεπρωμένην τύχην,

ταύτην κατακτάς· εἶτ᾽ ἐμὴν ἀψυχίαν

λέγεις, γυναικὸς, ὦ κάκισθ᾽, ἡσσημένος,

ἢ τοῦ καλοῦ σοῦ προύθανεν νεανίου;

Σοφῶς δ᾽ ἐφεῦρες, ὥστε μὴ θανεῖν ποτὲ,   715

εἰ τὴν παροῦσαν κατθανεῖν πείσεις ἀεὶ

γυναῖχ᾽ ὑπὲρ σοῦ· κᾆτ᾽ ὀνειδίζεις φίλοις

τοῖς μὴ θέλουσι δρᾷν τάδ᾽, αὐτὸς ὢν κακός;

Σίγα· νόμιζε δ᾽, εἰ σὺ τὴν σαυτοῦ φιλεῖς

ψυχὴν, φιλεῖν ἅπαντας· εἰ δ᾽ ἡμᾶς κακῶς   720

ἐρεῖς, ἀκούσει πολλὰ κοὐ ψευδῆ κακά.

ΧΟ. Πλείω λέλεκται νῦν τε καὶ τὰ πρὶν κακά·

παῦσαι δὲ, πρέσβυ, παῖδα σὸν κακορροθῶν.

THE ORDER, AND ENGLISH ACCENTUATION.

Χαίρεις ὁρῶν φως, δε δοκεῖς πάτερα ου χαίρειν; Η μην λογίζομαι τον χρόνον κάτω γε πόλυν, δε το ζην σμίκρον, ἀλλα ὅμως γλύκυ. Συ ουν αναιδως γε διεμάχου το μη θάνειν, και ζης παρέλθων την πεπρώμενην τύχην, κατάντας ταύτην· εἰτα λέγεις ἐμην αψύχιαν, ω κακίστε, ἡσσήμενος γυναίκος, ἡ προ-έθανε σου του κάλου νεάνιου; Δε εφεύρες σόφως, ὥστε μη ποτε θάνειν, εἰ πείσεις την ἀει παροῦσαν γυναίκα κάτθανειν ὑπερ σου· και εἰτα ονειδίζεις φίλοις τοις μη θελούσι δραν τάδε, ων αὐτος κάκος; Σίγα· δε νομίζε, εἰ συ φίλεις την ψύχην σαυτου, ἀπάντας φίλειν· δε εἰ ἐξεις κάκως ἥμας, ακούσει πόλλα κάκα και ου ψεύδη. ΧΟ. Πλείω κάκα λελέκται τε νυν και τα πριν· δε παύσαι, πρέσβυ, κακόρροθων σον παίδα.

TRANSLATION.

Thou joyest beholding the light, and dost thou think that thy father joys not? I for certain count the time we must spend beneath indeed long, but life is short, — yet nevertheless sweet. Thou, however, didst shamelessly at least fight off from dying, and thou livest, having passed over thy destined fate, by [*Pointing to the corse.*] slaying her: after that dost thou [*With a frown of scorn.*] talk of my nothingness of soul, O most vile one,—when thou hast been conquered by a woman who died for thee [*Sneeringly.*] the handsome youth? But thou hast made a grand discovery, so as never to die, if thou wilt persuade the wife that is thine from-time-to-time to die in thy stead : and then reproachest thou thy friends who are not willing to do this, being thyself a coward?

Hold thy peace:—and consider, if thou lovest thine own life, that all persons love theirs : and if thou wilt speak evilly against us, thou shalt hear many reproaches and not false ones.

CHORUS. [*Interruptingly and frowningly.*] Too many reproaches have been uttered both [*Looking at Phérës.*] now, — and [*Looking at Admétus.*] before: so [*To Phérës.*] desist, old man, from reproaching thy son !

---

707. Aristóphanês in his Clouds, 1415, has the following parody on this verse: κλαίουσι παῖδες, πατέρα δ᾽ οὐ κλαίειν δοκεῖς;

708. For ἢ, Elmsley gives καὶ.

713. ἡσσημένος, literally, *being worsted.* Monk quotes ἡσσώμενος, Hec. 1234: ἡσσηθήσομαι, Hipp. 724 and 980,—&c.

715—16. *Thou hast cleverly discovered, so as not to die ever, if thou wilt always persuade the wife present* (that is, *thy wife for the time being*) *to die for thee.* For πείσεις ἀεὶ, most editions have πείσειας ἄν. Monk rightly explains τὴν παροῦσαν ἀεὶ γυναῖκα, by "*uxórem quæ pro témpore fúerit.*".

56   724. ΕΥΡΙΠΙΔΟΥ

ΑΔ. Λέγ᾽, ὡς ἐμοῦ λέξαντος· εἰ δ᾽ ἀλγεῖς κλύων
τἀληθὲς, οὐ χρῆν σ᾽ εἰς ἔμ᾽ ἐξαμαρτάνειν.   725

ΦΕ. Σοῦ δ᾽ ἂν προθνήσκων μᾶλλον ἐξημάρτανον.

ΑΔ. Ταὐτὸν γὰρ ἡβῶντ᾽ ἄνδρα καὶ πρέσβυν θανεῖν;

ΦΕ. Ψυχῇ μιᾷ ζῆν, οὐ δυοῖν, ὀφείλομεν.

ΑΔ. Καὶ μὴν Διός γε μείζονα ζώης χρόνον.

ΦΕ. Ἀρᾷ γονεῦσιν, οὐδὲν ἔκδικον παθών;   730

ΑΔ. Μακροῦ βίου γὰρ ᾐσθόμην ἐρῶντά σε.

ΦΕ. Ἀλλ᾽ οὐ σὺ νεκρὸν ἀντὶ σοῦ τόνδ᾽ ἐκφέρεις;

ΑΔ. Σημεῖα τῆς σῆς, ὦ κάκιστ᾽, ἀψυχίας.

ΦΕ. Οὔτοι πρὸς ἡμῶν γ᾽ ὤλετ᾽· οὐκ ἐρεῖς τόδε.

ΑΔ. Φεῦ. Εἴθ᾽ ἀνδρὸς ἔλθοις τοῦδέ γ᾽ εἰς χρείαν ποτέ.

ΦΕ. Μήστευε πολλὰς, ὡς θάνωσι πλείονες.   736

ΑΔ. Σοὶ τοῦτ᾽ ὄνειδος· οὐ γὰρ ἤθελες θανεῖν.

ΦΕ. Φίλον τὸ φέγγος τοῦτο τοῦ θεοῦ, φίλον.

THE ORDER, AND ENGLISH ACCENTUATION.

ΑΔ. Λέγε, ὡς ἐμου λεξάντος· δε ει ἀλγεις κλύων το ἀληθες, ου χρην σε εξαμάρτανειν εις εμε. ΦΕ. Δε αν εξημάρτανον μᾶλλον προθνήσκων σου. ΑΔ. Γαρ το αὐτον ἡβῶντα ἀνδρα και πρέσβυν θάνειν; ΦΕ. Οφείλομεν ζην μια ψύχη, ου δυοιν. ΑΔ. Και μην γε ζώης μείζονα χρόνον Διός. ΦΕ. Ἀρα γονεύσι, πάθων οὐδεν ἐκδικον; ΑΔ. Γαρ ᾐσθομην σε ἐρωντα μάκρου βίου. ΦΕ. Ἀλλα ου συ ἐκφερεις τόνδε νέκρον ἀντι σου; ΑΔ. Σημεία, ω κακίστε, της σης ἀψύχιας. ΦΕ. Οὔτοι ὤλετο προς ἡμων γε· ουκ ἐρεις τόδε. ΑΔ. Φευ. Είθε ποτε γε ἐλθοις εις χρείαν τουδε ἀνδρος. ΦΕ. Μνηστεύε πόλλας, ὡς πλείονες θανώσι. ΑΔ. Τουτο ονειδος σοι· γαρ ουκ ήθελες θάνειν. ΦΕ. Φίλον το τουτο φέγγος του θεου, φίλον.

TRANSLATION.

ADMETUS. [*To his father.*] Speak, since I have spoken :—and if thou art vexed at hearing the truth, thou shouldest not err respecting me! PHERES. But I should have erred more if I had died for thee! ADMETUS. For is it the same thing for a man in the prime of life, and for an old man, to die? PHERES. We ought to live with one life, not with two. ADMETUS. [*Scoffingly.*] And may thou for troth live then a longer time than Jove! PHERES. Cursest thou thy parents, having suffered no injustice? ADMETUS. For I perceived thou lovedst a long life! PHERES. But art thou not bearing forth this corse in lieu of thyself? ADMETUS. [*Angrily.*] A proof this, O thou most cowardly one, of thy nothingness-of-soul! PHERES. She died not at our hand at least:—thou wilt not say this! ADMETUS. [*Affected.*] Hey! I wish thou may sometime at least come to the need of this man! [*Meaning himself.*] PHERES. [*With scorn.*] Wed many wives, in order that more may die! ADMETUS. This is a reproach to thee, for thou wast not willing to die! PHERES. [*Placidly.*] Dear is this light of the God, dear!

724. One MS. has λέγοντος: Wakefield on the conjecture of Reiske edited λέξοντος: Markland in a precisely similar instance gives ᾽λέγξαντος—conceiving it to be the reading of the Scholiast.

729. Ita Matthiæ: caéteri μείζον᾽ ἂν ζώοις χρόνοις, praéter Lascar. qui ζώης. Quóniàm véro impreeántis est orátio deléndum ésse ἂν monuère plúres. MONK.

733. Aldus edited σημεῖά γ᾽, ὦ κάκισ-

τε, ταῦτ᾽ ἀψυχίας. Musgrave, from Láscar and MSS., restored the true lection.

734. Lascar, Aldus, and several MSS. have ὄυτι,—but the metre as well as the sense requires οὖτοι.

738. τοῦ θεοῦ, *of the god,* viz. *of Phœbus* or *the Sun:*—the article, as Monk justly observes, is much oftener omitted than expressed with θεὸς in this sense:—φίλον, *dear—delightful—sweet.*

ΑΔ. Κακὸν τὸ λῆμα, κοὐκ ἐν ἀνδράσιν, τὸ σόν.

ΦΕ. Οὐκ ἐγγελᾷς γέροντα βαστάζων νεκρόν.   740

ΑΔ. Θανεῖ γε μέντοι δυσκλεὴς, ὅταν θάνῃς.

ΦΕ. Κακῶς ἀκούειν οὐ μέλει θανόντι μοι.

ΑΔ. Φεῦ, φεῦ· τὸ γῆρας ὡς ἀναιδείας πλέων.

ΦΕ. Ἥδ᾽ οὐκ ἀναιδής· τήνδ᾽ ἐφεῦρες ἄφρονα.

ΑΔ. Ἄπελθε, καί με τόνδ᾽ ἔα·θάψαι νεκρόν.   745

ΦΕ. Ἄπειμι· θάψεις δ᾽ αὐτὸς ὢν αὐτῆς φονεύς.

Δίκας δὲ δώσεις σοῖσι κηδεσταῖς ἔτι,

ἢ τἄρ᾽ Ἄκαστος οὐκέτ᾽ ἔστ᾽ ἐν ἀνδράσιν,

εἰ μή σ᾽ ἀδελφῆς αἷμα τιμωρήσεται.

ΑΔ. Ἔῤῥοις νυν αὐτὸς, χ᾽ ἡ ξυνοικήσασά σοι·   750

ἄπαιδε παιδὸς ὄντος, ὥσπερ ἄξιοι,

γηράσκετ᾽· οὐ γὰρ τῷδ᾽ ἔτ᾽ εἰς ταὐτὸν στέγος

νεῖσθ᾽· εἰ δ᾽ ἀπειπεῖν χρῆν με κηρύκων ὕπο

τὴν σὴν πατρῴαν ἑστίαν, ἀπεῖπον ἄν.

THE ORDER, AND ENGLISH ACCENTUATION.

ΑΔ. Κάκον το λῆμα το σον, και ουκ εν ἀνδρασι. ΦΕ. Ουκ ἐγγελᾳς βαστάζων γεροντα νέκρον. ΑΔ. Μέντοι θάνει δύσκλενης γε, ὅταν θάνῃς. ΦΕ. Ακούειν κάκως ου μέλει μοι θανόντι. ΑΔ. Φευ, φευ· ὡς πλέων αναιδείας το γήρας. ΦΕ. Ἥδε ουκ αναιδὴς· τήνδε εφεύρες ἄφρονα. ΑΔ. Ἀπέλθε, και ἐα με θάψαι τόνδε νέκρον. ΦΕ. Απείμι· δε θάψεις αὐτος ων φόνευς αὐτης. Δε δώσεις δίκας ἔτι σοῖσι κηδέσταις· η τοι ἄρα Ακάστος ἐστι οὐκετι εν ἀνδρασι, ει μη τιμωρήσεται σε αἱμα αδέλφης. ΑΔ. Ἔῤῥοις νυν αὐτος και ἡ ξυνοικησάσα σοι· ἀπαιδε, ὥσπερ ἄξιοι, γηράσκετε, παιδος ὄντος· γαρ ουκ ἔτι νείσθε εις το αὐτο στέγος τῶδε· δε ει χρην με απείπειν την σην πατρῴαν ἔστιαν ὑπο κηρύκων, αν απείπον.

TRANSLATION.

ADMETUS. [*Sneeringly.*] Base is thy spirit, and unworthy of a man! PHERES. Thou sneerest not, carrying an aged corse! ADMETUS. Thou however wilt die inglorious at least when thou diest! PHERES. To hear reproaches, matters not to me when dead! ADMETUS. Alas! alas! how full of shamelessness is old age! PHERES. [*Pointing to the corpse.*] She was not shameless:— her thou foundest mad! ADMETUS. Begone, and suffer me to bury the dead! PHERES. I will go:— but thou wilt bury her, being thyself her murderer. However thou wilt render satisfaction yet to thy wife's relatives, else assuredly Acástus ranks no longer among men—if that he avenge not himself on thee for the blood of his sister! [*Exit Phérës.*] ADMETUS. Get thee gone now thyself, and she who dwells with thee: childless, as ye deserve, wax ye old, your child still living:—for ye no more come into the same house with me: and if it were necessary for me to renounce thy paternal hearth by heralds, I would renounce it.

---

739. οὐκ ἐν ἀνδράσι, literally, *not among men*, that is, *not of masculine stamp*. The phrase ἐν ἀνδράσι occurs again below, v. 748, and in several other plays.

743. The vulgate reading here is πλέ-ον:—Lascar has πλέων, the Attic form.

747. κηδεσταῖς, *by brothers in law:* the word κηδεστὴς has several meanings, but it originally signifies "*a manager*, or one *who has the care of any thing.*"

748. The more common lection is ἔτ᾽

ἄρ᾽, but Monk defends ἢ τἄρ᾽, viz. ἢ τοι ἄρα, as in verse 658 above.

750. Aldus from MSS. printed ἔῤῥου: Musgrave from three MSS. and consentingly with Lascar, edited ἔῤῥοις.

752. The reading of all editions (Matthiæ's excepted,) is, τῷδ᾽ ἔτ᾽ εἰς ταὐτὸ στέγος:—Matthiæ has τῷδέ γ᾽. Monk says, "ταὐτὸν usitátius est quàm ταὐτό."

753. νεῖσθε, *ibitis*, praésens pro futúro, quod in hôc vérbo solénne est. MONK.

H

Ἡμεῖς δὲ (τοὺν ποσὶν γὰρ ὀιστέον κακὸν)   755

στείχωμεν, ὡς ἂν ἐν πυρᾷ θῶμεν νεκρόν.

ΧΟ. Ἰώ. Ἰώ. Σχετλία τόλμης·

ὦ γενναία, καὶ μέγ' ἀρίστη,

χαῖρε· πρόφρων σε χθόνιός θ' Ἑρμῆς,

Ἅιδης τε δέχοιτ'· εἰ δέ τι κἀκεῖ   760

πλέον ἔσσ' ἀγαθοῖς, τούτων μετέχουσ'

Ἅιδου νύμφη παρεδρεύοις.

ΘΕΡΑΠΩΝ.

Πολλοὺς μὲν ἤδη, κἀπὸ παντοίας χθονὸς

ξένους μολόντας οἶδ' ἐς Ἀδμήτου δόμους,

οἷς δεῖπνα προύθηκ'· ἀλλὰ τοῦδ' οὔπω ξένου   765

κακίον' εἰς τήνδ' ἑστίαν ἐδεξάμην.

Ὃς πρῶτα μὲν, πενθοῦντα δεσπότην ὁρῶν,

εἰσῆλθε, κἀτόλμησ' ἀμείψασθαι πύλας·

ἔπειτα δ' οὔτι σωφρόνως ἐδέξατο

τὰ προστυχόντα ξένια, συμφορὰν μαθών·   770

ἀλλ' εἴ τι μὴ φέροιμεν, ὤτρυνεν φέρειν.

THE ORDER, AND ENGLISH ACCENTUATION.

Δε ἥμεις (γαρ το κάκον εν πόσι οιστεον) στειχώμεν, ὡς αν θώμεν νέκρον εν πύρα. ΧΟ. Ἰω. Ἰω. Σχέτλια τόλμης· ω γενναία, και μέγα αρίστη, χαῖρε· πρόφρων δε ει και ἐκει ἐστι τι πλέον ἀγαθοις, μετεχούσα τούτων παρεδρεύεις νύμφη Αἰδου. ΘΕ. Ἡδη μεν οἰδα πόλλους ξένους, και ἀπο παντοίας χθόνος, μολόντας ες δόμους Αδμήτου, οἰς προ-εθηκα δεῖπνα· ἀλλα ουπω εδεξαμην εις τήνδε ἐστιαν κακίονα τούδε ξένου. Ὁς πρωτα μεν, ὁρων δέσποτην πενθοῦντα, εισῆλθε, και ετολμήσε αμείψασθαι πύλας· δε επειτα ουτι σώφρενως εδεξατο τα ξένια προστυχόντα, μάθων σύμφοραν· αλλα ει μη φεροιμεν τι, ὠτρυνε φέρειν.

TRANSLATION.

But let us (for the evil before us must be borne) proceed, that we may place the corse upon the funeral pyre. [*Exit Admétus in procession, followed by the Chorus chanting the benedictory hymn.*]

CHORUS. [*Chanting most mournfully.*] Alas! Alas! Unhappy because of thy bold-deed: O noble, and by far most excellent, farewell:—may both Mércury below the Earth, and Hádës, receive thee kindly:—and if in that kingdom too there be any distinction for the good, partaking of it may thou sit beside the bride of Plúto. [*The Chorus following up the procession disappears; but the chanting is heard for a few seconds.*]

MAN-SERVANT. [*Entering.*] Prior to now, indeed, have I known many guests, and from all parts of the world, come to the house of Admétus, before whom I have spread the feast:—but never yet did I receive into this abode a worse-one than this guest. Who in the first place indeed, though he saw my master in grief, came in, and had the assurance to pass the gates:—and next, he nowise in a becoming manner received the regalement which there chanced to be, knowing of the calamity: but if we did not bring aught, he hurried us to bring it.

---

755. ἐν ποσὶ, *at our feet*, a very common mode of expressing "*just before us.*"

757. Monk has followed Lascar; but in Aldus and most of the early editions we find ὦ σχετλία τόλμης, γενναία.

760. ἐκεῖ, *there* or *yonder*, that is, *in the* regions below. So in the Medéa, 1069, ἐυδαιμονοῖτον· ἀλλ' ἐκεῖ, *blessed be ye: but yonder* viz. *in the kingdom of Plúto.*

761. πλέον, *more favor* or *indulgence.*

762. The Chorus now leaves the stage to attend the funeral of Alcéstis.

Ποτῆρα δ᾽ ἐν χείρεσσι κίσσινον λαβὼν,

πίνει μελαίνης μητρὸς εὔζωρον μέθυ,

ἕως ἐθέρμην᾽ αὐτὸν ἀμφιβᾶσα φλὸξ

οἴνου· στέφει δὲ κρᾶτα μυρσίνης κλάδοις,   775

ἄμουσ᾽ ὑλακτῶν· δισσὰ δ᾽ ἦν μέλη κλύειν·

ὁ μὲν γὰρ ᾖδε, τῶν ἐν Ἀδμήτου κακῶν

οὐδὲν προτιμῶν, οἰκέται δ᾽ ἐκλαίομεν

δέσποιναν· ὄμμα δ᾽ οὐκ ἐδείκνυμεν ξένῳ

τέγγοντες· Ἀδμήτος γὰρ ὧδ᾽ ἐφίετο.   780

Καὶ νῦν ἐγὼ μὲν ἐν δόμοισιν ἑστιῶ

ξένον, πανοῦργον κλῶπα καὶ λῃστήν τινα.

Ἡ δ᾽ ἐκ δόμων βέβηκεν, οὐδ᾽ ἐφεσπόμην,

οὐδ᾽ ἐξέτεινα χεῖρ᾽, ἀποιμώζων ἐμὴν

δέσποιναν, ἥ ᾽μοὶ πᾶσί τ᾽ οἰκέταισιν ἦν   785

μήτηρ· κακῶν γὰρ μυρίων ἐρρύετο,

ὀργὰς μαλάσσουσ᾽ ἀνδρός. Ἆρα τὸν ξένον

στυγῶ δικαίως, ἐν κακοῖς ἀφιγμένον;

THE ORDER, AND ENGLISH ACCENTUATION.

Δε λάβων εν χειρέσσι ποτῆρα κίσσινον, πίνει ευζώρον μέθυ μελαίνης μήτρος, ἕως φλοξ οίνευ αμφιβάσα αύτον εθερμήνε· δε στέφει κρᾶτα κλάδοις μύρσινης, ὑλάκτων αμούσα· δε ην δίσσα μέλη κλύειν· γαρ ὁ μεν ἦδε, προτίμων ουδεν των κάκων εν Αδμήτου, δε οίκεται εκλαίομεν δεσποίναν· ξένω δε ουκ εδεικνύμεν τεγγόντες ὅμμα· γαρ ὧδε Αδμήτος εφίετο. Και νυν εν δομοίσι μεν εγω ἑστιω ξένον, τίνα πανούργον κλῶπα και λήστην. Δε ἡ βέβηκε εκ δόμων, ουδε εφέσπομην, ουδε εξετεινα χείρα, αποιμώζων εμην δεσποίναν, ἡ ην εμοί τε πᾶσι οικεταῖσι μήτηρ· γαρ ερρύετο μύριων κάκων, μαλασσούσα οργας άνδρος. Ἀρα δικαίως στύγω τον ξένον, αφίγμενον εν κάκοις;

TRANSLATION.

And having taken in his hands the cup wreathed-with-ivy, he quaffs the neat juice of the purple mother, until the fumes of the wine coming upon him inflamed him: and he crowns his head with branches of myrtle, howling discordantly: and there were two strains to hear; for he in troth was singing—concerned in no degree about the afflictions in the family of Admétus,—and we domestics were bewailing our mistress:—to the guest, however, we shewed not that we were bedewing our eyes,—for thus had Admétus commanded.

And now in the house indeed am I entertaining this stranger, some deceitful thief and robber!

But she [*Shedding tears.*] is gone from the palace, nor did I follow; neither stretched I forth my hand, lamenting my mistress, who was to me and to all the domestics a mother; for she saved us from ten thousand ills, softening the anger of her husband.

Do I not justly then hate this guest, who is come in our miseries?

772. Ita ómnes (says Monk) praéter Lascárem, qui corrúptè dédit δ᾽ ἐχείρεσσι. Dúbito aútèm ánnon réctiùs ésset "ποτήριον δ᾽ ἐν χερσὶ κίσσινον λαβών." Scholiásta cértè habet ποτῆρα δ᾽ ἐν χερσὶ, et suspécta est, in diálogo, poética fórma χείρεσσι. Sóphocles quídèm, Antig. 1297, hábet ἔχω μὲν ἐν χείρεσσιν ἀρτίως τέκνα,—sed éum mélicis interjéctum. Vócem ποτήρ non álibì vidísse mémini praéter Cycl. 151.

773. μελαίνης μητρός· τῆς ἀμπέλου· ὁ γὰρ μέλας οἶνος ἰσχυρότερός ἐστι. SCHOLIAST. 775. Several MSS. and almost all the early editions have μυρσίνοις. 783. The more common (but certainly less correct) reading, is, ἥδ᾽ ἐκ δόμων. Both Wakefield and Matthiæ give ἡ δ᾽ ἐκ δόμων, rightly. 787. ἆρα, nónne, ut súprà ver. 351. Inútilis ígitur corréctió est, ἆρ᾽ ὄν. MONK.

<table>
<tr><td>ΗΡ. Οὗτος, τί σεμνὸν καὶ πεφροντικὸς βλέπεις;</td><td>– – | ⏑ – || – – | ⏑ – || ⏑ – | ⏑ –</td></tr>
<tr><td>Ου χρὴ σκυθρωπὸν τοῖς ξένοις τὸν πρόσπολον</td><td>– – | ⏑ – || – – | ⏑ – || – – | ⏑ ⏑</td></tr>
<tr><td>εἶναι, δέχεσθαι δ' ἐυπροσηγόρῳ φρενί.</td><td>– – | ⏑ – || – – | ⏑ – || ⏑ – | ⏑ ⏑</td></tr>
<tr><td>Σὺ δ', ἄνδρ' ἑταῖρον δεσπότου παρόνθ' ὁρῶν,</td><td>⏑ – | ⏑ – || – – | ⏑ – || ⏑ – | ⏑ –</td></tr>
<tr><td>στυγνῷ προσώπῳ καὶ ξυνωφρυωμένῳ</td><td>– – | ⏑ – || – – | ⏑ – || ⏑ – | ⏑ –</td></tr>
<tr><td>δέχει, θυραίου πήματος σπουδὴν ἔχων.</td><td>⏑ – | ⏑ – || – – | ⏑ – || – – | ⏑ –</td></tr>
<tr><td>Δεῦρ' ἔλθ', ὅπως ἂν καὶ σοφώτερος γένῃ.</td><td>– – | ⏑ – || – – | ⏑ – || ⏑ – | ⏑ –</td></tr>
<tr><td>Τὰ θνητὰ πράγματ' οἶδας, ἣν ἔχει φύσιν;</td><td>⏑ – | ⏑ – || ⏑ – | ⏑ – || ⏑ – | ⏑ ⏑</td></tr>
<tr><td>Οἶμαι μὲν, ὀύ· πόθεν γάρ; Ἀλλ' ἄκουέ μου·</td><td>– – | ⏑ – || ⏑ – | ⏑ – || ⏑ – | ⏑ –</td></tr>
<tr><td>Βροτοῖς ἅπασι κατθανεῖν ὀφείλεται·</td><td>⏑ – | ⏑ – || ⏑ – | ⏑ – || ⏑ – | ⏑ ⏑</td></tr>
<tr><td>κὀυκ ἔστιν αὐτῶν, ὅστις ἐξεπίσταται</td><td>– – | ⏑ – || – – | ⏑ – || ⏑ – | ⏑ ⏑</td></tr>
<tr><td>τὴν αὔριον μέλλουσαν ἐι βιώσεται·</td><td>– – | ⏑ – || – – | ⏑ – || ⏑ – | ⏑ ⏑</td></tr>
<tr><td>τὸ τῆς τύχης γὰρ ἀφανὲς, οἶ προβήσεται,</td><td>⏑ – | ⏑ – || ⏑ ⏑ ⏑ | ⏑ – || ⏑ – | ⏑ ⏑</td></tr>
<tr><td>κἄστ' ὀυ διδακτὸν, ὀυδ' ἁλίσκεται τέχνῃ.</td><td>– – | ⏑ – || ⏑ – | ⏑ – || ⏑ – | ⏑ –</td></tr>
<tr><td>Ταῦτ' οὖν ἀκούσας, καὶ μαθὼν ἐμοῦ πάρα,</td><td>– – | ⏑ – || – – | ⏑ – || ⏑ – | ⏑ ⏑</td></tr>
<tr><td>εὔφραινε σαυτὸν, πῖνε, τὸν καθ' ἡμέραν</td><td>– – | ⏑ – || – – | ⏑ – || ⏑ – | ⏑ –</td></tr>
<tr><td>βίον λογίζου σὸν, τὰ δ' ἄλλα τῆς Τύχης.</td><td>⏑ – | ⏑ – || – – | ⏑ – || ⏑ – | ⏑ –</td></tr>
</table>

THE ORDER, AND ENGLISH ACCENTUATION.

ΗΡ. Ούτος, τι βλέπεις σέμνον και πεφρόντικος; Ου χρη τον πρόσπολον είναι σκυθρώπον τοις ξένοις, δε δεχέσθαι ευπροσήγορῳ φρένι. Δε συ, ὅρων άνδρα ἑταίρον δέσποτου παρόντα, δέχει στύγνῳ και ξυνωφρυώμενῳ προσώπῳ, έχων σπούδην θυραίου πήματος. Ἔλθε δεύρο, ὅπως αν και γένη σοφώτερος. Οίδας τα θνήτα πράγματα, ἡν φύσιν έχει; Οίμαι μεν, ου· γαρ πόθεν; Ἄλλα ακούε μου· Κάτθανειν οφείλεται άπάσι βρότοις· και ουκ έστι αύτων, ὅστις εξεπίσταται ει βιώσεται την μελλούσαν αύριον· γαρ το της τύχης άφανες, όι προβήσεται, και ουκ έστι διδάκτον, ούδε άλίσκεται τέχνῃ. Ακούσας ταύτα ουν, και μάθων πάρα έμου, ευφραίνε σαύτον, πίνε, λογίζου τον βίον κάτα ἥμεραν σον, δε τα άλλα της Τύχης.

TRANSLATION.

Hercules. [*Entering in gladsome mood accosts the servant.*] Ho there! Why lookest thou grave and thoughtful? It becomes not a servant to be of woful countenance before guests, but to receive them with cheerful mind! But thou, though thou seest a man the companion of thy lord present, receivest him with a morose and clouded countenance, fixing thy attention on an extrinsic calamity. [*Beckoning.*] Come hither, that thou mayest in fact be made wiser! [*The servant approaches Hérculës.*] Knowest thou mortal affairs, of what nature they are? I think indeed, not: for whence shouldest thou? But hear me:—" *To die is a debt that must be paid by all men:—and there is not one of them who knows whether he shall be alive the coming morrow: for whatever depends upon fortune is uncertain, how it will turn out—and is not to be learnt, neither is it detected by art.*" Having heard these things, then, and having learnt them from me, make thyself merry,—drink,—consider the life granted thee from day to day thine own, but the rest Fortune's.

789. οὗτος, *heus tu*,—a common mode of calling the attention of any one unceremoniously addressed:—τί σεμνὸν βλέπεις, *why lookest thou reverently* or *sanctifiedly?* In Greek nothing is more common than the use of nouns adjective in the neuter gender for adverbs.

794. θυραίου πήματος σπουδὴν ἔχων, *having anxiety* or *concern of mind about a misfortune wherewith thou hast nothing to do: a disaster with which thou hast not any business: an unlucky event foreign to thee.*

795. ὅπως ἂν καὶ σοφώτερος γένῃ, literally, *that thou mayest become even the wiser.*

796. Non ádmodùm fréquens est fórma οἶδας pro commúni οἶσθα. Monk.

799. For ἔστιν αὐτῶν, some MSS., and editions not a few, have ἔστι θνητῶν.

Τίμα δὲ καὶ τὴν πλεῖστον ἡδίστην θεῶν

Κύπριν βροτοῖσιν· εὐμενὴς γὰρ ἡ θεός.

Τὰ δ᾽ ἄλλ᾽ ἔασον ταῦτα, καὶ πιθοῦ λόγοις

ἐμοῖσιν, εἴπερ ὀρθά σοι δοκῶ λέγειν·

ὄιμαι μέν. Οὔκουν, τὴν ἄγαν λύπην ἀφεὶς,   810

πιεῖ μεθ᾽ ἡμῶν, τάσδ᾽ ὑπερβαλὼν πύλας,

στεφάνοις πυκασθείς; Καὶ σάφ᾽ οἶδ᾽, ὅθ᾽ οὕνεκα

τοῦ νῦν σκυθρωποῦ καὶ ξυνεστῶτος φρενῶν

μεθορμιεῖ σε πίτυλος ἐμπεσὼν σκύφου.

Ὄντας δὲ θνητοὺς θνητὰ καὶ φρονεῖν χρεών·   815

ὡς τοῖς γε σεμνοῖς καὶ ξυνωφρυωμένοις

ἅπασίν ἐστιν, ὡς γ᾽ ἐμοὶ χρῆσθαι κριτῇ,

ὃν βίος ἀληθῶς ὁ βίος, ἀλλὰ συμφορά.

ΘΕ. Ἐπιστάμεσθα ταῦτα· νῦν δὲ πράσσομεν

οὐχ οἷα κώμου καὶ γέλωτος ἄξια.   820

ΗΡ. Γυνὴ θυραῖος ἡ θανοῦσα· μὴ λίαν

πένθει, δόμων γὰρ ζῶσι τῶνδε δεσπόται.

THE ORDER, AND ENGLISH ACCENTUATION.

Δε τίμα και Κύπριν την πλείστον ἡδίστην θεῶν βροτοῖσι· γαρ ἡ εὔμενης θέος. Δε εάσον ταῦτα τα άλλα, και πίθου ἐμοίσι λόγοις, εἴπερ δόκω σοι λέγειν ὀρθα· οἰμαι μεν. Οὔκουν, ἀφεις την άγαν λύπην, πίει μέτα ἡμων, πυκάσθεις στέφανοις, ὑπέρβαλων τάσδε πύλας; Και σάφα οἰδα ὅτι πίτυλος σκύφου ἐμπέσων μεθόρμιει σε ούνεκα το νυν σκυθρώπου και ξυνεστώτος φρέναν. Δε χρέαν ὄντας θνήτους φρόνειν και θνήτα· ὡς τοις ἀπάσι σέμνοις· γε και ξυνωφρευώμενοις, ὡς χρήσθαι ἐμοι γε κρίτη, ὁ βίος ουκ ἐστι ἀλήθως βίος, ἀλλα σύμφορα. ΘΕ. Ἐπισταμέσθα ταῦτα· δε νυν πράσσομεν ουκ ὄια ἄξια κώμου και γελώτος. ΗΡ. Γύνη ἡ θανοῦσα θυραῖος· μη πένθει λίαν, γαρ δέσποται τῶνδε δόμων ζώσι.

TRANSLATION.

And honor also Vénus, incomparably the sweetest of deities to mortals, for she is a benign goddess. So forego those other considerations, and obey my words, if I appear to thee to speak rightly : I, indeed, am of this opinion !

Wilt thou not, therefore, abandoning thy excessive grief, drink with us, crowned with garlands, having thrown-open these doors? And well know I that the trickling of the cup gliding down will divert thee from thy present cloudy and pent state of mind.

For it behoves us as we are mortals to think also as mortals : since to all demure persons, indeed, and to those of woful countenance, if they take me at least as judge, life is not truly life, but misery !

MAN-SERVANT. We know it :—but at the present time we are in circumstances, not such as are adapted to revelry and mirth !

HERCULES. The lady who is dead was a stranger :—grieve not so excessively,—for the lords of this house live !

---

806. τὴν πλεῖστον ἡδίστην θεῶν, the most sweetest of deities, a double superlative.

808. πάντα pro ' ταῦτα' cónjicit Marklándus,—fortásse réctè. Deínde ómnes πείθου,—sed álterum præferéndum, ubicúnque per métrum lícet. MONK.

811. For πιεῖ, which was given for the first time of all by Wakefield, MSS. not a few and Lascar have πίη,—which Mus-

grave approved. In Aldus and many others we find πίης. All editions prior to Musgrave's have τύχας, although MSS. partially offer πύλας. The Scholiast acknowledges both readings. Wakefield gives πτύχας from conjecture.

818. Aldus and his followers have ὁ βίος ἀληθῶς ὁ βίος, faultily in respect of the metre, as the fourth foot is an anapæst.

ΘΕ. Τί ζῶσιν; Ου κάτοισθα τὰν δόμοις κακά;
ΗΡ. Εἰ μή τι σός με δεσπότης ἐψεύσατο.
ΘΕ. Ἄγαν ἐκεῖνος ἔστ᾽ ἄγαν φιλόξενος.   825
ΗΡ. Ου χρῆν μ᾽ ὀθνείου γ᾽ οὕνεκ᾽ εὖ πάσχειν νεκροῦ;
ΘΕ. Ἦ κάρτα μέντοι καὶ λίαν οἰκεῖος ἦν.
ΗΡ. Μῶν ξυμφοράν τιν᾽ οὖσαν ουκ ἔφραζέ μοι;
ΘΕ. Χαίρων ἴθ᾽· ἡμῖν δεσποτῶν μέλει κακά.
ΗΡ. Ὅδ᾽ ου θυραίων πημάτων ἄρχει λόγος.   830
ΘΕ. Ου γάρ σε κωμάζοντ᾽ ἂν ἠχθόμην ὁρῶν.
ΗΡ. Ἀλλ᾽ ἢ πέπονθα δεῖν᾽ ὑπὸ ξένων ἐμῶν;
ΘΕ. Ουκ ἦλθες ἐν δέοντι δέξασθαι δόμοις,
πένθος γὰρ ἡμῖν ἐστι, καὶ κουρὰν βλέπεις,
μελαμπέπλος στολμούς τε. ΗΡ. Τίς δ᾽ ὁ κατθανών;
Μῶν ἢ τέκνων τις φροῦδος, ἢ γέρων πατήρ;   836

THE ORDER, AND ENGLISH ACCENTUATION.

ΘΕ. Τι ζῶσι; Ου κατοῖσθα τα κάκα εν δόμοις; ΗΡ. Εἰ μη σος δέσποτης εψεύσατο με τι. ΘΕ. Εκεῖνος ἐστι άγαν άγαν φιλόξενος. ΗΡ. Ου χρην με ευ πάσχειν οὕνεκα γε οθνείου νέκρου; ΘΕ. Η μέντοι ην κάρτα και λίαν οικεῖος. ΗΡ. Μων ουκ εφράζε μοι τίνα ξύμφοραν οὔσαν; ΘΕ. Ἰθι χαίρων· ἡμιν κάκα δέσποτων μέλει. ΗΡ. Ὁδε λόγος ουκ άρχει θυραίων πήματων. ΘΕ. Γαρ ουκ αν ἡχθομην ὁρων σε κωμαζόντα. ΗΡ. Αλλα η πεπόνθα δεινα ὑπο εμων ξένων; ΘΕ. Ουκ ἦλθες εν δεοντι δόμοις δεξάσθαι, γαρ ἐστι πένθος ἡμιν, και βλέπεις κούραν τε μελάμπεπλους στόλμους. ΗΡ. Δε τις ὁ κάτθανων; Μων η τις τέκνων φρούδος, η γέρων πάτηρ;

TRANSLATION.

MAN-SERVANT. What live? Knowest thou not of the ills in the family? HERCULES. Unless thy master has told me aught falsely. MAN-SERVANT. He is too, too hospitable! HERCULES. Was it not meet that I should fare nobly because forsooth of a stranger's death? MAN-SERVANT. [*Greatly affected.*] Surely however she was singularly and exceedingly near! HERCULES. [*Conjecturingly and with interrogation.*] Has he not told me of some disaster there is? MAN-SERVANT. Depart faring-happily:—to us the afflictions of our lords is of care! HERCULES. This speech is not the prelude of a foreign loss! MAN-SERVANT. For if so, I should not have been grieved at seeing thee revelling.

HERCULES. But have I really experienced ill-usage from mine host?

MAN-SERVANT. Thou camest not in a fit time for the house to receive thee,—for there is grief amongst us; and thou seest our shorn-hair and our sable garments!

HERCULES. [*Pressingly.*] But who is it that is dead? Is either some one of the children gone, or his aged father?

---

824. For εἰ μή τι in this line, Elmsley would have εἰ μή γε.

825. In most MSS. and, consentingly with them, in editions very generally we find γ᾽ between ἄγαν and ἐκεῖνος, but this particle Matthiæ expunged—considering it as an intruder that had corruptly found its way into the text here and in many other passages after ἄγαν and λίαν followed by a vowel. See the note at v. 695, above.

826. Aldus edited οὔκουν᾽ ὀθνείου γὰρ οὕνεκ᾽ εὖ πάσχει νεκροῦ, most corruptly. For

οὕνεκα, Barnes has ἕνεκα. Monk facetiously translates this verse, "*ought I to be illtreated on account of a stranger's death?*"

827. Both Lascar and Matthiæ have λίαν θυραῖος ἦν: — Aldus and most others λίαν γ᾽ οἰκεῖος ἦν.

828. For ξυμφοράν τιν᾽ οὖσαν, Markland conjectured ξυμφορὰν τήν οὖσαν.

829. Monk translates χαίρων ἴθι, "*váde et vále,*" correctly indeed, though not literally. In most editions we find δὲ, unnecessarily and faultily, after ἡμῖν.

833. The common reading is δόμους.

ˊΘΕ. Γυνὴ μὲν οὖν ὅλωλεν Ἀδμήτου, ξένε.

ΗΡ. Τί φής; Ἔπειτα δῆτά μ᾿ ἐξενίζετε;

ΘΕ. Ἠδεῖτο γάρ σε τῶνδ᾿ ἀπώσασθαι δόμων.

ΗΡ. ῍Ω σχέτλι᾿, οἵας ἤπλακες ξυναόρου.   840

ΘΕ. Ἀπωλόμεσθα πάντες, οὐ κείνη μόνη.

ΗΡ. Ἀλλ᾿ ἠσθόμην μὲν, ὄμμ᾿ ἰδὼν δακρυῤῥοοῦν,

κουράν τε, καὶ πρόσωπον· ἀλλ᾿ ἔπειθέ με

λέγων θυραῖον κῆδος εἰς τάφον φέρειν·

βίᾳ δὲ θυμοῦ τάσδ᾿ ὑπερβαλὼν πύλας,   845

ἔπινον ἀνδρὸς ἐν φιλοξένου δόμοις,

πράσσοντος οὕτω, κἀπεκώμαζον, κάρα

στεφάνοις πυκασθείς. Ἀλλὰ σοῦ τὸ μὴ φράσαι,

κακοῦ τοσούτου δώμασιν προσκειμένου.

Ποῦ καί σφε θάπτει; Ποῖ νιν εὑρήσω μολών;   850

ΘΕ. Ὀρθὴν παρ᾿ οἶμον, ἣ ᾿πὶ Λάρισσαν φέρει,

τύμβον κατόψει ξεστὸν ἐκ προαστίου.

THE ORDER, AND ENGLISH ACCENTUATION.

ΘΕ. Γύνη ουν Αδμήτου μεν ολώλε, ξένε. ΗΡ. Τι φης; Επείτα δῆτα εξενίζετε με; ΘΕ. Γαρ ηδεῖτο απωσάσθαι σε τώνδε δόμων. ΗΡ. Ω σχέτλιε, οίας ξυναόρου ήπλακες. ΘΕ. Απωλομέσθα πάντες, ου κείνη μόνη. ΗΡ. Ἀλλα ησθομην μεν, ιδων ομμα δακρυῤῥοουν, τε κούραν, και πρόσωπον· αλλα επείθε με λέγων φέρειν εις τάφον θυραίον κῆδος· δια θυμου υπέρβαλων τάσδε πύλας, επίνεν εν δόμοις φιλόξενου ανδρος, ούτω πρασσόντος, και επεκωμάζον, πυκάσθεις κάρα στέφανοις. Ἀλλα σου το μη φράσαι, τοσούτου κάκου προσκείμενου δώμασι. Και που θάπτει σφε; Ποι μόλων ευρήσω νιν; ΘΕ. Πάρα ορθην οίμον, ἡ φέρει επι Λαρίσσαν, κατόψει ξέστον τύμβον εκ προάστιου.

TRANSLATION.

MAN-SERVANT. [*Sighing.*] The wife, then, of Admétus indeed is dead, stranger. HERCULES. What sayest thou? Yet notwithstanding this ye admitted me? MAN-SERVANT. For he was-out-of-respect-loath to turn thee from his house! HERCULES. [*Raising his hands.*] Oh! unhappy man, what a wife thou hast lost! MAN-SERVANT. We have perished all,—not she alone. HERCULES. [*Sighing.*] But I perceived it indeed, when I saw his eye streaming-with-tears,—and his cropped-hair, and his countenance: however he persuaded me by saying he was conducting to the tomb the funeral of a stranger: and in spite of my will having entered within these gates, I drank in the house of the hospitable man, while he was thus circumstanced,—and I revelled, crowned as to my head with garlands. But it was thine not to acquaint me, when such a calamity was present in the family. [*Distressedly.*] And where is he burying her? To what place repairing can I find him? MAN-SERVANT. Hard by the high road that leads to Laríssa thou wilt see the polished tomb beyond the suburbs. [*Exit Man-Servant, returning into the palace.*]

---

838. ἔπειτα δῆτα, *and yet after all—and nevertheless.*—In place of ἐξενίζετε, some have conjectured ἐξενίζετο, but (as Monk very justly observes,) ξενίζεσθαι is never used in the sense of " *hospitio excipere.*"

840. The Scholiast explained σχέτλιε, by ἄθλιε, *infélix* vel *míser*, and this seems to be its true meaning here.

841. For μόνη, Gaisford edited μόνον.

842. Blomfield suspected (but causelessly, I think,) that ἠσθόμην μὲν should

be ἠσθόμην ἂν, *I might have known or perceived*, and not " *I perceived* or *knew.*"

847. In this verse two other readings are met with, namely, κἆτ᾿ ἐκώμαζον, and κᾆτα κωμάζω,—both faultless.

850. For ποῦ all editions have ποῦ.

851. ὀρθὴν παρ᾿ οἶμον, strictly, *by the direct road.* In lieu of Λάρισσαν Monk proposes Λαρίσσας. The Larissa here meant is the famous Thessálian Laríssa, called also Cremásté or Pénsilis.

853. ΕΥΡΙΠΙΔΟΥ

ΗΡ. Ὦ πολλὰ τλᾶσα καρδία, ψυχή τ' ἐμὴ,

νῦν δεῖξον, οἷον παῖδά σ' ἡ Τιρυνθία

ἐγείνατ' Ἠλεκτρύωνος Ἀλκμήνη Διί.   855

Δεῖ γάρ με σῶσαι τὴν θανοῦσαν ἀρτίως

γυναῖκα, κεἰς τόνδ' αὖθις ἱδρῦσαι δόμον,

Ἄλκηστιν, Ἀδμήτῳ θ' ὑπουργῆσαι χάριν.

Ἐλθὼν δ' ἄνακτα τὸν μελάμπεπλον νεκρῶν

Θάνατον φυλάξω· καί νιν εὑρήσειν δοκῶ   860

πίνοντα τύμβου πλησίον προσφαγμάτων.

Κἄνπερ λοχήσας αὐτὸν, ἐξ ἕδρας συθεὶς,

μάρψω, κύκλον δὲ περιβάλω χεροῖν ἐμαῖν,

οὐκ ἔστιν ὅστις αὐτὸν ἐξαιρήσεται

μογοῦντα πλευρὰ, πρὶν γυναῖκ' ἐμοὶ μεθῇ.   865

Ἢν δ' οὖν ἁμάρτω τῆσδ' ἄγρας, καὶ μὴ μόλῃ

πρὸς αἱματηρὸν πέλανον, εἶμι τὴν κάτω,

Κόρης ἄνακτός τ' εἰς ἀνηλίους δόμους,

THE ORDER, AND ENGLISH ACCENTUATION.

ΗΡ. Ω πόλλα τλάσα κάρδια, τε έμη ψύχη, νυν δείξον, δίον παίδα ή Τιρύνθια Αλκμήνη Ηλεκτρυώνος εγείνατο σε Διΐ. Γαρ δεῖ με σώσαι Αλκήστιν την γυναίκα άρτιως θανούσαν, και ιδρύσαι αύθις εις τόνδε δόμον, τε υπουργήσαι χάριν Αδμήτω. Δε έλθων φυλάξω τον μελάμπεπλον ανάκτα νέκρων, Θάνατον· και δόκω ευρήσειν νιν πίνοντα προσφάγματων πλησίον τύμβου. Και εάνπερ λοχήσας αύτον, σύθεις εξ έδρας, μάρψω, δε περιβάλω κύκλον έμαιν χέροιν, ουκ εστι όστις εξαιρήσεται αύτον μογούντα πλεύρα, πριν μέθη έμοι γυναίκα. Δε ην ουν αμάρτω τήσδε άγρας, και μη μόλη προς αιματήρον πέλανον, είμι την κάτω, εις ανήλιους δόμους Κόρης τε ανάκτος,

TRANSLATION.

Hercules. [Solus.] O my much daring heart, and my soul, now exhibit what manner of son the Tirýnthian Alcména, daughter of Eléctryon, bare thee to Jove! For I must rescue Alcéstis the lady lately dead, and establish her again in this house,—and do a kindness to Admétus. So, going I will watch for the sable-robed king of the departed, Death: and methinks I shall find him drinking of the libations near the tomb. And if indeed, having discovered him by lying in wait for him, I can, by rushing from mine ambush, lay hold of him, and form a clasp about him with my two-arms, there is no one who shall release him, panting as to his sides, before he give up to me the lady. But if, however, I fail of this caption, and he come not to the clottered mass of blood, I will go the road beneath, unto the sunless mansions of the virgin and her king,

---

853. For ψυχή τ' ἐμὴ in this line, some have καὶ χεὶρ ἐμή.

855. Several different readings of this verse occur: whereof the two chief are, Ἠλεκτρυῶνος γείνατ'°Ἀλκμήνη Διΐ-Ἠλεκτρύωνος ἐγείνατ' Ἀλκμήνη Διΐ. On these Monk says, "utrumcúnque léges, in consuetúdinem tragicórum peccábis:—néque omítti pótest augméntum, néque anapæstus in tértio lóco stáre. Fácile conjícias ἔτεκεν pro ἐγείνατ',—sed hoc periculósius est." In the reading adopted by Monk, Ἠλεκτρύωνος is pronounced as four syllables, by the coalescence of υω into one.

861. πίνοντα προσφαγμάτων, drinking of the libations,—understand μέρος τι, some part or portion of— a certain lot or share.

863. For κύκλον, Aldus and all editors, (with the exception of Wakefield,) have κύκλῳ. In one MS. κύκλιον is the reading. Instead of περιβάλω, MSS. and editions in general have περιβαλῶ,—which Monk greatly condemns.

865. πρὶν γυναῖκ' ἐμοὶ μεθῇ, before he let go the woman to me: here the particle ἂν (absolutely necessary indeed to the integrity of the construction,) is suppressed, but clearly understood.

868. Κόρης, of the maid, for κόρης Δήμητρος, of Cérës's girl or daughter, namely, Próserpine, whom Plúto, king of hell, is said to have carried off and married.

αἰτήσομαί τε· καὶ πέποιθ' ἄξειν ἄνω
Ἄλκηστιν, ὥστε χερσὶν ἐνθεῖναι ξένου, 870
ὅς μ' εἰς δόμους ἐδέξατ', οὐδ' ἀπήλασε,
καίπερ βαρείᾳ ξυμφορᾷ πεπληγμένος,
ἔκρυπτε δ', ὢν γενναῖος, αἰδεσθεὶς ἐμέ.
Τίς τοῦδε μᾶλλον Θεσσαλῶν φιλόξενος ;
Τίς Ἑλλάδ' οἰκῶν ; Τοιγὰρ οὐκ ἐρεῖ κακὸν 875
εὐεργετῆσαι φῶτα, γενναῖος γεγώς.

ΑΔΜΗΤΟΣ.

Ἰώ. Ἰώ. Στυγναὶ πρόσοδοι,
στυγναὶ δ' ὄψεις χήρων μελάθρων.
Ἰώ μοι, αῖ, αῖ.
Ποῖ βῶ ; Πῇ στῶ ; Τί λέγω ; Τί δὲ μή ; 880
Πῶς ἂν ὀλοίμην ;
Ἦ βαρυδαίμονα μήτηρ μ' ἔτεκεν.
Ζηλῶ φθιμένους, κείνων ἔραμαι,
κεῖν' ἐπιθυμῶ δώματα ναίειν·
οὔτε γὰρ αὐγὰς χαίρω προσορῶν, 885
οὔτ' ἐπὶ γαίας πόδα πεζεύων·

THE ORDER, AND ENGLISH ACCENTUATION.

τε αἰτήσομαι· καὶ πεποῖθα ἄξειν Ἄλκηστιν ἄνω, ὥστε ἐνθεῖναι χέρσι ξένου, ὃς ἐδέξατο με εἰς δόμους, οὐδὲ ἀπήλασε, καίπερ πεπλήγμενος βαρείᾳ ξύμφορα, δὲ ἐκρύπτε, ὢν γενναῖος, αἰδεσθεὶς ἐμε. Τίς Θέσσαλων μᾶλλον φιλόξενος τοῦδε ; Τίς οἴκων Ἑλλαδα ; Τοιγαρ οὐκ ἐρεῖ εὐεργετῆσαι κάκον φῶτα, γέγως γενναῖος. ΑΔ. Ἰω. Ἰω. Στύγναι πρόσοδοι, δὲ στύγναι ὄψεις χήρων μέλαθρων. Ἰω μοι, αι, αι. Ποι βω ; Πη στω ; Τι λέγω ; Δε τι μη ; Πως αν ολοιμην ; Η μήτηρ ἔτεκε με βαρυδαίμονα. Ζήλω φθίμενους, κείνων ἐραμαι, κείνα δώματα ἐπιθύμω ναίειν· γαρ οὔτε πρόσοραν αὔγας χαίρω, οὔτε πεζεύων πόδα ἐπι γαίας·

TRANSLATION.

and will prefer my request:—and I trust I shall bring Alcéstis up, so as to place her in the hands of that host, who received me into his house, nor sent me away, although struck with a heavy misfortune—but concealed it, being a generous man, impressed with respect for me. [*Ad- miringly.*] Who of the Thessálians is more hospitable than he? What one inhabiting Greece? Wherefore he shall not say he did a service to a worthless fellow, being himself noble. [*Exit Hérculës.*]

ADMETUS.[*Entering mournfully on his way home—followed by the Cho- rus.*] Alas! Alas! O hateful approach, and hateful view of this widowed house! Ah me! Hey! hey! Whither can I go? Where can I rest? What can I say? And what can I not? How gladly I could perish! Surely my mother brought me forth destined to a heavy fate! I account the dead happy, them I long for, those mansions I desire to dwell in: for neither looking on the sun-beams do I joy, nor treading my foot on the earth:

---

877. For στυγναὶ, the Scholiast's read- ing, and which Musgrave edited on the authority of three MSS. and consenting- ly with Lascar, Aldus printed στυγεραί.
880. On ποῖ and πῆ, Monk (after Por- son) says, " ποῦ quiétem nótat : ποῖ mó- tum : πῆ in utrámque pártem súmitur."

881.πῶς ἂν ὀλοίμην; *útinàm péream:* má- lè vértit Meláncthon, *quómodò quéam pe- ríre?* Ὀλοίμαν ómnes. MONK.
883.ζηλῶ, *I praise* or *commend—I deem happy* or *fortunate.*
885. αὐγὰς for αὐγὰς ἡλίου, *beams,* sim- ply,—for the "*sun's beams* or *light.*"

1

τοῖον ὅμηρόν μ' ἀποσυλήσας |–∪∪|––||∪∪–|––

Αἴδη θάνατος παρέδωκεν. ||––|∪∪–||∪∪–|∪*

ΧΟ. Πρόβα, πρόβα· βᾶθι κεῦθος οἴκων. [Στροφὴ α'.] ∪–|∪ ⸱⸱||–∪|–∪||––   α'

ΑΔ. 'Αῖ, αῖ.   890 |––   β'

ΧΟ. Πέπονθας ἄξι' ἀιαγμάτων. |∪–∪–||∪––∪–   γ'

ΑΔ. Ἐ, ἔ. |∪∪   δ'

ΧΟ. Δι' ὀδύνας ἔβας, σάφ' οἶδα. |∪∪∪––∪–||∪–∪   ε'

ΑΔ. Φεῦ, φεῦ. |––   ζ'

ΧΟ. Τὰν νέρθεν οὐδὲν ὠφελεῖς.   895 |––|∪–||∪–|∪–   η'

ΑΔ. 'Ιώ μοι μοι. |––|––   θ'

ΧΟ. Τὸ μήποτ' εἰσιδεῖν φιλίας ἀλόχου |∪–|∪–||∪||–∪∪|–∪∪|– ι'

πρόσωπον * ἄντα, λυπρόν. |∪––*–||∪––   κ'

ΑΔ. Ἔμνησας, ὅ μου φρένας ἥλκωσεν· |––|∪∪–||∪∪–|––

τί γὰρ ἀνδρὶ κακὸν μεῖζον, ἁμαρτεῖν   900 |∪∪–|∪∪–||∪∪|––

πιστῆς ἀλόχου; Μή ποτε γήμας |––|∪∪–||–∪∪|––

ὤφελον οἰκεῖν μετὰ τῆσδε δόμους. |–∪∪|––||∪∪–|∪∪–

THE ORDER, AND ENGLISH ACCENTUATION.

τοίον ὁμήρον θάνατος παρέδωκέ με ἀποσυλήσας 'Αἴδη. ΧΟ. Πρόβα, πρόβα· βᾶθι κεῦθος οἴκων. ΑΔ. Αἰ, αι. ΧΟ. Πεπόνθας ἄξια αιάγματων. ΑΔ. Ε, ε. ΧΟ. Ἔβας δία ὀδύνας, σάφα οἶδα. ΑΔ. Φεv, φεv. ΧΟ. Οὐδὲν ὠφελεις ταν νέρθεν. ΑΔ. 'Ιω μοι μοι. ΧΟ. Τὸ μήποτε εἰσιδειν προσώπον φίλιας ἀλόχου ἄντα, λύπρον. ΑΔ. Εμνήσας, ὁ ἡλκωσε φρένας μου· γαρ τι μεῖζον κάκον ἀνδρι, ἁμάρτειν πίστης ἀλόχου; Μήποτε γήμας ὤφελον οἰκειν μέτα τῆσδε δόμους.

TRANSLATION.

of such a pledge [*Groaning deeply.*] has death robbed me, delivering it up to Plúto. [*The king wrings his hands, and appears in great agony.*]

CHORUS. [*To Admétus, who has not heart to enter the palace.*] Advance, advance: go into seclusion of the house.

ADMETUS. [*Groaning.*] Wo! Wo!

CHORUS. Thou hast suffered a loss deserving of groans!

ADMETUS. [*Sobbing.*] Hey! bey! CHORUS. Thou hast passed through grief, I well know! ADMETUS. Alas! alas! CHORUS. Thou nothing advantagest her that is beneath! ADMETUS. Ah me! me! CHORUS. Never to see thy dear wife's face again before thee is a sad thing!

ADMETUS. Thou hast mentioned that which hath ulcerated my soul: for what can be a greater ill to a man, than to lose his faithful wife? Never ought I, having married her, to have dwelt with her in the palace!

---

889. κεῦθος, *hiding place* or *recess—privacy* or *retirement*.

891. πέπονθας ἄξι' ἀιαγμάτων, literally, *thou hast suffered things worthy of groans.* Musgrave and Wakefield inserted γ' after πέπονθας for the metre's sake.

897. This verse, as Monk very rightly observes, is an *Iambélegus*, that is, it consists of an iambic penthémimer; followed by a dactylic penthémimer. Such are verses 931 and 932 of the Hécuba: and many more examples indeed of this species of metre might be quoted from the

writings as well of Eurípidës,—as of Sóphoclés, particularly his Ajax.

898. A syllable is wanting in this line to render it of equal time with ver. 919, viz. the corresponding line of the antístrophë. Musgrave to supply this defect inserted τιν' before ἄντα. In place of λυπρὸν, Aldus and some others have λυπηρόν.

900. We must here understand either ἢ or τοῦ before ἁμαρτεῖν,—else we must with Schaefer make this infinitive to depend on ἔμνησας, inclosing τί γὰρ ἀνδρὶ κακὸν μεῖζον in a parénthesis.

Ζηλῶ δ' ἀγάμους ἀτέκνους τε βροτῶν·

μία γὰρ ψυχή· τῆσδ' ὑπεραλγεῖν,

μέτριον ἄχθος.   905

Παίδων δὲ νόσους, καὶ νυμφιδίους

εὐνὰς θανάτοις κεραϊζομένας,

ὃν τλητὸν ὁρᾷν, ἐξὸν ἀτέκνοις

ἀγάμοις τ' εἶναι διὰ παντός.

ΧΟ. Τύχα, τύχα δυσπάλαιστος ἥκει. ['Αντιστρ. α'.]   α'

ΑΔ. Αἶ, αἶ.   β'

ΧΟ. Πέρας δ' οὐδὲν τίθης ἀλγέων;   γ'

ΑΔ. Ε, ἔ.   δ'

ΧΟ. Βαρέα μὲν φέρειν, ὅμως δὲ—   ε'

ΑΔ. Φεῦ, φεῦ.   915   ζ'

ΧΟ.—τλᾶθ'· ὃν σὺ πρῶτος ὤλεσας—   η'

ΑΔ. Ἰώ μοι μοι.   θ'

ΧΟ.—γυναῖκα· συμφορὰ δ' ἑτέρους ἑτέρα   ι'

πιέζει φανεῖσα θνατῶν.   κ'

ΑΔ. Ὦ μακρὰ πένθη, λῦπαί τε φίλων   920

τῶν ὑπὸ γαίας.

Δε ζήλω ἀγάμους τε ἀτέκνους βρότων· γαρ μία ψύχη· ὑπεράλγειν τῆσδε, μέτριον ἄχθος. Δε ὅ-ραν νόσους παίδων, και νυμφίδιους εὔνας κεραϊζόμενας θάνατοις, ου τλήτον, ἐξόν εἶναι ἀτέκνοις τε ἀγάμοις δια πάντος. ΧΟ. Τύχα, τύχα δυσπαλαίστος ἥκει. ΑΔ. Αι, αι. ΧΟ. Δε τίθης οὔδεν πέ-ρας ἀλγεων; ΑΔ. Ε, ε. ΧΟ. Βαρεία μεν φέρειν δε ὅμως—ΑΔ. Φευ, φευ. ΧΟ.—τλάθε· συ ου πρώ-τος ὤλεσας— ΑΔ. Ἰω μοι μοι. ΧΟ.—γυναῖκα· δε σύμφορα φανείσα πιέζει ἔτερους θνάτων ἕ-τερα. ΑΔ. Ω μάκρα πένθη, τε λύπαι φίλων των ὕπο γαίας.

TRANSLATION.

But I count the unwedded and childless of mortals happy, in as much as theirs is one life: to grieve for that is a moderate burden! But to behold the diseases of children, and the bridal bed laid waste by death, is not supportable,—it being in men's power to be without children, and to continue unmarried through the whole of life.

CHORUS. Fate,—fate hard-to-be-struggled-with, hath come! ADMETUS. [*Groaning.*] Wo! Wo! CHORUS. But settest thou no bounds to thy sorrows! ADMETUS. [*Sobbing.*] Hey! hey! CHORUS. Heavy indeed are they to bear, but still—ADMETUS. [*Sighing.*] Alas! alas! CHORUS.—bear with them: thou art not the first man who hast lost—ADMETUS. [*Most sorrowfully and interruptingly.*] Ah me! me! CHORUS.——thy consort: but calamity appearing affects different persons differently. ADMETUS. O lasting griefs, and sorrows for our friends beneath the earth! [*To the*

904. Lascar, Aldus, and indeed all the early editions have ψυχῇ δὲ μιᾷ.

905. Monk contrary to every authority, and to sound taste, transposed these two words, and edited ἄχθος μέτριον.

907. Imitátur Homérum Il. x'. 63, καὶ θαλάμους κεραϊζομένους. BLOMFIELD.

909. In most editions, διαπαντὸς is giv-

en (though less correctly) as one word.

912. Both Lascar and Aldus have τι-θεῖς:—most others before Musgrave, τι-θεὶς. Gaisford, on surmise, edited τιθεῖσ'. Matthiæ, following Markland, gives τί-θης, rightly, according to the Attic form.

921. For ὑπὸ γαίας, all, with the exception of Monk, read ὑπὸ γαῖαν.

Τί μ' ἐκώλυσας ῥῖψαι τύμβου

τάφρον εἰς κοίλην, καὶ μετ' ἐκείνης

τῆς μέγ' ἀρίστης κεῖσθαι φθίμενον ;

Δύο δ' ἀντὶ μιᾶς Ἅιδης ψυχὰς   925

τὰς πιστοτάτας γε συνέσχ' ἂν ὁμοῦ

χθονίαν λίμνην διαβάντε.

XO. Ἐμοὶ τὶς ἦν   [Στροφὴ β'.]   α'

ἐν γένει, ᾧ κόρος ἀξιό-   β'

θρηνος ᾤχετ' ἐν δόμοισιν   930   γ'

μονόπαις· ἀλλ' ἔμπας   δ'

ἔφερε κακὸν ἅλις, ἄτεκνος ὤν,   ε'

πολιὰς ἐπὶ χαίτας   ζ'

ἤδη προπετὴς ὤν, βιότου τε πόρσω.   η'

ΑΔ. Ὦ σχῆμα δόμων, πῶς εἰσέλθω ;   935

Πῶς δ' οἰκήσω, μεταπίπτοντος

δαίμονος ; Οἴμοι· πολὺ γὰρ τὸ μέσον·

τότε μὲν πεύκαις ξὺν Πηλιάσι,

ξύν θ' ὑμεναίοις ἔστειχον ἔσω,

THE ORDER, AND ENGLISH ACCENTUATION.

Τι εκωλυσας με ῥιψαι εις κοιλην ταφρον τυμβου, και κεισθαι φθιμενον μετα εκεινης της μεγα αριστης ; Δε Αιδης γε αν συνεσχε, αντι μιας, δυο ψυχας τας πιστοτατας ὁμου διαβαντε χθονιαν λιμνην. XO. Ην τις εν γενει εμοι, ᾧ κορος αξιοθρηνος μονοπαις ᾠχετο εν δομοισι· αλλα εμπας εφερε κακον ἁλις, ατεκνος ων, ων ηδη προπετης επι πολιας χαιτας, τε πορσω βιοτου. ΑΔ. Ω σχημα δομων, πως εισελθω ; Δε πως οικησω, δαιμονος μεταπιπτοντος ; Οιμοι· γαρ πολυ το μεσον· τοτε μεν ξυν Πηλιασι πευκαις, τε ξυν ὑμεναιοις εστειχον εσω,

TRANSLATION.

Chorus.]Why didst thou hinder me from throwing myself into the hollow pit of her grave—and from lying dead with her the by far most excellent woman? And Plúto, troth, would have retained, instead of one, two souls the most faithful having together crossed the infernal lake.

CHORUS. There was a certain person of kin to me, whose son, worthy to be lamented, an only child, died in his house:—but nevertheless he bore his misfortune with moderation,—bereft of child as he was, being already hastening on to grey hairs, and far-advanced in life.

ADMETUS.[*Looking on his own palace.*] O mansion's form, how can I enter in? And how can I dwell in thee—my fortune having undergone this change? Alas me! for there is a wide difference between this and that:—then indeed with Pélian torches and bridal songs entered I in,

---

922. ῥῖψαι, *from rushing headlong :* else understand ἐμαυτόν.

927. On διαβάντε Monk remarks thus : "éadem erat Atticis partícipii feminíni duális fórma ac masculíni."

931. ἔμπας καὶ ἔμπα, Ἀττικῶς· ἔμπης δὲ, Ἰωνικῶς· δηλοῖ δὲ τὸ ὅμως. ZONARAS.

932. The Scholiast interprets ἅλις in this verse by μετρίως, *moderately,* that is, *well enough.* For ἔφερε Lascar has ἔφερεν.

934. In lieu of πόρσω, most MSS. and all the earlier editions have πρόσω :—but Barnes, displeased with this method of spelling, gave πρόσσω. Matthiæ's reading is βιότου πρόσσω τε. Monk has followed Gaisford, in the belief that πόρσω was the original form of the later Atticism πόρρω : and he adds, "non áliter differébant ἄρσην et ἄρρην, Θάρσος et Θάρρος, &c."

937. The Scholiast rightly explained τὸ μέσον in this passage, by τὸ διάφορον τῆς νῦν τύχης καὶ τῆς παλαιᾶς.

Φιλίας ἀλόχου χέρα βαστάζων,　940　∪∪-|∪∪-‖∪∪-|-

πολυήχητός 9' εἴπετο κῶμος,　∪∪-|--‖-∪∪|--

τήν τε θανοῦσαν κἄμ' ὀλβίζων,　-∪∪|--‖--|--

ὡς εὐπατρίδαι, κἀπ' ἀμφοτέρων　--|∪∪-‖--|∪∪-

ὄντες ἀρίστων, ξύζυγες εἶμεν·　-∪∪|--‖-∪∪|--

νῦν δ' ὑμεναίων γόος ἀντίπαλος,　945　-∪∪|--‖∪∪-|∪∪-

λευκῶν τε πέπλων μέλανες στολμοὶ　--|∪∪-‖∪∪-|--

πέμπουσί μ' ἔσω,　--|∪∪-

λέκτρων κοίτας ἐς ἐρήμους.　--|-‖∪∪-|-*

ΧΟ. Παρ' εὐτυχῆ　['Αντιστροφὴ β'.]　∪-|∪-　　α'

σοι πότμον ἦλθεν ἀπειροκά-　950　-∪∪|-∪∪|-∪∪　β'

κῳ τόδ' ἄλγος· ἀλλ' ἔσωσας　-∪|-∪‖-∪|--　γ'

βίοτον καὶ ψυχάν.　∪∪--‖--　δ'

Ἔθανε δάμαρ, ἔλιπε φιλίαν·　∪∪∪|∪∪∪‖∪∪∪|∪-　ε'

τί νέον τόδε; Πολλοὺς　∪∪-|∪∪-‖-　ζ'

ἤδη παρέλυσεν θάνατος δάμαρτος.　955　--∪∪‖---∪∪‖-∪|-∪η'

ΑΔ. Φίλοι, γυναικὸς δαίμον' εὐτυχέστερον　∪-|∪-‖--|∪-‖∪-|∪∪

τοὐμοῦ νομίζω, καίπερ οὐ δοκοῦνθ', ὅμως·　--|∪-‖--|∪-‖∪-|∪-

τῆς μὲν γὰρ οὐδὲν ἄλγος ἅψεταί ποτε,　--|∪-‖∪-|∪-‖∪-|∪∪

THE ORDER, AND ENGLISH ACCENTUATION.

βαστάζων χέρα φίλιας ἀλόχου, τε εἴπετο πολυηχήτος κώμος ὀλβίζων τε την θανούσαν και ἐμε, ὡς ὄντες εὐπάτριδαι, και ἀπο ἀρίστων ἀμφότερων, εἶμεν ξύζυγες· δε νυν γόος ἀντίπαλος ὑμεναίων, τε μέλανες στόλμοι λευκων πέπλων πεμπούσι με ἔσω, ἐς κοίτας ἐρήμους λέκτρων. ΧΟ. Πάρα εὐτυχη πότμον ἦλθε τόδε ἄλγος σοι ἀπειρόκακω· ἀλλα εσώσας βίοτον και ψυχάν. Δάμαρ ἔθανε, φίλιαν ἔλιπε· τι νέον τόδε; Θάνατος ἤδη παρελύσε πόλλους δαμάρτος. ΑΔ. Φίλοι, νομίζω δαίμονα γυναίκος εὐτυχέστερον του ἐμου, καίπερ ου δοκούντα ὅμως· γαε της μεν ουδέν άλγος πότε ἅψεται,

TRANSLATION.

holding the hand of my beloved wife, and there followed us a sonórous company hailing as happy both her that is dead and me,—forasmuch as being noble, and of illustrious parents on both sides, we were united together: but now the groan in lieu of nuptial-hymns, and black array instead of white robes, usher me in, to my chamber's deserted couch.

Chorus. [To Admétus.] Quick upon happy fortune came this grief over thee unschooled-in-wo: but thou hast saved thy life and soul. Thy spouse is dead,—her love she left behind: what new thing this? Death ere now has robbed many a one of his wife!

Admetus. [Most sorrowfully unto the Chorus.] My friends, I deem the fortune of my consort more happy than my own, and though it appears not so, yet nevertheless : — for, her, in sooth, no grief shall ever touch,

941. Monk, contrary indeed to all editions prior to his own, has given πολυήχητός 9' in lieu of πολυάχητος δ'.

944. Some have here ἥμεν, and others ἐιμὲν,—both of them faulty.

948. λέκτρων κοίτας ἐς ἐρήμους, into the solitary or forsaken cubicularies of the bed.

949-50. Aldus's reading is παρ' εὐτυχεῖ σοι πότμος. Wakefield changed πότμον in

this verse to πότμῳ,—but indefensibly.

953. For ἔλιπε φιλίαν, Wakefield sillily conjectured ἔλιπέ τε φλίαν.

954. Most editions have πολλοῖς in this line, and παρέλυσε in the next.

957. I have placed a comma between δοκοῦνθ' and ὅμως—because by this punctuation the sense appears more perfect than without the comma.

πολλῶν δὲ μόχθων εὐκλεὴς ἐπαύσατο.

Ἐγὼ δ᾽, ὃν οὐ χρῆν ζῆν, παρεὶς τὸ μόρσιμον,   960
λυπρὸν διάξω βίοτον· ἄρτι μανθάνω.

Πῶς γὰρ δόμων τῶνδ᾽ εἰσόδους ἀνέξομαι;

Τίν᾽ ἂν προσειπών, τοῦ δὲ προσρηθεὶς ὕπο,

τερπνῆς τύχοιμ᾽ ἂν εἰσόδου; Ποῖ τρέψομαι;

Ἡ μὲν γὰρ ἔνδον ἐξελᾷ μ᾽ ἐρημία,   965

γυναικὸς εὐνὰς εὖτ᾽ ἂν εἰσίδω κενὰς,

θρόνους τ᾽, ἐν οἷσιν ἷζε, καὶ κατὰ στέγας

αὐχμηρὸν οὖδας, τέκνα δ᾽ ἀμφὶ γούνασι

πίπτοντα κλαίη μητέρ᾽, οἱ δὲ δεσπότιν

στένωσιν, οἵαν ἐκ δόμων ἀπώλεσαν.   970

Τὰ μὲν κατ᾽ οἴκους, τοιάδ᾽· ἔξωθεν δέ με

γάμοι τ᾽ ἐλῶσι Θεσσαλῶν καὶ ξύλλογοι

γυναικοπληθεῖς· οὐ γὰρ ἐξανέξομαι

λεύσσων δάμαρτος τῆς ἐμῆς ὁμήλικας.

Ἐρεῖ δέ μ᾽, ὅστις ἐχθρὸς ὢν κυρῇ, τάδε·   975

THE ORDER, AND ENGLISH ACCENTUATION.

δὲ εὐκλεὴς ἐπαύσατο πόλλων μόχθων. Δὲ ἐγὼ, ὃν οὐ χρην ζην, πάρεις το μόρσιμον, διάξω λύπρον βίοτον· ἄρτι μάνθανω. Γαρ πως ανέξομαι εἰσόδους τωνδε δόμων; Τίνα αν προσείπων, δὲ ὕπο του προσρήθεις, αν τυχοίμι τέρπνης εἰσόδου; Ποι τρέψομαι; Γαρ ἡ ερημια ἔνδον μεν ἐξελα με, εὔτε αν εἰσιδω εὔνας γυναικος κένας, τε θρόνους, εν οἶσι ἴζε, και οὔδας κάτα στέγας αὐχμηρον, δὲ τέκνα πιπτόντα ἀμφι γούνασι κλαιη μητέρα, δὲ οἱ στενῶσι δέσποτιν, οἵαν απώλεσαν εκ δόμων. Τοιάδε μεν τα κάτα οἴκους· δὲ ἐξώθεν τε γάμοι Θέσσαλων και ξύλλογοι γυναικοπληθεις ἐλῶσι με· γαρ οὐκ ἐξανέξομαι λεύσσων ὁμήλικας της ἐμης δαμάρτος. Δὲ ὅστις κύρη ων ἐχθρος ερει με τάδε·

TRANSLATION.

and she hath with glory ceased from many toils. But I, who ought not to have lived, shall, having escaped my destiny, lead a bitter life: I now perceive it! For how can I bear my entry into this house? Whom addressing, and by whom addressed, can I have joy in entering? Whither shall I turn me? For the solitude within will in troth drive me forth, when I see the sleeping-place of my wife empty, and the seat whereon she used to sit, and the floor throughout the house dirty, and when my children falling about my knees weep for their mother, and when these [*Looking distressedly on the servants about the doors.*] lament their mistress,—what a lady they have lost out of the house! Such, indeed, the state of things within the palace: and abroad the nuptials of the Thessálians, and the assemblies full of women will torture me: for I shall not be able [*Sobbing and shedding tears.*] to look on the companions of my wife! And whoever happens to be mine enemy will speak thus of me:

960. χρὴ ómnes: sed proculdúbio repónendum χρῆν, *oportébat,*— quod réctè vértunt intérpretes. MONK.

961. ἄρτι μανθάνω, *I recently discover or learn — I am now finding out.* Aldus and most others give μανθάνω, corruptly.

965. Vúlgo légitur, ut in Aldínâ, ἐξολεῖ μ᾽. Repósuit Wakefiéldius ἐξελᾷ μ᾽ ex MSS. et Lascáre, sequéntibus Gaisfórdio et Matthiáeo. MONK.

967. Aldus has ἴζες most faultily, yet which Canter by some mistake adopted.

969. In the greatest part of editions before Musgrave's, the reading is κλαίει. The subjunctive mood, however, is unquestionably necessary after εὖτ᾽ ἄν.

972. In place of τ᾽ ἐλῶσι, the Florentine Copy and Lascar have γελῶσι: Aldus, γ᾽ ἐλῶσι. The Attic future of ἐλαύνω, is ἐλῶσι: Iónicè, ἐλάσουσι.

975. In many editions the sense is destroyed by the interposition of a comma between δὲ and μ᾽:—all before Monk's have κυρεῖ, instead of κυρῇ.

Ἰδοῦ τὸν αἰσχρῶς ζῶνθ', ὃς οὐκ ἔτλη θανεῖν,
ἀλλ', ἣν ἔγημεν ἀντιδοὺς, ἀψυχίᾳ
πέφευγεν Ἅιδην, (κᾆτ' ἀνὴρ εἶναι δοκεῖ;)
στυγεῖ δὲ τοὺς τεκόντας, αὐτὸς οὐ θέλων
θανεῖν. Τοιάνδε πρὸς κακοῖσι κληδόνα   980
ἕξω· τί μοι ζῆν δῆτα κύδιον, φίλοι,
κακῶς κλύοντι, καὶ κακῶς πεπραγότι;

ΧΟ. Ἐγὼ καὶ διὰ μούσας   [Στροφὴ α'.]   α'
καὶ μετάρσιος ᾖξα, καὶ   β'
πλεῖστον ἀψάμενος λόγων,   985   γ'
κρεῖσσον οὐδὲν Ἀνάγκας   δ'
εὗρον· οὐδέ τι φάρμακον   ε'
Θρᾴσσαις ἐν σανίσιν, τὰς   ζ'
Ὀρφεία κατέγραψεν   η'
γᾶρυς, οὐδ' ὅσα Φοῖβος Ἀ-   990   θ'
σκληπιάδαις ἔδωκε   ι'
φάρμακα πολυπόνοις   κ'
ἀντιτεμὼν βροτοῖσιν.   λ'

THE ORDER, AND ENGLISH ACCENTUATION.

Ἰδου τον αἰσχρως ζωντα, ὁς οὐκ ἔτλη θάνειν, ἀλλα, ἀντιδους ἡν ἐγῆμε, πεφευγε Ἅιδην ἀψύχια, (και εἰτα δόκει εἰναι ἀνηρ;) δε στυγει τους τεκόντας, αὑτος ου θέλων θάνειν. Τοιάνδε κληδόνα ἕ-ξω προς κακοῖσι τι δῆτα κύδιον μοι, φίλοι, ζην κλυόντι κάκως, και πεπραγοτι κάκως; ΧΟ. Ἐγω και, και ᾖξα μετάρσιος δια μούσας, και πλεῖστον ἀψάμενος λόγων, εὑρον οὐδεν κρεῖσσον Ἀνάγκας· οὐδε τι φάρμακον εν Θρᾴσσαις σάνισι, τας Ορφεια γαρυς κατεγράψε, οὐδε ὁσα φάρμακα Φοίβος ἐδωκε Ασκληπιάδαις, ἀντιτεμων πολυπονοις βροτοῖσι.

TRANSLATION.

"Look at that one ingloriously alive, who had not the courage to die, but, by giving in his stead her whom he married, escaped Death through cowardice, (and yet seems he to be a man?) and he hates his parents, himself unwilling to die." Such ill-language shall I have in addition to my woes:—why then is it better for me, my friends, to live hearing reproach, and suffering wretchedness?

CHORUS. I too have both been borne aloft through song,—and, having very much handled arguments, have found nothing more powerful than Necessity:—nor is there any cure in the Thracian tablets which Orpheus's voice inscribed; nor among all the many medicines which Apóllo has given to the sons of Æsculápius, dispensing them to wretched mortals.

984. For ᾖξα, the reading of both Lascar and Aldus, several editions have ἔξη-α, most corruptly. Barnes restored ᾖξα.

985. MSS. for the most part and Lascar have πλεῖστον—agreeing with λόγων, instead of πλεῖστον assumed adverbially.

988. The more common lection here, is Θρήσσαις: nor (I imagine) is the Doric form, as Monk appears to think, invariably preferable in the Choruses. Lascar edited Θρηίσσαις.—On σανίσιν Musgrave says: "conservátas ad Haémum, Thrá-

ciæ móntem, trádit Scholiástes ad Hécubam. Quícquid hújus fúerit, Euripides haud dúbiè réspicit scrípta, quæ súâ, et Platónis ætáte, Orpheo tríbui solébant." In this verse the poet has usurped τὰς, those, for ἃς, which.

989-90. Ὀρφεία γᾶρυς, literally, the Orphéan voice, a periphrase for "Orpheus."

991. In the early editions, Lascar's alone excepted, the reading is Ἀσκληπιάδαισιν παρέδωκε. Lascar has Ἀσκληπιάδης. Musgrave gives ἔδωκε, correctly.

Μόνας δ' οὔτ' ἐπὶ βωμοὺς   ['Αντιστροφὴ α'.]   ᴗ –‖– ᴗ ᴗ –‖–   α'
ἐλθεῖν, οὔτε βρέτας θεᾶς   995   – –‖– ᴗ ᴗ –‖ᴗ –   β'
ἐστίν· ὃυ σφαγίων κλύει.   – ᴗ‖– ᴗ ᴗ –‖ᴗ –   γ'
Μή μοι, πότνια, μείζων   – –‖– ᴗ ᴗ –‖–   δ'
ἔλθοις, ἢ τὸ πρὶν ἐν βίῳ.   – –‖– ᴗ ᴗ –‖ᴗ –   ε'
Καὶ γὰρ Ζεὺς, ὅ τι νεύσῃ,   – –‖– ᴗ ᴗ –‖–   ϛ'
ξὺν σοὶ τοῦτο τελευτᾷ·   1000   – –‖– ᴗ ᴗ –‖–   η'
καὶ τὸν ἐν Χαλύβοις δαμά-   – ᴗ‖– ᴗ ᴗ –‖ᴗ –   θ'
ζεις σὺ βίᾳ σίδαρον·   – ᴗ ᴗ –‖ᴗ –‖ᴗ   ι'
ἐνδέ τις ἀποτόμου   – ᴗ ᴗ‖– ᴗ ᴗ‖   κ'
λήματός ἐστιν αἰδώς.   – ᴗ ᴗ –‖ᴗ –‖   λ'

Καὶ σ' ἐν ἀφύκτοισι χερῶν   [Στροφὴ β'.] 1005   – ᴗ ᴗ –‖– ᴗ ᴗ –   α'
εἷλε θεὰ δεσμοῖς·   – ᴗ ᴗ –‖– –   β'
τόλμα δ', οὐ γὰρ ἀνάξεις ποτ' ἔνερθεν   – –‖– ᴗ ᴗ –‖– ᴗ ᴗ –‖–   γ'
κλαίων τοὺς φθιμένους ἄνω.   – –‖– ᴗ ᴗ –‖ᴗ –   δ'
Καὶ θεῶν σκότιοι φθίνουσι   – – ᴗ ᴗ‖– ᴗ‖– ᴗ   ε'
παῖδες ἐν θανάτῳ.   1010   – ᴗ‖– ᴗ ᴗ –   ϛ'
Φίλα μὲν, ὅτ' ἦν μεθ' ἡμῶν,   ᴗ – ᴗ ᴗ‖– ᴗ‖– –   η'
φίλα δ' ἔτι καὶ θανοῦσα.   ᴗ – ᴗ ᴗ‖– ᴗ‖– ᴗ   θ'

THE ORDER, AND ENGLISH ACCENTUATION.

Δε θέας μόνας οὔτε ἐστι ἐλθειν ἐπι βώμους, οὔτε βρέτας· ου κλύει σφάγιων. Μη, πότνια, ἐλθοις μοι μείζων, η το πριν εν βίῳ. Γαρ και Ζευς, ὅ τι νεύσῃ, ξυν σοι τελευτᾳ τούτο· και συ βίᾳ δαμάζεις τον σιδάρον εν Χαλύβοις· ουδε απότομου λήματος ἐστι τις αιδως. Και σε θέα εἷλε εν αφυκτοῖσι δέσμοις χερων· δε τόλμα, γαρ οὔποτε κλαίων ανάξεις άνω τους φθίμενους ενέρθεν. Και σκότιοι παιδες θέων φθίνουσι εν θάνατῳ. Φίλα μεν, ὅτε ην μέτα ἡμων, δε φίλα ἔτι και θανοῦσα.

TRANSLATION.

But of this Goddess alone it is not of avail to approach either the altars, or the image:—she listens not to victims! [*Prayingly.*] Do not, O revered one, come on me more severe than heretofore in my life. For on the one hand Jove, whatever he may have assented to, with thee brings this to pass,—and on the other thou by force subduest the iron among the Chálybi: nor of thy fierce spirit is there any remorse. And [*Looking at Admétus.*] thee the Goddess hath seized in the inevitable grasp of her hand: but bear up, for thou wilt never by weeping bring upon Earth the dead from below. Even the stealth-begotten sons of the Gods perish in death! [*With pathos.*] Dear indeed was she, while she was with us, and dear is she still, although dead!

995. θεᾶς, *of this Goddess*, namely, *Necessity:* but she was not the only Deity that was deaf to the voice of victims.

999. Ita ómnes ánte Musgrávium, qui ex tribus MSS. dédit νεύσει,—pérperam ut opínor:—νεύσῃ est subjunctívus aorísti, subaudíto ἄν. MONK.

1001. Barnes edited Χαλύβεσσι silently: forgetting, perhaps, that both Χάλυβοι and Χάλυβες were in use. It cannot, however, be denied that the latter form was by far the more common.

1002. Aldus has ὁυ for σὺ in this line;

most likely by an error at press; owing to the great similarity between ὁ and σ. Barnes here adopted Canter's supposed emendation, δαμάζει σου βίᾳ.

1003-04. *Nor is there any blush or feeling of shame appertaining to thy abrupt or headlong disposition.*

1009. σκότιοι, *illegitimate—illicit.*

1011. Ita Lascáris: ἦν γε μεθ' ἡμῶν Aldus cæterique, et in antistróphico vérsu 1021 ínfrà, πρόὔθανεν,—míro cérte consénsu: únde ómnis numérorum suávitas omnínò subláta est. MONK.

Γενναιοτάταν δὲ πασᾶν

ἐζεύξω κλισίαις ἄκοιτιν.

—

Μηδὲ νεκρῶν ὡς φθιμένων   ['Αντιστρ. β'.] 1015   α'

χῶμα νομιζέσθω   β'

τύμβος σᾶς ἀλόχου, θεοῖσι δ' ὁμοίως   γ'

τιμάσθω, σέβας ἐμπόρων·   δ'

καί τις, δοχμίαν κέλευθον   ε'

ἐμβαίνων, τόδ' ἐρεῖ·   1020   ζ'

'Αὔτα ποτὲ πρόὔθαν' ἀνδρὸς,   η'

νῦν δ' ἐστὶ μάκαιρα δαίμων·   θ'

χαῖρ', ὦ πότνι', εὖ δὲ δοίης.   ι'

Τοῖαί νιν προσεροῦσι φᾶμαι.   κ'

—

Καὶ μὴν ὅδ', ὡς ἔοικεν, 'Αλκμήνης γόνος, 1025

"Αδμητε, πρὸς σὴν ἑστίαν πορεύεται.

ΗΡ. Φίλον πρὸς ἄνδρα χρὴ λέγειν ἐλευθέρως,

"Αδμητε, μομφὰς δ' οὐχ ὑπὸ σπλάγχνοις ἔχειν

σιγῶντ'. 'Εγὼ δὲ σοῖς κακοῖσιν ἠξίουν

ἐγγὺς παρεστὼς ἐξετάζεσθαι φίλος· 1030

THE ORDER, AND ENGLISH ACCENTUATION.

Δε κλίσιαις εζεύξω ακοίτιν γενναιόταταν πάσαν. Μήδε τύμβος σας άλοχου νομιζέσθω ως χώμα νέκρων φθίμεναν, δε τιμάσθω ομοίως θεοίσι, σέβας έμπορων· και τις, εμβαίνων δόχμιαν κελεύθον, έρει τόδε· 'Αύτα πότε προ-έθανε άνδρος, δε νυν έστι μακαίρα δαίμων· χαίρε, ω πότνια, δε δοίης ευ. Τοίαι φάμαι προσεροῦσι νιν. Και μην όδε, ώς εοίκε, πορεύεται γόνος Αλκμήνης προς σην έστιαν, Αδμήτε. ΗΡ. Χρη, Αδμήτε, λέγειν ελευθέρως προς άνδρα φίλον, δε ου σιγώντα έχειν ύπο σπλάγχνοις μόμφας. Δε εγώ ήξιουν παρέστως φίλος έγγυς σοις κακοίσι εξεταζέσθαι·

TRANSLATION.

For to thy bed thou didst join a wife the noblest of all women! Nor let the tomb of thy spouse be accounted as the mound over the dead that perish, but let it be honored equally with the Gods, an object of adoration to travellers: and some one, going along the direct road, will speak thus: *"She once upon a time died for her husband, but is now a blessed divinity:—hail, O adored one, and be propitious!"* Such words will be addressed to her! [*Looking round.*] And lo! here, as it seems, comes the son of Alcména to thy dwelling, Admétus.

HERCULES. [*Entering, with a lady in a robe and hood leaning on his arm, accosts Admétus in a tone of displeasure and rebuke.*] It is right, Admétus, to speak unreservedly to a person who is one's friend, and not in silence to retain in our bosoms what we blame. Now I thought myself worthy, standing as a friend near thee in thy afflictions, to enquire into them:

1015. Sic Suppl. 44, φθιμέναν νεκύων: et 558, τοὺς ὀλωλότας νεκρούς. Flúxit, ut vidétur, ab Homérico, Odyss. Λ'. 490, νεκύεσσι καταφθιμένοισι. MONK.

1017. Hîc animadvértant vélim tirónes θεοῖσι dissýllabon ésse: métrum est ex êâ spécie antispástici hendecasýllabi, cújus exémpla indicávit Porsónus in Addéndis, ad Hécubæ 1169, p. 82, editiónis secúndæ. MONK.

1020. Gaisford and Matthíæ have ἐμβαίνων, rightly—as have also two of the Parisian MSS. collated by Musgrave: in all others the lection is ἐκβαίνων.

1021. Lascar has αὐτά,—most others, αὐτά: and for πρόὔθαν', all have πρόὔθανεν.

1023. εὖ δὲ δοίης, literally, *and give well*, that is, *and grant to us success*: Tyrwhitt conjectured εὖ διδοίης, for the εὖ δὲ διδοίης of Lascar's text.

K

σὺ δ' οὐκ ἔφραζες σῆς προκείμενον νέκυν
γυναικός· ἀλλά μ' ἐξένιζες ἐν δόμοις,
ὡς δὴ θυραίου πήμματος σπουδὴν ἔχων.
Κᾆστεψα κρᾶτα, καὶ θεοῖς ἐσπεισάμην
σπονδὰς ἐν οἴκοις δυστυχοῦσι τοῖσι σοῖς.   1035
Καὶ μέμφομαι δὴ, μέμφομαι παθὼν τάδε·
οὐ μήν σε λυπεῖν γ' ἐν κακοῖσι βούλομαι.
Ὧν δ' οὕνεχ' ἥκω, δεῦρ' ὑποστρέψας πάλιν,
λέξω. Γυναῖκα τήνδε μοι σῶσον λαβών,
ἕως ἂν ἵππους δεῦρο Θρηκίας ἄγων   1040
ἔλθω, τύραννον Βιστόνων κατακτανών.
Πράξας δ' ὃ μὴ τύχοιμι, (νοστήσαιμι γὰρ,)
δίδωμι τήνδε σοῖσι πρόσπολον δόμοις.
Πολλῷ δὲ μόχθῳ χεῖρας ἦλθεν εἰς ἐμάς·
ἀγῶνα γὰρ πάνδημον εὑρίσκω τινὰς   1045
τιθέντας ἀθληταῖσιν, ἄξιον πόνου,
ὅθεν κομίζω τήνδε, νικητήρια

THE ORDER, AND ENGLISH ACCENTUATION.

δε συ ουκ εφραζες νέκυν σης γυναικος προκείμενον· ἀλλα εξενιζες με εν δόμοις, ὡς ἔχων σπουδὴν πήματος δη θυραίου. Καὶ ἐσ τ ἔψα κρᾶτα, και ἐσπεισαμην σπόνδας θεοις εν τοις σοις οικοις δυστυχοῦσι. Καὶ δη μέμφομαι, μεμφομαι παθὼν τάδε· μην ου βούλομαι λύπειν σε γε εν κακοισι. Δε ούνεκα ὧν ἥκω, ὑποστρέψας πάλιν δευρο, λέξω. Λάβων τήνδε γυναικα σώσον μοι, ἕως αν ἔλθω δευρο ἄγων Θρηκιας ἵππους, κατάκτανων τυράννον Βιστονων. Δε πράξας ὃ μη τυχοίμι, γαρ νοστήσαιμι, διδώμι τήνδε πρόσπολον σοισι δόμοις. Δε πόλλω μόχθω ἦλθε εις εμας χειρας· γαρ ευρισκω τινας τιθεντας πανδημον αγῶνα αθληταισι, άξιον πόνου, όθεν κομίζω τήνδε, νικητήρια

TRANSLATION.

however thou didst not tell me that it was thy wife's corse that was laid out; but receivedst me into thy mansion,—as though feeling concern for a calamity actually foreign. And I crowned my head, and poured out libations to the Gods in this house of thine that was in distress.

And I certainly blame thee, I blame thee, having experienced from thee this treatment : yet I wish not to grieve thee, at least in thy misfortunes. But for what reason I am come,—having turned back again hither, I will tell thee.

Receiving at my hands this woman, take care of her for me, until I come back bringing with me the Thrácian mares, having slain the king of the Bistónians. But if I meet with what I pray I may not chance to meet with, (for may I return,) I give her to thee as an attendant in thy palace. And by much toil did she come into my hands : for I find some persons who had proposed a public contest for wrestlers, worthy of my exertion,—from whence I bear her off, having, as the prize of victory,

---

1033. Monk notices that θυραίου πήματος σπουδὴν ἔχων, occurred above, v. 794.

1034. Several MSS. and Lascar have ἐλειψάμην for ἐσπεισάμην,—and this Tyrwhitt praises, but Monk condemns. The latter quotes the Eléctra, 511–12, σπονδάς τε, λύσας ἀσκὸν ὃν φέρω ξένοις, ἔσπεισα.

1037. The γ' in this verse owes its insertion to Monk.

1039. For σῶσον in this line, Aldus and his followers have σῶσαι :—and for τήνδε μοι Matthiæ gives τήνδ' ἐμοί : this, Monk styles more emphatic.

1042. Wakefield interpreted the first five words of this verse, most clearly indeed, although not very literally, as follows—" si támèn id páliar, quod útinàm mihi non contíngat páti."

1044. Lascar and Aldus printed πολλᾶν δὲ μόχθων ἦλθε χεῖρας εἰς ἐμάς.

λαβών· τὰ μὲν γὰρ κοῦφα τοῖς νικῶσιν, ἦν

ἵππους ἄγεσθαι, τοῖσι δ᾽ αὖ τὰ μείζονα

νικῶσι, πυγμὴν καὶ πάλην, βουφόρβια·   1050

γυνὴ δ᾽ ἐπ᾽ αὐτοῖς εἵπετ᾽· ἐντυχόντι δὲ

αἰσχρὸν παρεῖναι κέρδος ἦν τόδ᾽ εὐκλεές.

Ἀλλ᾽, ὥσπερ εἶπον, σοὶ μέλειν γυναῖκα χρή·

οὐ γὰρ κλοπαίαν, ἀλλὰ σὺν πόνῳ λαβὼν

ἥκω· χρόνῳ δὲ καὶ σύ μ᾽ αἰνέσεις ἴσως.   1055

ΑΔ. Οὗτοι σ᾽ ἀτίζων, οὐδ᾽ ἐν ἐχθροῖσιν τιθείς,

ἔκρυψ᾽ ἐμῆς γυναικὸς ἀθλίους τύχας·

ἀλλ᾽ ἄλγος ἄλγει τοῦτ᾽ ἂν ἦν προσκείμενον,

εἴπερ πρὸς ἄλλου δώμαθ᾽ ὡρμήθης ξένου·

ἅλις δὲ κλαίειν τοὐμὸν ἦν ἐμοὶ κακόν.   1060

Γυναῖκα δ᾽, εἴ πως ἐστὶν, αἰτοῦμαί σ᾽, ἄναξ,

ἄλλον τιν᾽, ὅστις μὴ πέπονθεν οἷ᾽ ἐγώ,

σώζειν ἄνωχθι Θεσσαλῶν· πολλοὶ δέ σοι

ξένοι Φεραίων· μή μ᾽ ἀναμνήσῃς κακῶν.

THE ORDER, AND ENGLISH ACCENTUATION.

λαβων· γαρ τοις μεν νικωσι τα κουφα, ην αγεσθαι ἵππους, δε τοισι αυ νικωσι τα μειζονα, πυγμην και παλην, βουφόρβια· δε επι αυτοις γύνη εἵπετο· δε ευτυχόντι ην αισχρον παρειναι τόδε ευκλεες κέρδος. Ἀλλα, ὥσπερ ειπον, χρη γυναικα μέλειν σοι· γαρ ἥκω ου λάβων κλοπαίαν, αλλα συν πόνω· δε χρόνω και συ ισως αινεσεις με. ΑΔ. Ουτοι ατίζων σε, ουδε τιθεις εν εχθροίσι, εκρύψα αθλιους τύχας εμης γυναικος· αλλα τουτο αν ην αλγος προσκειμενον αλγει, ειπερ ωρμηθης προς δώματα αλλου ξένου·'δε εμοι ην ἁλις· κλαιειν το εμον κάκον. Δε γυναικα, αιτουμαι σε, αναξ, ει πως εστι, ανώχθι τινα αλλον Θεσσαλων, ὁστις μη πεπονθε οἱα εγω, σώζειν, (δε Φεραίων πόλλοι ξένοι σοι), μη αναμνήσῃς με κάκων.

TRANSLATION.

received her:—for to those indeed who conquered in the lighter exercises, it was to obtain horses; but to those again who proved victorious in the greater, (pugilism and wrestling,) herds of cattle: and to these a woman was added: — now in me, who succeeded, it would have been base to neglect this glorious prize. But, as I said, it is fit the woman be a care unto thee: for I am come not having obtained her clandestinely, but with labor: and in time thou too wilt perhaps commend me for it.

ADMETUS. Not by any means slighting thee, neither accounting thee among mine enemies, did I conceal from thee the unhappy fate of my wife: but this would have been grief added to grief, if thou hadst gone to the house of another host:—and to me it was enough to weep over mine own misfortune. But as to this woman, I beseech thee, O king, if it be in any way possible, bid some other of the Thessálians, (who has not suffered what I have,) take care of her, (for amongst the people of Phéræ thou hast many friends,) lest thou remind me of my woes.

1056. ἀτιμάζων Scholiástes, Lascáris, Aldus, et ómnes ánte Barnésium. Corrigéndum ἀτίζων vidérunt et Scáliger et Pórtus, et hoc scriptum est in Fragménto MSti hújus fábulæ in Muséo Británnico. Deínde, pro ἐχθροῖσιν, ómnes editiónes Musgraviánam præcedéntes éxhibent αἰσχροῖς: álteram servávit únus Códex Parisiénsis, 2713. MONK.

1057. ἄθλιος being either of two, or of three terminations, gave to the poet the means of choosing between ἀθλίας and ἀθλίους: he preferred the latter, that the concord might be decidedly with τύχας.

1058. Monk quotes the Tróadës, 591, ἐπὶ δ᾽ ἄλγεσιν ἄλγεα κεῖται. Similar, too, is an expression in the Phœnissæ, ver.382, ἐκ γὰρ ἄλγους ἄλγος αὖ.

Ὀυκ ἂν δυναίμην, τήνδ' ὁρῶν ἐν δώμασιν,   1065

ἄδακρυς εἶναι· μὴ νοσοῦντί μοι νόσον

πρόσθης· ἅλις γὰρ ξυμφορᾷ βαρύνομαι.

Ποῦ καὶ τρέφοιτ' ἂν δωμάτων νέα γυνή;

Νέα γὰρ, ὡς ἐσθῆτι καὶ κόσμῳ πρέπει.

Πότερα κατ' ἀνδρῶν δῆτ' ἐνοικήσει στέγην;   1070

Καὶ πῶς ἀκραιφνὴς ἐν νέοις στρωφωμένη

ἔσται; Τὸν ἡβῶνθ', Ἡράκλεις, οὐ ῥᾴδιον

εἴργειν· ἐγὼ δέ σου προμηθίαν ἔχω.

Ἢ τῆς θανούσης θάλαμον εἰσβήσας τρέφω;

Καὶ πῶς ἐπεισφρῶ τήνδε τῷ κείνης λέχει;   1075

Διπλῆν φοβοῦμαι μέμψιν, ἔκ τε δημοτῶν,

μή τίς μ' ἐλέγξῃ, τὴν ἐμὴν εὐεργέτιν

προδόντ', ἐν ἄλλης δεμνίοις πίτνειν νέας·

καὶ τῆς θανούσης (ἀξία δέ μοι σέβειν)

πολλὴν πρόνοιαν δεῖ μ' ἔχειν. Σὺ δ', ὦ γύναι,   1080

THE ORDER, AND ENGLISH ACCENTUATION.

Ουκ αν δυναίμην, έχων τήνδε εν δώμασι, είναι αδάκρυς· μη πρόσθης νόσον μοι νοσούντί· γαρ άλις βαρύνομαι ξύμφορα. Και που δώματων αν νέα γύνη τρεφοίτο; Γαρ νέα, ως πρέπει εσθήτι και κόσμω. Πότερα ενοικήσει δήτα κάτα στέγην άνδρων; Και πως, στρωφώμενη εν νέοις, έσται ακραίφνης; Τον ηβώντα, Ηράκλεις, ου ράδιον είργειν· δε εγω έχω προμήθιαν σου. Η τρέφω εισβήσας θάλαμον της θανούσης; Και πως επείσφρω τήνδε τω λέχει κείνης; Φοβούμαι διπλην μέμψιν, τε εκ δήμοτων, μη τις ελέγξη με, προδόντα την εμήν ευεργέτιν, πίτνειν δέμνιοις άλλης νέας· και της θανούσης, δε άξια σέβειν μοι, δει με έχειν πόλλην προνοίαν. Δε συ, ω γύναι,

TRANSLATION.

[*Heaving a heavy sigh.*] I should not be able, beholding her in the palace, to refrain from tears: add not a sore to me already sore: for I am sufficiently weighed down with misery!

Besides, where in the house can a young woman be lodged? For she is young, as she evinces by her garb and attire. Shall she reside then in the men's apartment? And how, abiding among young men, will she remain undefiled? A man in the prime of life, Herculës, it is not easy to restrain:—but I have fore-consideration for thee.

Or can I provide for her, having made her enter the chamber of her who is dead? And how [*With an air expressive of the greatest unwillingness.*] can I introduce this woman into that one's bed? I fear twofold blame; first from the citizens, lest any one convict me (having betrayed my benefactress) of lying in the bed of another youthful-one;—next, towards the dead, (for she is worthy of veneration from me,) I ought to entertain great respect.—[*Addressing the female.*] But do thou, O lady,

1066. ἀδακρυς εἶναι, literally, *to be tearless*, that is, *to refrain from shedding tears* or *to abstain from weeping*.

1067. Matthïæ, contrary to all others, has συμφοραῖς in the plural number.

1068. ποῦ τρέφοιτ' ἂν, literally, *how can she be nourished* or *fed? Where can she be boarded and lodged? In what place can she be disposed of*, or *maintained?* Wakefield conjectured στρέφοιτ' ἂν,—speciously enough indeed with allusion to στρωφαμένη in verse 1071, below.

1069. Lascar and Aldus give νέα, badly:—most others have νέα γὰρ ὡς, ἐσθῆτι, &c., faulty in the punctuation only.

1073. Subandítur (ut vidétur) præpositio ἀμφὶ, hîc et infrà, v. 1079. MONK.

1074. Aldus's text, and that of his followers, is here most corrupt, their reading being—εἰς θάλαμον εἰσβήσας. Musgrave edited—θάλαμον εἰσβήσας, consentingly with Lascar, and several MSS.

1078. For πίτνειν, the common lection here is πιτνεῖν.

ἥτις ποτ᾽ εἶ σὺ, ταύτ᾽ ἔχουσ᾽ Ἀλκήστιδι

μορφῆς μέτρ᾽ ἴσθι, καὶ προσήϊξαι δέμας.

Οἴμοι· κόμιζε πρὸς θεῶν ἀπ᾽ ὀμμάτων

γυναῖκα τήνδε, μή μ᾽ ἔλῃς ᾑρημένον.

Δοκῶ γὰρ, αὐτὴν εἰσορῶν, γυναῖχ᾽ ὁρᾷν   1085

ἐμήν· θολοῖ δὲ καρδίαν· ἐκ δ᾽ ὀμμάτων

πηγαὶ κατερρώγασιν. Ὦ τλήμων ἐγὼ,

ὡς ἄρτι πένθους τοῦδε γεύομαι πικροῦ.

ΧΟ. Ἐγὼ μὲν οὐκ ἔχοιμ᾽ ἂν εὖ λέγειν τύχην·

χρὴ δ᾽, ὅστις εἶ σὺ, καρτερεῖν θεοῦ δόσιν.   1090

ΗΡ. Εἰ γὰρ τοσαύτην δύναμιν εἶχον, ὥστε σὴν

εἰς φῶς πορεῦσαι νερτέρων ἐκ δωμάτων

γυναῖκα, καί σοι τήνδε πορσῦναι χάριν.

ΑΔ. Σάφ᾽ οἶδα βούλεσθαί σ᾽ ἂν· ἀλλὰ ποῦ τόδε;

Οὐκ ἔστι τοὺς θανόντας εἰς φάος μολεῖν.   1095

ΗΡ. Μή νυν ὑπέρβαλλ᾽, ἀλλ᾽ ἐναισίμως φέρε.

THE ORDER, AND ENGLISH ACCENTUATION.

ἥτις πότε συ ει, ἴσθι ἐχούσα τα αὐτα μέτρα μόρφης Ἀλκήστιδι, και προσήϊξαι δέμας. Οἴμοι· κόμιζε προς θεῶν τήνδε γυναῖκα ἀπο ὀμμάτων, μη ἔλῃς με ᾑρημένον· γαρ δόκω εἰσορων αὐτην, ὁραν ἐμην γυναῖκα· δε θόλοι· καρδιαν· δε ἐκ ὀμμάτων πήγαι κατερρωγάσι. Ὦ τλήμων ἐγω, ὡς ἄρτι γεύομαι τοῦδε πίκρου πένθους. ΧΟ. Ἐγω οὐκ αν ἐχοίμι μεν λέγειν ευ τύχην· δε χρη, ὅστις συ ει, κάρτερειν δόσιν θέου. ΗΡ. Γαρ ει εἶχον τοσαύτην δύναμιν, ὥστε πορεύσαι σην γυναῖκα εκ νέρτερων δώματων εις φως, και πορσύναι σοι τήνδε χάριν. ΑΔ. Σάφα οἶδα σε αν βουλέσθαι· ἀλλα που τόδε; Ουκ ἔστι τους θανόντας μόλειν εις φάος. ΗΡ. Μη νυν ὑπερβάλλε, ἀλλα φέρε ἐναισίμως.

TRANSLATION.

whosoever at all thou art, know, that thou hast the same size of person with Alcéstis, and resemblest her in shape. [*Bursts into tears.*]

[*To Hérculës.*] Ah! me! Remove, by the Gods, this woman from before mine eyes, lest thou destroy me already destroyed. For methinks, when I look upon her, that I behold my wife : and it agitates my heart; and from mine eyes the streams break forth! O unhappy me, how lately have I been made to taste this bitter grief! [*Sighs and laments.*]

CHORUS. [*Consolingly to Admétus.*] I cannot indeed speak well of thy fortune : but it behoves thee, whatever thou art, to bear-with-firmness the dispensation of heaven.

HERCULES. [*Wishingly.*] For would that I had such power, as to bring thy consort back from the infernal mansions into the light, and to render thee this service!

ADMETUS. Well know I that thou hast the will: but how can this be? It is not possible for the dead to come back into the light. [*Weeps.*]

HERCULES. Do not, now, exceed all bounds,—but bear it decently.

1081. Most MSS. and all the early editions have ταῦτ᾽,— Musgrave and Gaisford, τὰυτ᾽. Matthiæ here edited τἀυτ᾽, *eadem*, rightly.

1084. Lascar has ᾑρτημένον—a reading Tyrwhitt approved. Wakefield proposed ᾑσσημένον, but edited ἔχῃς ᾑρημένον.

1086. Hesýchius explains θολῶσαι by ταράξαι, σκοτίσαι:—deriving the verb θολόω, *turbo*, from θολός, of which he gives the signification to be—τὸ τῆς σηπίας μέλαν, *the black juice of the cuttle-fish*.

1090. For εἶ σὺ, Tyrwhitt conjectured ἐστί. In Lascar's text σὺ is wanting.

1091. Aldus and some others have εἶχον ἐκ Διός. Monk notices that the meaning of εἰ γὰρ εἶχον is, "*nàm útinàm habérem*," whereas εἰ γὰρ ἔχοιμι, would signify, "*nàm útinàm hábeam*."

1096. Lascar and Aldus have ὑπέρϐαιν᾽.

78   1097. ΕΥΡΙΠΙΔΟΥ

ΑΔ. Ῥᾷον παραινεῖν, ἢ παθόντα καρτερεῖν. |--|⏑-||--|⏑-||⏑-|⏑-

ΗΡ. Τί δ' ἂν προκόπτοις, εἰ θέλοις ἀεὶ στένειν; |⏑-|⏑-||--|⏑-||⏑-|⏑-

ΑΔ. Ἔγνωκα κἀυτός· ἀλλ' ἔρως τίς μ' ἐξάγει. |⏑-|⏑-||⏑-|⏑-||--|⏑-

ΗΡ. Τὸ γὰρ φιλῆσαι τὸν θανόντ' ἄγει δάκρυ. 1100 |⏑-|⏑-||--|⏑-||⏑-|⏑-

ΑΔ. Ἀπώλεσέν με, κἄτι μᾶλλον ἢ λέγω. |⏑-|⏑-||⏑-|⏑-||⏑-|⏑-

ΗΡ. Γυναικὸς ἐσθλῆς ἤπλακες· τίς ἀντερεῖ; |⏑-|⏑-||--|⏑-||⏑-|⏑-

ΑΔ. Ὥστ' ἄνδρα τόνδε μηκέθ' ἥδεσθαι βίῳ. |--|⏑-||⏑-|⏑-||--|⏑-

ΗΡ. Χρόνος μαλάξει, νῦν δ' ἔθ' ἡβᾷ σοι, κακόν. |⏑-|⏑-||--|⏑-||--|⏑⏑

ΑΔ. Χρόνον λέγοις ἄν, εἰ χρόνος τὸ κατθανεῖν. 1105 |⏑-|⏑-||⏑-|⏑-||⏑-|⏑-

ΗΡ. Γυνή σε παύσει, καὶ νέου γάμου πόθος. |⏑-|⏑-||--|⏑-||⏑-|⏑-

ΑΔ. Σίγησον· οἷον εἶπας; Οὐκ ἂν ᾠόμην. |--|⏑-||⏑⏑-|⏑-||⏑-|⏑-

ΗΡ. Τί δ'; Οὐ γαμεῖς γάρ, ἀλλὰ χηρεύσεις μόνος; |⏑-|⏑-||⏑-|⏑-||⏑-|⏑⏑

ΑΔ. Οὐκ ἔστιν ἥτις τῷδε συγκλιθήσεται. |--|⏑-||⏑-|⏑-||--|⏑⏑

ΗΡ. Μῶν τὴν θανοῦσαν ὠφελεῖν τι προσδοκᾷς; 1110 |--|⏑-||⏑-|⏑-||⏑-|⏑-

ΑΔ. Κείνην, ὅπου πέρ ἐστι, τιμᾶσθαι χρεών. |--|⏑-||⏑-|⏑-||--|⏑-

THE ORDER, AND ENGLISH ACCENTUATION.

ΑΔ. Ῥᾷον παραίνειν, η παθόντα κάρτερειν. ΗΡ. Δε τι αν προκόπτοις, ει θέλοις στένειν άει; ΑΔ. Εγνώκα και αὐτός· άλλα τις έρως εξάγει με. ΗΡ. Γαρ το φιλῆσαι τον θανόντα άγει δάκρυ. ΑΔ. Απώλεσε με, και έτι μᾶλλον η λέγω. ΗΡ. Ήπλακες ἐσθλῆς γυναίκος· τις αντερει; ΑΔ. Ὥστε τόνδε ἄνδρα μήκετι ἡδέσθαι βίω. ΗΡ. Χρόνος μαλάξει κάκον, δε νυν ἔτι ἡβᾷ σοι. ΑΔ. Χρόνον λέγοις, ει το κάτθανειν χρόνος. ΗΡ. Γύνη παύσει σε, και πόθος νέου γάμου. ΑΔ. Σιγήσον· οἷον εἶπας; Οὐκ αν ᾠόμην. ΗΡ. Δε τι; Γαρ ου γάμεις, άλλα χηρεύσεις μόνος; ΑΔ. Οὐκ ἐστι ἥτις συγκλιθήσεται τῷδε. ΗΡ. Μων πρόσδοκας ὠφέλειν τι την θανοῦσαν; ΑΔ. Κείνην, ὅπου περ ἐστι, χρέων τιμάσθαι.

TRANSLATION.

ADMETUS. It is easier to exhort, than in suffering to endure! HERCULES. But what advantage canst thou reap, even if thou like to groan for ever? ADMETUS. I know that too, myself:—but a certain liking impels me. HERCULES. Ay, love for one who is dead draws the tear. ADMETUS. [Beating his bosom.] She has destroyed me, and still more than I can express! HERCULES. Thou hast lost an excellent wife:—who will deny it? ADMETUS. So that this man [Meaning himself.] is no longer delighted with life! HERCULES. Time will soften the evil, but at present it is still in its vigor on thee! ADMETUS. [Sighing.] Time thou mayest say, if to die be time! HERCULES. A wife will cure thee, and the desire of a new marriage. ADMETUS. Hold thy peace:—what saidest thou? I could not have supposed it! HERCULES. But why? For wilt thou not wed, but lead a widowed life alone? ADMETUS. There is not a woman who shall lie with this man! HERCULES. Dost thou imagine that thou art in aught benefiting her who is dead? ADMETUS. Her, wheresoever she is, I am bound to honor!

1099. Elmsley rejected μ',—avowedly for no other reason than that the fifth foot might be an iambus, and the whole verse a pure iambic. Monk says: 'fáteor iámbum fóre numerosiórem : nec tamen aúsus essem ómnes hujásmodi versículos sollicitáre quod fécit Elmsleíus.'

1104. In Lascar, Aldus, and editions generally, as well as in MSS., there is no comma inserted between σοι and κακὸν. The want of this comma occasions κακ-

ὸν to be the nominative to ἡβᾷ,—instead of the accusative after μαλάξει. Valckenaer and Porson contend for the comma :--Blomfield advocates its omission, contrary to the opinion of Monk.

1108. Some MSS. have χηρεύσει λέχος: Lascar, Aldus, and all other editors except Musgrave, Gaisford, and Matthiæ, give χηρεύεις μόνος. Monk prefers the future tense,—instancing the "carpére" of Virgil, Æn. iv. 32.

ΗΡ. Αἰνῶ μὲν, αἰνῶ· μωρίαν δ᾽ ὀφλισκάνεις. |--|∪-‖--|∪-‖∪-|∪-

ΑΔ. Ὡς μήποτ᾽ ἄνδρα τόνδε νυμφίον καλῶν. |--|∪-‖∪-|∪-‖∪-|∪-

ΗΡ. Ἐπήνεσ᾽, ἀλόχῳ πιστὸς οὕνεκ᾽ εἶ φίλος. |∪-|∪∪∪‖--|∪-‖∪-|∪∪

ΑΔ. Θάνοιμ᾽, ἐκείνην, καίπερ οὐκ οὖσαν, προδούς. |∪-|∪-|∪-‖--|∪-‖--|∪-

ΗΡ. Δέχου νυν εἴσω τήνδε γενναίαν δόμων.   1116 |∪-|∪-‖--|∪-‖--|∪-

ΑΔ. Μὴ, πρὸς σὲ τοῦ σπείραντος ἄντομαι Διός. |--|∪-‖--|∪-‖∪-|∪∪

ΗΡ. Καὶ μὴν ἁμαρτήσει γε, μὴ δράσας τάδε. |--|∪-‖--|∪-‖--|∪-

ΑΔ. Καὶ δρῶν γε, λύπη καρδίαν δηχθήσομαι. |--|∪-‖--|∪-‖--|∪∪

ΗΡ. Πιθοῦ· τάχ᾽ ἂν γὰρ εἰς δέον πέσοι χάρις.   1120 |∪-|∪-‖∪-|∪-‖∪-|∪-

ΑΔ. Φεῦ. Εἴθ᾽ ἐξ ἀγῶνος τήνδε μὴ ᾽λαβές ποτε.   -‖--|∪-‖--|∪-‖∪-|∪∪

ΗΡ. Νικῶντι μέντοι καὶ σὺ συννικᾷς ἐμοί. |--|∪-‖--|∪-‖--|∪-

ΑΔ. Καλῶς ἔλεξας· ἡ γυνὴ δ᾽ ἀπελθέτω. |∪-|∪-‖∪-|∪-‖∪-|∪-

ΗΡ. Ἄπεισιν, εἰ χρή· πρῶτα δ᾽, εἰ χρεὼν, ὅρα. |∪-|∪-‖--|∪-‖∪-|∪-

ΑΔ. Χρή, σοῦ γε μὴ μέλλοντος ὀργαίνειν ἐμέ.   1125 |--|∪-‖--|∪-‖--|∪∪

ΗΡ. Εἰδώς τι κἀγὼ τήνδ᾽ ἔχω προθυμίαν. |--|∪-‖--|∪-‖∪-|∪-

THE ORDER, AND ENGLISH ACCENTUATION.

ΗΡ. Αἴνω μεν, αἴνω· δε οφλισκανεις μώριαν. ΑΔ. Ὡς μήποτε κάλων τόνδε ἄνδρα νύμφιον. ΗΡ. Επήνεσα, οὕνεκα ει πίστος φίλος ἀλοχῳ. ΑΔ. Θανοίμι, πρόδους εκείνην, καίπερ ουκ ούσαν. ΗΡ. Δέχου νυν τήνδε γενναίαν εἴσω δόμων. ΑΔ. Μη, ἀντομαι σε προς Διος του σπειράντος. ΗΡ. Και μην γε ἁμαρτήσει, μη δράσας τάδε. ΑΔ. Και δρων γε, δηχθήσομαι κάρδιαν λύπη. ΗΡ. Πίθου· γαρ τάχα χάρις αν πέσοι εις δέον. ΑΔ. Φευ. Είθε μήποτε ελαβες τήνδε εξ αγώνος. ΗΡ. Μέντοι εμοι νικώντι και συ συννίκας. ΑΔ. Ελέξας κάλως· δε ἡ γύνη απέλθετω. ΗΡ. Απείσιν, ει χρη· δε πρώτα ὅρα, ει χρέων. ΑΔ. Χρη, σου γε μη μελλόντος οργαίνειν εμε. ΗΡ. Ειδώς τι εγω έχω και τήνδε προθύμιαν.

TRANSLATION.

Hercules. I commend thee indeed, I commend thee: but thou wilt incur the imputation of folly!

Admetus. [*With the utmost indifference.*] As being never about to call this man bridegroom!

Hercules. I do commend thee, because thou art a faithful friend to thy wife! Admetus. May I die when I forsake her, although she is not!

Hercules. [*Presenting the lady to Admétus.*] Receive, now, this noble woman into thy house. Admetus. [*Refusing to receive her.*] Do not, I beseech thee by Jove thy sire. Hercules. And yet, in sooth, wilt thou be acting wrong, if thou doest not this! Admetus. And by doing it indeed, I shall gnaw my heart with sorrow! Hercules. [*Entreatingly.*] Be persuaded: for perhaps this favor may prove in season! Admetus. Alas! Would that thou hadst never borne her off from the contest! Hercules. And yet with me conquering, thou also art victorious! Admetus. Thou hast spoken handsomely: but let the lady depart! Hercules. She shall depart, if it be requisite:—but first see whether it be requisite! Admetus. It is requisite, if at least thou art not going to provoke me! Hercules. Possessing a certain knowledge I have in fact this inclination!

1116. Editions not a few indeed have νῦν, contrary to the metre:—Matthíæ in common with some MSS. gives γενναίων agreeing with δόμων—*take this woman into thy noble mansion,* instead of, *take this noble woman into thy mansion.*

1117. μὴ, *nay*: or understand βιάζου, *do not insist—do act against my wish.*

1121. Lascar edited μὴ ᾽λαβές: Aldus,

μὴ λάβοις: Musgrave, Gaisford, and Matthíæ, μὴ ᾽λάβες. Tyrwhitt was the first editor who gave μὴ ᾽λαβες, rightly.

1123. καλῶς ἔλεξας, *thou hast nobly spoken—thou hast prettily said.*

1124. In MSS. partially and Matthíæ we find ἄθρει in room of ὅρα.

1125. For ἐμὲ in this line, all except Monk have ἐμοί.

ΑΔ. Νίκα νυν· οὐ μὴν ἀνδάνοντά μοι ποιεῖς.

ΗΡ. Ἀλλ᾽ ἔσθ᾽ ὅθ᾽ ἡμᾶς αἰνέσεις· πιθοῦ μόνον.

ΑΔ. Κομίζετ᾽, εἰ χρὴ τήνδε δέξασθαι δόμοις.

ΗΡ. Οὐκ ἂν μεθείην τὴν γυναῖκα προσπόλοις. 1130

ΑΔ. Σὺ δ᾽, αὐτὸς αὐτὴν εἴσαγ᾽, εἰ δοκεῖ, δόμους.

ΗΡ. Εἰς σὰς μὲν οὖν ἔγωγε θήσομαι χέρας.

ΑΔ. Οὐκ ἂν θίγοιμι· δῶμα δ᾽ εἰσελθεῖν πάρα.

ΗΡ. Τῇ σῇ πέποιθα χειρὶ δεξιᾷ μόνῃ.

ΑΔ. Ἄναξ, βιάζει μ᾽ οὐ θέλοντα δρᾶν τάδε. 1135

ΗΡ. Τόλμα προτείνειν χεῖρα, καὶ θιγεῖν ξένης.

ΑΔ. Καὶ μὴν προτείνω, Γοργόν᾽ ὡς καρατόμῳ.

ΗΡ. Ἔχεις; ΑΔ. Ἔχω. ΗΡ. Ναὶ, σῶζέ νυν· καὶ τὸν Διὸς

φήσεις ποτ᾽ εἶναι παῖδα γενναῖον ξένον.

Βλέψον δ᾽ ἐς αὐτὴν, εἴ τι σῇ δοκεῖ πρέπειν   1140

γυναικί· λύπης δ᾽ εὐτυχῶν μεθίστασο.

ΑΔ. Ὦ θεοί, τί λέξω; Θαῦμ᾽ ἀνέλπιστον τόδε.

THE ORDER, AND ENGLISH ACCENTUATION.

ΑΔ. Νίκα νυν· μην ποίεις ουκ ανδανόντα μοι. ΗΡ. Ἀλλα ἐστι ὁτε αίνεσεις ἡμας· μόνον πίθου. ΑΔ. Κομίζετε, ει χρη δεξάσθαι τήνδε δόμοις. ΗΡ. Ουκ αν μεθείην την γυναίκα πρόσπολοις. ΑΔ. Δε συ αυτος εἴσαγε αύτην δόμους, ει δόκει. ΗΡ. Μεν εις σας χέρας ουν εγώγε θήσομαι. ΑΔ. Ουκ αν θιγοίμι· δε πάρα εισέλθειν δώμα. ΗΡ. Τη ση δέξιᾳ χείρι μόνη πεποίθα. ΑΔ. Ἀναξ, βιάζει με ου θελόντα δραν τάδε. ΗΡ. Τόλμα προτείνειν χείρα, και θιγειν ξένης. ΑΔ. Και μην προτείνω, ὡς καρατόμῳ Γόργονι. ΗΡ. Ἔχεις; ΑΔ. Ἔχω. ΗΡ. Ναι, σώζε νυν· και πότε φήσεις τον παιδα Διος είναι γεννάιον ξένον. Δε βλέψον ες αύτην, ει δόκει τι πρέπειν ση γυναίκι· δε εὐτυχων μεθίστασο λύπης. ΑΔ. Ω θέοι, τι λέξω; Ανελπίστον θαύμα τόδε.

TRANSLATION.

ADMETUS. Succeed then: however thou art doing what is not gratifying to me! HERCULES. But it may be thou wilt some time or other praise us: only be advised! ADMETUS. [*To his Pages.*] Conduct her in, if I must receive her into my house! [*The Pages prepare.*] HERCULES. [*To Admétus.*] I will not deliver over the lady to servants. ADMETUS. But do thou thyself conduct her into the palace, if it seem meet to thee! HERCULES. Indeed into thy hands then at least will I deliver her! ADMETUS. I will not touch her :—but she is at liberty to enter the house. HERCULES. In thy right hand alone do I confide! [*Hérculës hands the lady to Admétus.*]

ADMETUS. O king, thou compellest me against my inclination to do this! HERCULES. [*Catching hold of Admétus by the arm.*] Dare to stretch forth thine hand, and to touch the stranger. [*Hérculës guides Admétus's hand.*] ADMETUS. And in troth I stretch it forth, as to the Gorgon with severed head! HERCULES. Hast thou her? ADMETUS. [*Sighing.*] I have! HERCULES. Well, keep her fast :—and sometime or other thou wilt say that the son of Jove is a generous guest. [*Removing the hood.*] But look on her, whether she seems in aught to resemble thy wife: and, proving blest, be released from sorrow. ADMETUS.[*Gazing on Alcestis.*]O! Gods, what shall I say! [*With keen amazement.*] An unexpected wonder this!

1130. Some MSS. have μεθείμην σοῖς. Monk notices that μεθιέναι takes an accusative, but μεθίεσθαι a genitive—and he wonders that Valckenaer could commend, and Matthiæ edit σοῖς for τήν.

1131. In editions the reading is δόμοις.

1136. Omnes éditi conséntiunt in θίγειν, viz., à θίγω, quod vérbum est nihili. Aliam lectiónem éxhibet codex Florentínus, προτεινε χεῖρα και θίγε,—quam recépit Matthiaéus. MONK.

1138. MSS. assign ναὶ to Admétus.

Γυναῖκα λεύσσω τήνδ' ἐμὴν ἐτητύμως,

ἢ κέρτομός με θεοῦ τις ἐκπλήσσει χαρά;

ΗΡ. Ουκ ἔστιν· ἀλλὰ τήνδ' ὁρᾷς δάμαρτα σήν. 1145

ΑΔ. Ὅρα γε, μή τι φάσμα νερτέρων τόδ' ᾖ.

ΗΡ. Ου ψυχαγωγὸν τόνδ' ἐποίησω ξένον.

ΑΔ. Ἀλλ', ἢν ἔθαπτον, εἰσορῶ δάμαρτ' ἐμήν;

ΗΡ. Σάφ' ἴσθ'· ἀπιστεῖν δ' ὀύ σε θαυμάζω τύχη.

ΑΔ. Θίγω, προσείπω ζῶσαν ὡς δάμαρτ' ἐμήν; 1150

ΗΡ. Πρόσειπ'· ἔχεις γὰρ πᾶν, ὅσονπερ ἤθελες.

ΑΔ. Ὦ φιλτάτης γυναικὸς ὄμμα, καὶ δέμας,

ἔχω σ' ἀέλπτως, οὔποτ' ὄψεσθαι δοκῶν;

ΗΡ. Ἔχεις· φθόνος δὲ μὴ γένοιτό τις θεῶν.

ΑΔ. Ὦ τοῦ μεγίστου Ζηνὸς εὐγενὲς τέκνον, 1155

εὐδαιμονοίης, καί σ' ὁ φιτύσας πατὴρ

σώζοι· σὺ γὰρ δὴ τἄμ' ἀνώρθωσας μόνος.

THE ORDER, AND ENGLISH ACCENTUATION.

Ἐτήτυμως λεύσσω τήνδε ἐμην γυναῖκα, η τις κέρτομος χάρα θέου ἐκπλήσσει με; ΗΡ. Ουκ ἐστι· ἀλλα ὅρᾳς τήνδε σην δαμάρτα. ΑΔ. Γε ὅρα, μη τόδε ἢ τι φάσμα νέρτερων. ΗΡ. Ουκ ἐποίησω τόνδε ξένον ψυχαγωγον. ΑΔ. Ἀλλα εἰσορω ἐμην δαμάρτα ἢν ἐθάπτον; ΗΡ. Σάφα ἴσθι· δε ου θαυμάζω σε ἀπιστειν τύχη. ΑΔ. Θίγω, προσείπω ὡς ἐμην ζώσαν δαμάρτα; ΗΡ. Προσείπε· γαρ ἔχεις παν, ὅσονπερ ἤθελες. ΑΔ. Ω ὄμμα, και δέμας, φίλτατης γυναικος, ἔχω σε ἀέλπτως, δόκων ουποτε οψέσθαι; ΗΡ. Ἔχεις· δε μη γενοίτο τις φθόνος θέων. ΑΔ. Ω εύγενες τέκνον του μεγίστου Ζήνος, ευδαιμονοίης, και πάτηρ ὁ φιτύσας σώζοι σε· γαρ συ μόνος δη ανωρθώσας τα ἐμα·

TRANSLATION.

[*Looking again.*] Do I really see here my wife, or does some mocking joy of the deity strike me? HERCULES. It is not so: but thou beholdest here thy wife.

ADMETUS. Yet see, whether this be not a phantom from the realms below. HERCULES. [*Smiling.*] Thou hast not made this guest of thine an invoker of spirits! ADMETUS. [*Disbelievingly and with emotion.*] But do I behold my wife whom I buried. HERCULES. Be well assured of it: but I wonder not that thou discreditest thy fortune.

ADMETUS. May I touch her—may I speak to her as my living wife? HERCULES. [*Smiling.*] Speak to her:—for thou art in possession of all that thou desirest.

ADMETUS. [*Addressing Alcéstis with extacy.*] O countenance, and person of my dearest wife, possess I thee beyond my hopes, when I thought never to see thee more? [*Alcéstis answers with a gentle nod of the head.*] HERCULES. [*To Admétus.*] Thou hast her:—but let there not be any envy of the Gods! ADMETUS. [*With a look of gratitude.*] O noble son of most mighty Júpiter, blessed be thou; and may the father, who begat thee, protect thee:—for thou alone in troth hast restored my condition.

1143. The early editions have λεύσσων for λεύσσω, and in the next verse ἢ for ἡ.

1145. Markland conjectured ἀλλ' ἀυτὴν ὁρᾷς δάμαρτα σὴν: rashly, indeed, and inelegantly. The demonstrative τήνδε in this verse, as in ver. 1143 above, has the force of the adverb ἐνθάδε, here—that is, " present, and near me."

1147. For ὃν, Wakefield conjectured σὺ, evidently against all sense. Ψυχαγω-

γὸς means "a person who holds familiar intercourse with spirits—exercising so much power over them as to make them appear at command":—a sorcerer.

1149. The vulgate lection here is τύχην: but Reiske changed this to τύχη, a reading which Wakefield, Matthíæ, and others have rightly adopted.

1157. Aldus and his several followers have σὺ γὰρ τἄμ' ἐξανώρθωσας μόνος.

L

Πῶς τήνδ᾽ ἔπεμψας νέρθεν εἰς φάος τόδε;   ‑‑|◡‑||‑‑|◡‑||◡‑|◡◡

ΗΡ. Μάχην ξυνάψας νερτέρων τῷ κοιράνῳ.   1159   ◡‑|◡‑||◡‑|‑‑||◡‑|◡‑

ΑΔ. Ποῦ τήνδε Θανάτῳ φὴς ἀγῶνα συμβαλεῖν;   ‑‑|◡◡◡||‑‑|◡‑||◡‑|◡‑

ΗΡ. Τύμβον παρ᾽ αὐτὸν ἐκ λόχου μάρψας χεροῖν.   ‑‑|◡‑||◡‑|◡‑||‑‑|◡‑

ΑΔ. Τί γάρ ποθ᾽ ἥδ᾽ ἄναυδος ἕστηκεν γυνή;   ◡‑|◡‑||◡‑|◡‑||‑‑|◡‑

ΗΡ. Οὔπω θέμις σοι τῆσδε προσφωνημάτων   ‑‑|◡‑||◡‑|◡‑||‑‑|◡‑

κλύειν, πρὶν ἂν θεοῖσι τοῖσι νερτέροις   ◡‑|◡‑||◡‑|◡‑||◡‑|◡‑

ἀφαγνίσηται, καὶ τρίτον μόλη φάος.   1165   ◡‑|◡‑||‑‑|◡‑||◡‑|◡◡

Ἀλλ᾽ εἴσαγ᾽ εἴσω τήνδε· καὶ, δίκαιος ὤν,   ‑‑|◡‑||‑‑|◡‑||◡‑|◡‑

τολοιπὸν, Ἄδμητ᾽, εὐσέβει περὶ ξένους.   ◡‑|◡‑||◡‑|◡‑||◡‑|◡‑

Καὶ χαῖρ᾽· ἐγὼ δὲ τὸν προκείμενον πόνον   ‑‑|◡‑||◡‑|◡‑||◡‑|◡◡

Σθενέλου τυράννῳ παιδὶ πορσυνῶ μολών.   ◡◡‑|◡‑||‑‑|◡‑||◡‑|◡‑

ΑΔ. Μεῖνον παρ᾽ ἡμῖν, καὶ ξυνέστιος γενοῦ.   1170   ‑‑|◡‑||‑‑|◡‑||◡‑|◡‑

ΗΡ. Αὖθις τόδ᾽ ἔσται· νῦν δ᾽ ἐπείγεσθαί με δεῖ.   ‑‑|◡‑||‑‑|◡‑||◡‑|◡‑

ΑΔ. Ἀλλ᾽ εὐτυχοίης, νόστιμον δ᾽ ἔλθοις ὁδόν.   ‑‑|◡‑||‑‑|◡‑||◡‑|◡◡

Ἀστοῖς δὲ πάσῃ τ᾽ ἐννέπω τετραρχίᾳ,   ‑‑|◡‑||‑‑|◡‑||◡‑|◡‑

THE ORDER, AND ENGLISH ACCENTUATION.

Πως ἐπέμψας τήνδε νέρθεν εἰς τόδε φάος; ΗΡ. Ξυνάψας μάχην τω κοιράνω νέρτερων. ΑΔ. Που φὴς συμβαλειν τόνδε ἀγῶνα Θανάτω; ΗΡ. Πάρα τύμβον, ἐκ λόχου μάρψας αὐτὸν χέροιν. ΑΔ. Γαρ τι πότε ἕστηκε ἥδε γυνη αναυδος; ΗΡ. Οὔπω θέμις σοι κλύειν προσφωνηματων τήσδε, πριν αν αφαγνισηται τοισι νέρτεροις θεοισι, και τρίτον φάος μόλη. Ἀλλα εἴσαγε τήνδε εἴσω· και τολοιπον, αν δικαιος, Αδμήτε, εὐσέβει πέρι ξένους. Και χαιρε· δε μόλων ἐγω πόρσυνω τον πόνον προκείμενον τυράννω παιδι Σθένελου. ΑΔ. Μεῖνον πάρα ἡμιν, και γένου ξυνέστιος. ΗΡ. Τόδε ἔσται αὐθις· δε νυν δει με ἐπείγεσθαι. Ἀλλα εὐτυχοίης, δε ἔλθοις νόστιμον ὁδόν. Δε ἀστοις, τε πάσῃ τετράρχια ἐννέπω,

TRANSLATION.

[With much amazement.] How didst thou bring her from beneath into the light? HERCULES. Having fought a battle-with-the prince of those below! ADMETUS. Where, dost thou say, hadst thou this conflict with Death? HERCULES. At the tomb,—having from ambush seized him in mine arms. ADMETUS. But why ever stands this woman speechless?

HERCULES. It is not yet allowable for thee to hear the sounds of her voice, before she is absolved-of-her-consecrations to the nether Gods, and the third day come. But conduct her in : and henceforward, being a righteous man, Admétus, shew respect to strangers. [Taking him by the hand.] And farewell : for proceeding-onward I will perform the task that is before me—for the royal son of Sthénelus. ADMETUS. [Entreatingly.] Remain with us, and be a companion of our fire-side.

HERCULES. [Politely.] This shall be at another time : but now I must haste.[Exit Hérculës, bowing respectfully, and Admétus waves his hand.]

ADMETUS. Wherefore may thou prosper, and may thou come the way back. But to the citizens, and all the tetrarchy I issue my commands,

---

1159. In most editions we find δαιμόνων in place of νερτέρων.

1160. ποῦ φὴς ἀγῶνα συμβαλεῖν; Where sayest thou to have joined combat?

1165. ἀφαγνίζειν non purificáre, sed desecráre, verténdum est. ΘΑΝΑΤΟΣ énim, quùm gládio totondísset Alcéstidis capíllos, éam Díis Mánibus sácram dicáverat, quod disértè ἥγνισαι appéllat nóster : víde vérsum 76, súprà. Contráriâ

igitur áliquâ ceremóniâ desecránda érat ántequàm Adméto éjus consuetúdine et collóquio frúi licéret. HEATH.

1166. Markand states quemádmodùm débes to be the sense of δίκαιος ὤν.

1172. Lascar and Aldus edited νόστιμον δ᾽ ἔλθοις δόμεν. Barnes has νόστιμος.

1173. In Lascar's text it is πᾶσιν ἐννέπω τετραρχίᾳ: and in Aldus's, πᾶσί τ᾽ ἐννέπω τετραρχίᾳ, corruptly both.

ΑΛΚΗΣΤΙΣ. 1174.   83

χορους ἐπ' ἐσθλαῖς ξυμφοραῖσιν ἱστάναι,

βωμούς τε κνισσᾶν βουθύτοισι προστροπαῖς· 1175

νῦν γὰρ μεθηρμόσμεσθα βελτίω βίον

τοῦ πρόσθεν· οὐ γὰρ εὐτυχῶν ἀρνήσομαι.

ΧΟ. Πολλαὶ μορφαὶ τῶν δαιμονίων,

πολλὰ δ' ἀέλπτως κραίνουσι θεοί,

καὶ τὰ δοκηθέντ' οὐκ ἐτελέσθη.   1180

Τῶν δ' ἀδοκήτων πόρον εὗρε θεός·

τοιόνδ' ἀπέβη τόδε πρᾶγμα.

                    ΤΕΛΟΣ.

THE ORDER, AND ENGLISH ACCENTUATION.

ἵστανᾳι χόρους ἐπι ἐσθλαις ξυμφοραῖσι, τε κνισσαν βώμους βουθυτοῖσι πρόστροπαις·—γαρ νυν μεθηρμοσμέσθα βέλτιω βίον του πρόσθεν· γαρ ουκ αρνήσομαι εὐτύχων. ΧΟ. Πόλλαι μόρφαι των δαιμόνιων, δε πόλλα θέοι κραινοῦσι αέλπτως, και τα δοκηθέντα ουκ ετελέσθη. Δε θέος εὑρε πόρον των αδοκήτων· τοιόνδε τόδε πράγμα απεβη.

TRANSLATION.

that they institute dances in honor of these happy events, and that they make the altars ódorous with the sacrifices of oxen which accompany their vows: seeing-that now we are placed in a better state of life than the former:—for I will not deny that I am happy. [*Exit Admétus, conducting Alcéstis into the palace, followed by a joyous retinue.*]

Chorus. Many are the forms of the deeds of the Gods—and many occurrences, contrary to expectation, do the deities bring about, while the things looked-for come not to pass. So Providence hath contrived the issue of unlikely incidents: in such wise has this affair terminated!

1175. On κνισσᾶν, Monk says :—'propéndeo in Blomfiéldii senténtiam, scribéntis κνίσα et κνισᾶν pro vulgátis κνίσσα et κνισσᾶν. Víde ad Æschyli Prometh. v. 505.'—For προστροπαῖς, most MSS. and Aldus have προτροπαῖς.

1178. Monk at this line remarks that no fewer than four others of the extant

plays of Euripídës, viz. the Medéa, Andrómachë, Bácchæ, and Hélena, terminate with the same anapæstic stanza as the Alcéstis, except that, instead of this first verse, the reading in the Medéa is, πολλῶν ταμίας Ζεὺς ἐν Ὀλύμπῳ.

1181. Aldus and most others have εὖρεν, causing θεὸς to be a monosyllable.

THE END.

MORAL INFERENCES.

1. *Every good man is humane, and indulgent to his dependants; but it does not follow that a man is (in the strict sense of the word) good, because he is indulgent and humane.* 2. *Hospitality is the mark of a noble mind, and has in many instances been crowned with the amplest reward.* 3. *Nothing insures the esteem and gratitude of servants more, than kind treatment from their masters.* 4. *Many a one, befriended in the hour of distress, has lived to do his benefactor an inestimable service.* 5. *Few persons love their friends to that degree, as to be willing (if required) to die for them.* 6. *A man may possess a very warm heart, and yet be withal a villain and an arrant coward.* 7. *Many bring up their children to their own sorrow: a calamity that originates in over-indulgence or neglect—so much depends on the early instilment of good principles, and on the force of example.* 8. *Unreasonable is the man who expects from others, what he in his turn would hesitate to grant.* 9. *Too frequently do parents meet with ingratitude from their offspring, in return for anxious care and unwearied kindness.* 10. *In prosperity Fortune ought to be feared, because her smile is generally of short duration.* 11. *In adversity it is better to hope than to despair, for, in cases even the most hopeless, relief has arisen.* 12. *Often unexpectedly and by extraordinary means hath succour come to the distressed.* 13. *The events of life are uncertain, seeing the ways of Providence are past finding out:—but the good man has nothing to fear, inasmuch as Piety goes not unrecompensed.*